Export Credit Insurance and Guarantees

Export Credit Insurance and Guarantees

A Practitioner's Guide

Zlatko Salcic

First published 2014 by
PALGRAVE MACMILLAN

Palgrave Macmillan in the UK is an imprint of Macmillan Publishers Limited, registered in England, company number 785998, of Houndmills, Basingstoke, Hampshire RG21 6XS.

Palgrave Macmillan in the US is a division of St Martin's Press LLC, 175 Fifth Avenue, New York, NY 10010.

Palgrave Macmillan is the global academic imprint of the above companies and has companies and representatives throughout the world.

Palgrave® and Macmillan® are registered trademarks in the United States, the United Kingdom, Europe and other countries.

ISBN 978–1–137–36680–1

This book is printed on paper suitable for recycling and made from fully managed and sustained forest sources. Logging, pulping and manufacturing processes are expected to conform to the environmental regulations of the country of origin.

A catalogue record for this book is available from the British Library.

A catalog record for this book is available from the Library of Congress.

Typeset by MPS Limited, Chennai, India.

Contents

List of Figures   xii

List of Abbreviations   xiv

Preface and Acknowledgements   xv

Part I   Subject Matter, Parties and Risks

1   Subject Matter and Basic Terms   3
   1.1   About the book   4
   1.2   Basic terms   5

2   ECAs and Users of the ECA Cover   9
   2.1   The Status of ECAs   9
   2.2   Purpose   10
   2.3   Official support   11
   2.4   Users of ECA cover   12
   2.5   Meaning of the term 'exporter'   12
   2.6   Meaning of the term 'bank'   13
   2.7   The insured under the ECA policy   14
   2.8   Beneficiary of the ECA policy   14

3   Political and Commercial Risks   16
   3.1   Time of occurrence of political and commercial events   17
   3.2   About definitions of political and commercial events   17
   3.3   Definitions of political events   18
   3.4   Definitions of commercial events   24
   3.5   Exclusion of documentation risk   28
   3.6   Distinction between documentation risk and legal risk   29
   3.7   Risk assessment procedures   29
   3.8   Assessment of political risks   30
   3.9   Assessment of commercial risks   31

Part II   Types of ECA Cover

4   Short-Term, Medium- to Long-Term and Partial Cover   35
   4.1   Basic classification of risks   35
   4.2   Characteristics of short-term credit transactions   36
   4.3   Characteristics of the short-term cover   36
   4.4   Short-term cover and international regulations   38

4.5 Characteristics of medium- to long-term credit transactions 40
4.6 Characteristics of the medium- to long-term cover 40
4.7 Medium- to long-term cover and international regulations 42
4.8 Characteristics of project finance transactions 43
4.9 Characteristics of cover for project finance risks 44
4.10 Cover for project finance risks and international regulations 44
4.11 Partial cover and different percentages of cover 45
4.12 Partial cover 45
4.13 Different percentages of ECA cover for political and commercial risks 46
4.14 Consequences of classification of risks as political or commercial 47

5 **Supplier Credit Cover** 49
5.1 Classification of transactions as supplier credit contracts 50
5.2 Limitations of supplier credit cover 50
5.3 Types of supplier credit cover 51
5.4 Cover for short-term supplier credit 51
5.5 Cover for medium- to long-term supplier credit 52

6 **Supplier Credit Cover with the Involvement of Banks** 53
6.1 The exporter's assignment of claim for payment and rights under ECA policy 54
6.2 The position of the bank after assuming rights under an ECA policy 56
6.3 The exporter's transfer of bill of exchange and assignment of rights under ECA policy 58
6.4 Insufficiency of the bank's position under ECA policy 58
6.5 Cover for bills of exchange (drafts) 59
6.6 Cover for promissory notes 61
6.7 Cover for account receivables 63

7 **Supplier Credit Cover in Complex Transactions** 65
7.1 Cover where several parties are involved on the exporter's side 66
7.2 Cover where the contract is between the exporter and its sub-supplier 66
7.3 Cover issued to the exporter when acting through an intermediary in a country of import 67
7.4 Cover issued to the exporter when acting through an intermediary in a third country 69
7.5 Cover issued to the exporter when acting through its subsidiary in a country of import 70
7.6 Difficulties covering credit risks in domestic transactions 71

7.7   Solutions for covering credit risks in domestic transactions
by foreign ECAs   72

7.8   Reinsuring of a domestic insurer by a foreign ECA   75

7.9   Global cover   75

7.10   Cover for political risks in transactions between exporters
and their foreign subsidiaries   76

8   Buyer Credit Cover   **77**

8.1   Purpose of the loan and payment of the loan amount   78

8.2   Separating the loan agreement from the commercial
contract   79

8.3   Limitations of buyer credit cover   79

8.4   ECA requirements for issuing cover for medium- to
long-term buyer credits   80

8.5   Other ECA requirements for issuing buyer credit cover   80

8.6   Buyer credit cover for bank-to-bank loans   81

8.7   Buyer credit cover issued to several banks in syndicate   82

8.8   Buyer credit cover and loan participation   83

8.9   Buyer credit cover and funded loan sub-participation   84

8.10   Buyer credit cover and unfunded loan sub-participation   85

8.11   Buyer credit cover issued to a multinational bank acting
through a local branch   86

9   Other Types of ECA Cover   **88**

9.1   Cover for manufacturing loss   88

9.2   Calculation of manufacturing loss   89

9.3   Cover for manufacturing loss combined with supplier
credit or buyer credit cover   90

9.4   Pre-shipment cover issued to banks   91

9.5   Cover for contract bonds and guarantees   92

9.6   Cover for justified and unfair calling of contract bonds
and guarantees   92

9.7   Cover for interconnected bonds and guarantees   93

9.8   Cover for counter indemnity issued to exporters   94

9.9   Cover for confirmed letters of credit   95

9.10   Applicability of OECD and EU regulations   96

10   Foreign Investment Cover   **98**

10.1   Political events that may cause loss of investment   99

10.2   Investments eligible for obtaining cover   101

10.3   Legal status of investment projects   102

10.4   Eligible investors   102

10.5   Highest amount of cover   103

10.6	Percentage of cover and partial cover	103
10.7	Duration of cover for foreign investments	104
10.8	Premium	104
10.9	Waiting period	104
10.10	Assignment of claim	104
10.11	Indemnification	105
10.12	Obligations of the insured investor	106

11   ECA Direct Loans   **107**
11.1	Purpose of direct loans	107
11.2	Misconceptions about direct loans	108
11.3	International regulations for direct loans	108
11.4	Minimum interest rates for direct loans	109
11.5	Application and offer for direct loans	110
11.6	Arranging direct loans by banks	110
11.7	Arranging direct loans by exporters	111
11.8	The ECA's recourse against a bank or an exporter	112
11.9	Charging a premium for credit risk	112
11.10	Tied aid	113

Part III   Procedures

12   Application, Offer, and Policy   **117**
12.1	Application for issuing cover	118
12.2	Offer for issuing the ECA policy	120
12.3	The ECA policy	121

13   Premium   **123**
13.1	Different premium rates for various types of cover	123
13.2	Basic elements for calculating the premium rate	124
13.3	Minimum premium rates	124
13.4	Buyer risk categories	125
13.5	Reducing minimum premium rate	126
13.6	Third party payment guarantee	126
13.7	Mitigation techniques	126
13.8	Enhancement of credit risk by providing security	127
13.9	Security and reducing the premium rate to the minimum	128
13.10	Increased premium rate	128
13.11	Payment of premium	129
13.12	Shifting the premium costs to foreign buyers	130
13.13	Indication of a premium rate	131

14   Foreign Content   **132**
| 14.1 | Determining the foreign content | 134 |
| 14.2 | National interest | 135 |

14.3   Determining the national interest   135
14.4   Reinsurance as a solution   137

15   Currency   **138**
15.1   Cover and currency risk   139
15.2   Contract denominated in the currency of the ECA country   139
15.3   Contract denominated in hard currency   140
15.4   Contract denominated in other convertible currency   141
15.5   Contract denominated in local currency   143

16   Confidentiality   **145**
16.1   Confidentiality in relations between exporters, banks
       and foreign buyers   145
16.2   Confidentiality in relations between exporters, banks
       and ECAs   146
16.3   Confidentiality in relations between ECAs and
       foreign buyers   147
16.4   Transparency requirements   149
16.5   Confidentiality in relations between ECAs and reinsurers   150

17   Security for Payment of Credits Covered by ECAs   **152**
17.1   Differences between security and the ECA cover   153
17.2   Security and the ECA cover provided for the same risk   154
17.3   Effects of security in export credit transactions covered
       by ECAs   154
17.4   Security in the initial stage of a contract   154
17.5   Security and renegotiation of credit   155
17.6   Enforcement of security   155
17.7   Uncertainty connected with security   156
17.8   Security in intercreditor agreements   157
17.9   Quasi-security   158
17.10 Negative pledge   159

18   Reinsurance   **160**
18.1   Reinsurance in ECA business   160
18.2   Reinsurance between ECAs   161
18.3   Other forms of cooperation between ECAs   162
18.4   Coinsurance between ECAs   162
18.5   Parallel insurance between ECAs   163
18.6   Percentage of foreign content covered by a single ECA   164
18.7   Reinsurance between ECAs and private reinsurance
       companies   164

19   Claims and Indemnification   **166**
19.1   Notification of non-payment, claim and waiting period   166
19.2   Payment of interest during the waiting period   168

19.3	Assignment of claim for payment of credit by insured to ECA	168
19.4	Distinction between assignment of claim and assignment of contract	170
19.5	Assignability of claim	170
19.6	Subrogation of claim	171
19.7	Enforcement of security and indemnification	172
19.8	Assignment of security to ECAs	174
19.9	Ascertainment of claim	174
19.10	Scope of indemnification	175
19.11	Indemnification method	175
19.12	Parties entitled to claim indemnification	177
19.13	Time limitation for claiming indemnification from ECAs	178
19.14	Rescheduling of foreign buyer's credit and right to indemnification	178
19.15	Disputed claim for payment against a foreign buyer	179

20 Recovery **181**
20.1	Classes of foreign buyers	181
20.2	Recovery of debt from sovereign foreign buyers	182
20.3	ECA methods for recovery of debt from sovereign buyers	184
20.4	The Paris Club	184
20.5	Recovery of debt from public buyers	185
20.6	ECA methods for recovery of debt from public buyers	187
20.7	Recovery of debt from private buyers	188
20.8	Negotiations with private buyers	188
20.9	Bilateral negotiations for recovery of a single debt	188
20.10	Multilateral negotiations involving the majority of creditors	189
20.11	Judicial reorganisation of foreign buyers	190
20.12	Legal action against foreign buyers	191
20.13	Sharing of recovery costs	192
20.14	Application of recovered amounts	192

Part IV   Legal Framework

21 OECD and EU Regulations in Terms of ECA Cover **197**
21.1	OECD Arrangement on Officially Supported Export Credits	197
21.2	Application of the Arrangement	198
21.3	Provisions on down payment, local costs, etc.	199
21.4	Maximum terms for payment of export credits	203
21.5	Payment of principal and interest	204
21.6	EU regulation	204

22 Other OECD Regulations and International Sanctions   **206**
  22.1   Combating bribery in international business transactions   206
  22.2   Environmental and social impacts   208
  22.3   Reviewing potential environmental and social impacts   209
  22.4   Sustainable lending practices   210
  22.5   International sanctions   210

23 Selected Standard Terms of ECA Cover   **212**
  23.1   Compensation of loss   213
  23.2   Disclosure of information to ECAs   213
  23.3   Increase of risk after issuing the ECA offer   214
  23.4   Permits for performance of commercial and loan contracts   215
  23.5   Variation of commercial and loan contracts   215
  23.6   Obligations of the insured at increased risk   216
  23.7   Retaining the non-covered percentage of risk by
       the insured   216
  23.8   Waivers and amendments of the ECA standard terms   217
  23.9   Governing law and jurisdiction for ECA policies   217

Bibliography   218

Index   219

List of Figures

2.1	ECA direct loan	12
3.1	Risks included in ECA cover	17
3.2	Ban on import as political event	19
3.3	Ban on export as political event	20
3.4	Prevention or delay in transfer of payment	21
3.5	Conversion and payment in local currency	23
4.1	ECA framework cover for several short-term credit risks	37
4.2	Restriction on ECAs from EU member states to issue short-term cover	39
4.3	Rights of ECAs from non-EU OECD countries to issue short-term cover	39
4.4	Nationality of bank in buyer credit transactions	41
4.5	Arrangement requirements for medium- to long-term transactions	42
4.6	Repayment of loan by the project company	43
6.1	Assignment of claim by exporter to bank	55
6.2	Assignment of rights under ECA policy by exporter to bank	55
6.3	ECA cover for bills of exchange	60
6.4	ECA cover for promissory notes	62
6.5	ECA cover for account receivables issued directly to bank	64
7.1	ECA cover issued to exporter when acting through foreign intermediary	68
7.2	Export transactions with subsidiaries acting as importers	70
7.3	Restriction on carrying on insurance business in foreign country	72
7.4	Shifting of credit risk by including 'if and when' payment terms	73
7.5	Shifting of credit risk by issuing a guarantee	74
8.1	ECA buyer credit cover	78
8.2	Requirements for issuing ECA cover in medium- to long-term transactions	81
8.3	ECA buyer credit cover for bank-to-bank loans	82

8.4	ECA buyer credit cover for syndicated loan	83
9.1	ECA pre-shipment cover issued to bank for loan to exporter	91
9.2	ECA cover issued to bank for contract bond or guarantee	93
9.3	ECA cover issued to bank for counter guarantee	94
9.4	ECA cover for confirmed letter of credit (L/C)	96
14.1	Foreign components added to exported goods	133
14.2	Entire manufacturing placed in third countries	133
14.3	National interest of country of export	136
15.1	Payment of credit in the currency of ECA country	140
15.2	Payment of credit in hard currency	141
15.3	ECA indemnification in hard currency	141
15.4	Payment of credit in other convertible currency	142
15.5	ECA indemnification in other convertible currency	142
15.6	Payment of credit in local currency	143
18.1	Reinsurance between ECAs	162
18.2	Quota-share reinsurance between an ECA and private reinsurer	164
18.3	Excess of loss reinsurance between an ECA and private reinsurer	165
19.1	Indemnification for the non-paid amount of credit	167
19.2	Assignment of claim for payment against foreign buyer	169
20.1	Non-payment of credit, assignment of claim and recovery	182
20.2	Foreign judgment or arbitration award, recognition and enforcement	183
20.3	Stages in the Paris Club procedure	186
20.4	Judicial reorganisation of foreign buyer company	191
20.5	Proportional application of the recovered amount	193
21.1	Example 1	200
21.2	Example 2	201

Abbreviations

BIT   bilateral investment treaty

CIRR   commercial interest reference rate

ECA   export credit agency

ESIA   environmental and social impact assessment

EU   European Union

IFC   International Finance Corporation

IMF   International Monetary Fund

OECD Organisation for Economic Co-operation and Development

UN   United Nations

WTO   World Trade Organization

Preface and Acknowledgements

When I started my work in the export insurance and guarantee business many years ago, I searched for a book that would guide me through the various types of export credit insurance and guarantees and the terms governing these transactions. I was surprised that such a book did not exist and that this important area of international trade had not been analysed or described in a systematic manner. Later, when I discussed this issue with exporters, bankers and experts from national export credit agencies, many of them said it would be good to have such a book to use in their daily work.

This book is my attempt to provide a practitioner's guide for parties that enter into international commercial and loan transactions, lawyers and other professionals involved in the export business. The book is based on the practice of export credit agencies, exporters, banks and foreign buyers, which I studied for more than a decade.

My intention was to explain the fundamental concepts of export credit insurance and guarantees, their variations and their connection to commercial and loan contracts used in international trade. I have tried to organise the material in a comprehensive way, describe the practical issues and add short theoretical explanations only when necessary. I have also tried to get directly to the point, simplify the complicated structures and, most importantly, provide a useful tool to practitioners.

The book reflects the practice and regulation available to me in early 2014. The views and opinions expressed in the book are my own.

I am grateful to Philip R. Wood QC of Allen & Overy for reviewing a part of the manuscript and Alexander R. Malaket, CITP, President of OPUS Advisory Services International Inc. for reviewing the complete manuscript. I am also grateful to the team my publisher engaged for their work on this project and to my editor, Aimee Dibbens, for her efficient work and professionalism.

Zlatko Salcic

Part I
Subject Matter, Parties and Risks

1
Subject Matter and Basic Terms

This book is about export credit insurance and guarantees provided by export credit agencies to exporters and banks to cover their export credit risks. An export credit risk arises when an exporter sells goods or services to a foreign buyer on credit terms or when a bank provides a loan to a foreign buyer for purchasing goods or services from a country of export. The purpose of export credit insurance and guarantees is to indemnify exporters and banks for losses incurred by non-payment of a credit by a foreign buyer. Export credit agencies are specialised institutions acting on behalf of a state and with the state's financial support. They are different from private insurance companies that conduct their business on their own account and without state support.

The export credit insurance and guarantees are in this book called the ECA cover. The abbreviation ECA is used in this book instead of the term export credit agency.

The ECA business and the benefits of obtaining the ECA cover are important for manufacturers, exporters, bankers, lawyers and other professionals engaged in international trade. They are also important for small and medium-sized companies whose representatives sometimes believe that the ECA cover is available only to large manufacturers selling capital equipment with a large value and multinational banks involved in such transactions. As a matter of fact, the ECA cover is available to companies of all sizes.

The first ECAs were established in several European countries directly after World War I. Today ECAs conduct their business in numerous countries of export covering a significant part of credit risks in the international trade. The importance of providing the ECA cover has increased due to the economic globalisation and global economic crises in which creditors seek state protection for credit risks in their export transactions.

Importance of export credit insurance and guarantees for international trade

According to the statistic provided by the Berne Union, the leading international association for the export credit and investment insurance industry, the volume of export credits and foreign direct investments insured by the members of Berne Union was USD$1.8 trillion in 2012. This means that more than 10% of international trade was covered by this type of insurance.

1.1 About the book

The book contains practical knowledge about the requirements for issuing the export credit insurance and guarantees, types of risks covered, types of policies available to exporters and banks, payment of claims, recovery procedures and the legal framework that governs this type of business. It is not about any particular export credit agency or country, but about common matters of providing the export credit insurance and guarantees globally. The book does not provide advice for any type of transaction and if a reader needs professional advice it should be always obtained from an expert.

The book consists of four parts, and each part consists of several chapters. The first part discusses ECAs, users of the ECA cover and the risks covered by ECAs. The second part is about two basic types of the ECA cover created to cover credit risks in commercial and loan transactions and other types of the ECA cover. The third part describes various procedures for obtaining the ECA cover, payment of claims by ECAs and recovery. Finally, the fourth part of the book discusses the legal framework that governs the ECA business.

The book is written as a practitioner's guide for all participants in international trade, including manufacturers, exporters, bankers and foreign buyers that enter into international commercial and loan transactions. It is also written for lawyers and other professionals that advise contractual parties, draft documentation and assist them in other ways. The book will also help small and medium-sized manufacturers in selling their goods and services abroad.

The book is structured in a way that helps even the average reader understand the subject matter. However, it does not necessarily need to be read from the first to the last chapter. A reader may find that some parts of the book are more interesting and read the book in another convenient way. Some readers will already know some aspects of the ECA cover and may complete their knowledge by reading about other aspects. The readers that are not familiar with this subject matter may read the short explanations of basic terms and then read the chapters they find more interesting and easier to understand.

The book is written using the generally known economic and legal terms only. The specific export credit insurance terminology and sophisticated financial and insurance terms used by specialists in the ECA business are avoided. Where a specific export credit term is used it is always explained in a way the average reader can understand. The illustrations included in the book are simple in order to make understanding of the subject matter easier.

1.2 Basic terms

Participants in export credit transactions use a number of specific terms, some of them known from other financial and commercial transactions and some of them developed for the purpose of providing export credit insurance and guarantees. Below are short explanations of the basic terms frequently used in this book, provided to help facilitate readers' understanding.

Credit

In the contractual context, 'credit' is defined as an agreement made between two parties by which some value is given by one party to another in exchange for a promise given by the other party to pay at a later date. Depending on the value given to the other party, credits may take two forms, the deferred payment of purchase price or the loan of money.

If a commercial contract for purchasing of goods or services provides payment of the contractual price at a later date, it is usually said that such a contract is entered on credit terms. The credit term constitutes a part of a commercial contract that normally contains several other terms. In loan contracts, where a lender provides a loan to a borrower in exchange for the borrower's promise to repay the loan at a later date, the credit is a basic contractual term.

Payment on credit terms is typical in commercial contracts but the contractual parties may agree on other ways of payment of the contractual price. Such payment can be made simultaneously with delivery of goods or services, usually called the payment on delivery. Some contracts provide advance payment where the buyer pays the contractual price to the seller in advance for a promise given by the seller to deliver goods or services at a later date.

Payment on delivery and advanced payments are not analysed in this book.

Export credit

Where a buyer of goods or services purchased on credit terms is from a country other than the supplier's country, such a credit is called the export credit. In the ECA context, the export credit agreed in a commercial contract is called the supplier credit.

The term 'export credit' includes a loan provided by a bank to a foreign buyer for purchasing goods or services from a country of export. In the ECA context, the export credit agreed in a loan agreement is called the buyer credit.

Export credit risk

The export credit risk is the risk that a credit will not be paid by a foreign buyer when due. Credit risks exist even in domestic credit transactions, but export credit risks are usually more complex than domestic credit risks. When the term 'credit risk' is used in this book, it always means export credit risk.

Exporter

In this book, the term 'exporter' is defined as a seller or supplier of goods or services supplied to a foreign buyer on credit terms. The exporter and foreign buyer may enter into various types of commercial contracts such as the contract on sale of goods or services, lease, construction, engineering and other contracts. The term 'exporter' emphasises the international character of export transactions that distinguishes them from domestic transactions. This book uses the term 'exporter' to mean a company, not an individual.

In this book the term 'exporter' is frequently used with the term 'bank', especially in the expression 'the insured exporter or bank', which describes them as creditors whose export credit risks are covered by export credit agencies.

Bank

In this book, the term 'bank' is used to mean a financial institution or other lender from a country of export or from a third country that provides a loan to a foreign buyer for purchasing goods or services from a country of export. When borrowing money from a bank, the foreign buyer acts in the capacity of borrower; however, the term 'foreign buyer' is used even in the loan context in order to emphasise the international character of a loan transaction and its connection with the commercial contract between the exporter and foreign buyer.

Foreign buyer

In this book, 'foreign buyer' has two meanings. In the first meaning, it is defined as a buyer of goods or services from a country different from the exporter's country. The second meaning defines 'foreign buyer' as a borrower from a country different from the bank's and exporter's country. A foreign buyer may borrow an amount of money from a bank to purchase goods or services from an exporter. In this book, the term 'foreign buyer' is used to mean a legal entity, not an individual.

ECAs differentiate between three categories of foreign buyers: sovereign, public and private. A sovereign buyer is a foreign state, government, ministry or other institution that can validly bind a state. The main characteristic of a sovereign buyer is that a state cannot be liquidated in a bankruptcy proceeding despite being unable to pay its debts. A public buyer is usually a company owned or controlled wholly or in majority by a state or government. Such companies can be declared bankrupt and liquidated in a bankruptcy procedure.

The public buyer cannot validly bind the state as its owner but it may receive financial support from the state. A private buyer is neither a sovereign nor a public buyer. Private foreign buyers are legal entities, usually organised and registered as companies in a country of import, and they are by far the largest group of foreign buyers with which export credit agencies deal.

Political and commercial events

The events that may cause non-payment of a credit by a foreign buyer can be of a political or commercial nature. Political events are normally out of the control of exporters, banks and foreign buyers. Commercial events affect the business of a foreign buyer, causing an inability to pay a credit. These events are usually called political and commercial risks.

Export credit insurance and export credit guarantees

In this book, the terms 'export credit insurance' and 'export credit guarantees' are defined as transactions by which export credit agencies insure export credit risks assumed by exporters or banks in their commercial or loan transactions with foreign buyers. Insurance and guarantees are similar transactions because both are used to transfer export credit risks from exporters or banks to export credit agencies. In return for providing export credit insurance or guarantees, export credit agencies charge a premium. An exporter or bank that has obtained export credit insurance or a guarantee from an ECA is called the insured.

ECA cover

In this book, the term 'ECA cover' is used for both export credit insurance and export credit guarantees.

Classification of a transaction as an export credit insurance or an export credit guarantee depends on the governing law of the transaction, but the terms of these transactions are similar and the transactions achieve the same economic effect. An export credit guarantee issued by an ECA in one country can be classified as an insurance contract in another and vice versa. In ordinary language both export credit insurance and export credit guarantees are called the export credit cover or the ECA cover, which is the term used in this book.

Export credit agency – ECA

An export credit agency (ECA) is a specialised institution that provides the ECA cover to exporters and banks. In providing the ECA cover, ECAs act on behalf of and with the financial support of their states. Therefore the state will compensate the loss incurred by an ECA in providing the ECA cover. The organisation and status of ECAs vary from country to country and they can be organised as a specialised bank, financial company, or insurance company acting on behalf of a state or an agency of state. The ECAs that are organised as banks or financial companies are wholly or partly owned by the state while insurance companies are usually privately owned but have a state mandate to act in the capacity of ECA.

Commercial or loan contract

In this book, the term 'commercial or loan contract' is defined as a contract in which the foreign buyer's payment obligation is agreed on credit terms and for which the ECA cover is issued. A commercial contract is entered into between an exporter and foreign buyer and a loan between a bank and a foreign buyer.

Claim and indemnification

The claim is a request for payment of indemnification made by an insured exporter or bank to an ECA. This book defines the term 'indemnification' as the payment made by an ECA to compensate for a loss caused to the insured exporter or bank by non-payment of credit by a foreign buyer.

Official support

Official support means providing the ECA cover with the financial support of a state. This means the risk of non-payment of export credit covered by an ECA is assumed by the state.

The Arrangement (Consensus)

The most important international document that regulates the provision of the ECA cover is the OECD (Organisation for Economic Co-operation and Development) Arrangement on Officially Supported Export Credits. Several OECD countries, called the participating countries, adopted this document. The Arrangement does not have formal status in law but it is considered binding by the participating countries, which are: Australia, Canada, the European Community (including all EU member states), Japan, Korea, New Zealand, Norway, Switzerland and the United States.

Premium

In this book, the term 'premium' is defined as a fee charged by ECAs for issuing the ECA cover for the risk of non-payment of credit by a foreign buyer. The premium charged by ECAs is expressed as a percentage of the amount of credit for which the ECA cover is issued. ECAs usually request the entire amount of premium to be paid in advance.

Security

The term 'security' is defined as a right provided by a foreign buyer to an exporter or bank in an asset owned by the foreign buyer, for the purpose of securing payment of a credit. It is also defined as a guarantee or surety provided by a third party for securing payment of a foreign buyer's credit.

2
ECAs and Users of the ECA Cover

The development of export credit agencies (ECAs) has followed development of world trade, globalisation of economies and the international regulation of officially supported export credits. Today, ECAs provide the ECA cover in a similar way, but there are still differences in their status and organisation. Some of these differences are the result of various historic developments of ECAs within their countries, but most are the result of differences in national economies and national exports they support.

The users of the ECA cover are exporters that sell goods or services to foreign buyers on credit terms and banks or other lending financial institutions that provide loans to foreign buyers to purchase goods or services from the countries of export. The terms 'exporter' and 'bank' are simple when analysed in the ECA context, but the status of exporters and banks is shifting because of changes in the global economy and the new ways of structuring export transactions. Many exporters no longer fit the classic picture of a national manufacturer and exporter, and the status and organisation of banks have changed to deal with international transactions. Changes of status and organisation of exporters and banks and the new ways in which they structure export transactions may affect their eligibility to obtain the ECA cover.

2.1 The Status of ECAs

Based on their legal status, ECAs can be classified into three groups. The first group includes the ECAs incorporated as banks or financial companies wholly or partly owned by a state. When incorporated as a bank they are organised according to the export–import bank model. The second group are the ECAs established as private insurance companies acting on behalf of a state. Such ECAs owe their duties to a ministry of finance or other ministries that provide official support to national export. The provision of the ECA cover by these ECAs is separated from their regular insurance business that is conducted without official support. The third group are ECAs that have the status of government agencies, acting in the capacity of the state when providing the ECA cover. When covering export credit risks through a government agency, the state acts in the capacity of insurer.

A common characteristic of all types of ECAs described above is that they receive, or may receive when necessary, financial support from their states.

Besides providing the ECA cover, some ECAs provide direct loans. These loans are provided by ECAs directly to foreign buyers to purchase goods or services from an ECA country. In some countries, a single ECA provides both the ECA cover and direct loans, while in other countries these two functions are separated in a way that one ECA issues the ECA cover and the other provides the ECA direct loans. This type of loan is analysed in Chapter 11.

Despite differences in their legal status and organisational forms, ECAs conduct their business in a very similar way. This is a result of similar commercial and loan contracts that ECAs cover, comprehensive international regulation applied in their business and similarity of standard terms governing the ECA policies issued to exporters and banks.

2.2   Purpose

Historically, the main purpose of establishing ECAs was to support national export. In the early nineteenth century, the governments of industrialised countries became aware that domestic private insurance companies were unwilling to provide credit insurance to national exporters when selling abroad on credit terms. Among other reasons for the unwillingness of private insurance companies to insure export credit risks were long payment terms of credits, difficulties in assessing the ability of foreign buyers to pay credits, and a lack of experience in recovering losses in foreign countries and assessing political developments in the world at that time. Since the lack of export credit insurance could negatively affect the economies of the industrialised countries that were oriented to export, some governments decided to insure the export credit risks themselves through special institutions called export credit agencies.

The private insurers' ability to insure export credit risks has improved since the early nineteenth century, but demand for the officially supported cover for export credit risks is still high and ECAs are still very active in providing it. Today's private insurers are willing to insure the short-term export credit risks while the medium- to long-term risks are still covered by ECAs with official support from their states.

Providing the ECA cover and direct loans to foreign buyers is regulated internationally. The international framework is applied by ECAs from the countries that participate in the OECD Arrangement and from the EU member states. The international legal framework applied by these ECAs is analysed in Chapters 21 and 22.

Terminology – ECA products

ECAs provide various types of insurance and guarantees to cover credit risks and other types of risks analysed in Part II of this book. These types of insurance and guarantees are sometimes called products, a modern term for financial services provided by banks and other financial institutions. Although the term 'product' is not inappropriate, the term 'ECA cover' is generally accepted and therefore is used in this book for all types of insurance and guarantees provided by ECAs.

2.3   Official support

The term 'official support', which indicates involvement of a state, can be unclear when used in the export credit context. There are two forms in which official support is provided by the governments in the countries of export: the first is insuring credit risks by providing the ECA cover and the second is providing the ECA direct loans to foreign buyers for purchasing goods or services from the countries of export.

A comparison between the private export credit insurance and the officially supported ECA cover for export credit risks is a good illustration of the term 'official support'. It is possible to obtain credit insurance for short-term export credits from private insurance companies in many exporting countries, but private insurance companies have limits for various credit risks and they are not willing to exceed them by insuring new risks. In addition, private insurers may not be willing to insure medium- to long-term export credit risks.

On the other hand, ECAs provide the ECA cover to national exporters on behalf of their states. One of the advantages of this type of insurance is that it is created to insure export credit risks only and the capacity of ECAs for insuring the short-term and medium- to long-term credit risks is considerably larger.

Another advantage of the ECA cover supported by a state is that a state cannot become bankrupt. This means that this type of insurance is safe even when a loss reserve of an ECA is not sufficient for payment of all claims to the insured exporters and banks. If such a situation occurs, the state will provide additional funds to the ECA to pay all claims, while if a private insurance company becomes insolvent and cannot pay claims, the state will not support it with additional funds. Private insurance companies can become insolvent or made bankrupt, which is a specific risk that must be taken into account when purchasing insurance from them.

The second form of official support is providing the ECA direct loans to foreign buyers for purchasing goods or services from the countries of export (Figure 2.1). These loans are provided with fixed interest rates that could be attractive for foreign buyers because the private lenders, commercial banks, usually are not willing to provide loans with fixed interest rates for financing

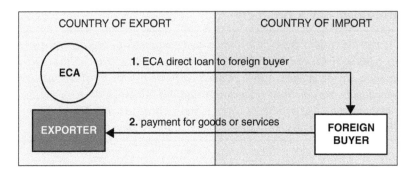

Figure 2.1   ECA direct loan

commercial transactions. The fixed interest rates cannot be agreed upon below an internationally accepted minimum and such fixed rates are sometimes less favourable than floating interest rates. However, an ECA direct loan with a fixed interest rate can be a better alternative and an incentive for a foreign buyer to purchase goods or services from a particular country of export. Besides fixed interest rates, official support is sometimes manifested in an ECA's willingness to provide a direct loan in a situation where commercial banks are not willing to do so.

2.4   Users of the ECA cover

The basic rule applied by ECAs provides that an exporter is eligible to obtain the ECA cover from the ECA in the country of its incorporation. This is because the ECA from the exporter's country has a mandate to support the national export and it will not provide cover to exporters from other countries. For the same reason, the exporter is not eligible for cover from ECAs from other countries. This rule seems clear but its interpretation may be uncertain because of the complexity of transactions and involvement of foreign participants on the exporter's side.

The mandate of an ECA may be restricted when requested to issue cover in transactions where both contractual parties are from the country of import, when the exported goods contain components purchased from third countries and when third parties are involved in an export credit transaction. These and other similar issues are analysed in more detail in Chapters 7, 8 and 14.

2.5   Meaning of the term 'exporter'

In the ECA context, the ordinary meaning of the term 'exporter' is a company incorporated in the country where goods are manufactured for export to a foreign buyer. An exporter of services may perform its services for a foreign buyer either in the country of its incorporation, the buyer's country or a third country. This is the classic meaning of the term 'exporter', which applies to numerous transactions covered by ECAs, especially where the exporter is a small or medium-sized company.

However, 'exporter' is more complex when analysing large manufacturers organised as multinational companies with subsidiaries in foreign countries. The export transactions entered into by multinational companies can be complicated because their foreign subsidiaries often act as their agents, distributors or intermediaries when selling goods or services to foreign buyers in the countries of import. Sometimes the goods are assembled or partly manufactured in the country of import and sold locally. Sometimes the goods are partly or completely manufactured in third countries and then shipped to the country of import without having any direct connection with the country where the company acting as a seller is incorporated. Structuring export transactions by involving subsidiaries from foreign countries is the result of economic globalisation and reorganisation of multinational companies in order to minimise manufacturing and transaction costs.

However, even multinational companies sell their goods or services on credit terms and they need the ECA cover for credit risks assumed in their export credit transactions. When asked to issue cover in a complex export transaction, an ECA has to analyse all aspects of a transaction before making a decision. This analysis includes elements such as identifying the company acting as an exporter and its relationship with the company acting as an importer, assessing the foreign content in goods or services to be supplied to a foreign buyer and the mandate of an ECA to issue cover for a particular transaction.

There are several issues that may arise when dealing with complex export credit transactions. One of these issues is the participation of ECAs from other countries in covering a credit risk. This may be arranged when some components are manufactured in other countries and later assembled as the final product exported from the country of export. If other ECAs are not willing or cannot participate in covering such export credit risks, the question of whether the ECA from the country of export should cover the entire risk will arise. When an ECA determines the cover cannot be issued for a particular transaction, the question is whether the exporter may structure the transaction in another way that is more acceptable to the ECA. These and other issues are analysed in Chapter 7.

2.6 Meaning of the term 'bank'

In the ECA context, the term 'bank' is used for a bank providing a loan to a foreign buyer for purchasing goods or services from a country of export. This term includes other financial lending institutions that provide loans without being registered as banks and without holding the bank licence. Unlike exporters, both banks and other financial institutions are usually under a special supervision of financial authorities in their countries of incorporation.

Due to economic globalisation, some large banks have expanded their businesses to numerous foreign countries around the world. These banks are called multinational or global banks. However, the way banks expand their businesses abroad is different from the way multinational companies expand. The difference is that banks usually set up branches, rather than subsidiaries, in foreign countries. Unlike a subsidiary, a branch is not an independent legal entity but an extension of the bank. In other words, the branch is an organisational part of a bank, acting under the same name as the bank and assuming the rights and liabilities in the bank's name and for the bank's account. However, the legal status of a branch of foreign bank can be regulated in various ways and in some jurisdictions a branch may be treated as an independent legal entity.

The provision of the ECA cover to the banks through their branches is another complex issue that is described in more detail in Chapter 8.

2.7   The insured under the ECA policy

The insured under an ECA policy is the entity to which the policy is issued and whose name is stated in the policy document. Such entity is either an exporter, established as a company, or a bank. Theoretically, individuals may be insured in the capacity of exporter but, in reality, it would be unusual that an individual applies for the ECA cover.

The term 'insured' is common in the ECA business, but the terms 'policy-holder' and 'guarantee-holder' are also used; to avoid confusion, only 'insured' is used this book. Similarly, the ECA policy is sometimes called the guarantee but the term ECA policy is used in the text for simplicity.

2.8   Beneficiary of the ECA policy

When an exporter obtains the ECA policy for a credit agreed upon in its commercial contract with a foreign buyer, it may sell its claim for payment to a bank at a discount before the due date for payment. When entering into such a transaction, the exporter is asked to assign its rights under the ECA policy to the bank that purchases the claim for payment against the foreign buyer. Once the rights under the ECA policy are assigned to the bank, it becomes the beneficiary under the ECA policy.

The capacity of a beneficiary under an ECA policy is distinguished from the capacity of an insured. The beneficiary assumes only the rights under the policy where the right to claim indemnification from the ECA is the most important. The insured assumes both rights and obligations when obtaining the ECA policy. After assigning the rights under the policy to a bank, the insured retains all obligations. This means that the insured is obligated to engage in avoiding or mitigating loss in a claim recovery from the foreign buyer, etc.

The assignment of rights under the ECA policy is sometimes called the security or the collateral, but for the purpose of simplicity, the term 'assignment of rights' is used in this book. Assignment of rights under an ECA policy is analysed in Chapter 6.

3
Political and Commercial Risks

The risks covered by ECAs are usually defined in ECA standard terms as political and commercial risks. However, in reality, ECAs actually cover the risk of non-payment of a credit caused by political and commercial events.

A classic example of a political event that may cause non-payment of a credit is war in the foreign buyer's country. War may affect the foreign buyer's business by destroying its facilities and making it impossible to continue the manufacturing process. The inability of the foreign buyer to manufacture and sell its products results in loss of its revenues and finally in non-payment of a credit to an exporter or bank. What ECAs cover in this example is the loss the exporter or bank incurs by non-receipt of the payment of credit, not the outbreak of war as such.

The occurrence of a political event covered by ECAs does not always cause non-payment of credit by a foreign buyer. It is possible the business of the foreign buyer is not affected by the war, which means that the buyer can continue the manufacturing process, sell its products, receive payments from its customers and make regular payments of the credit. In such a situation the exporter or bank receives payment of credit when due and no loss incurs. Consequently, the ECA that covers this credit risk cannot be claimed for indemnification on the grounds of occurrence of war only. In other words, the ECA in question has covered the risk of non-payment of the credit and not the risk of war as an event if it does not affect the foreign buyer's ability to pay the credit. This is an important distinction that is necessary to remember when analysing political risks that are actually political events.

The term 'commercial risk' can be explained in a similar way. If a foreign buyer becomes insolvent, the insolvency is just an event and the consequences may not be clear. Insolvency may be of a temporary nature, not affecting the foreign buyer's ability to pay the credit. When the insolvency of the foreign buyer is of a more permanent nature, causing non-payment of a credit and loss for an exporter or bank, such a loss is covered by ECAs. Insolvency that does not result in a loss for the exporter or bank is not covered by ECAs.

Although ECAs cover losses caused by political and commercial events, the expression that they cover political and commercial risks is still broadly used. The same expression is used in this book but it should always be understood that ECAs cover non-payment of a credit caused by political and commercial events (Figure 3.1).

The meaning of 'political risk' needs an additional explanation in this context. This book uses this term for political events only as they are described in this chapter. It is not used for the risk of non-payment of a credit by a state, also called a sovereign, when acting as a foreign buyer. This should be observed and these two meanings of the term political risk should be distinguished.

3.1 Time of occurrence of political and commercial events

As with insurance companies, ECAs cover losses caused by future uncertain events. A future event is an event that occurs after entering into a commercial or loan contract between the insured exporter or bank and the foreign buyer and after issuing the ECA policy. A loss caused by an event that occurred before issuing the ECA policy is not covered by ECAs. An event that occurred before issuing the ECA cover should have been known to an exporter or bank when applying for the ECA cover and disclosed to the ECA at that stage.

3.2 About definitions of political and commercial risks

The definitions of political and commercial risks ECAs provide in their standard terms are drafted in various ways, and some ECAs state they cover political and commercial risks without defining any of them. However, when comparing the existing definitions and the way ECAs apply them in practice, it appears that ECAs cover nearly the same political and commercial risks by applying definitions with different wording.

The common feature of all definitions used by ECAs is that their wording is very general and includes nearly all political and commercial risks known in international commercial and loan transactions. The general wording of these definitions makes the scope of the ECA cover very comprehensive, making it

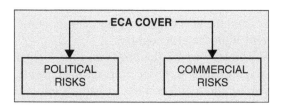

Figure 3.1   Risks included in ECA cover

safe and attractive for exporters and banks dealing with export credit risks. Overall, definitions of political risks are more comprehensive than definitions of commercial risks because political events may take many forms in different countries. However, even definitions of commercial risks, which are usually concise, can be interpreted in various ways, depending on where an event occurs.

It is difficult to select definitions of any single ECA as an example for analysis in this book because of the variety of definitions of political and commercial risks ECAs use. In addition, this book is not about any particular ECA or country but about common matters and aspects of providing ECA cover globally. Therefore, the analysis of definitions of political and commercial events that follows does not refer to any particular ECA. It is based on the Common Principles for Export Credit Insurance provided in the Annex to the EU Council Directive 98/29/EC of 7 May 1998 on harmonisation of the main provisions concerning export credit insurance for transactions with medium- and long-term cover. This book uses the definitions provided in the Common Principles as an example since they are not applied by the ECAs from the countries outside of the EU. However, the definitions used by other ECAs do not differ much from the definitions provided in the Common Principles.

The Common Principles contain definitions of six political and three commercial risks that are analysed below. These risks are called causes of loss, but they will be called risks in this book for the reason explained above. The definitions provided in the Common Principles also can be seen as specific guidelines for drafting standard terms for the ECAs from the EU member states. When included in the ECA standard terms, these definitions do not necessarily need to be structured in the same way or have identical wording.

3.3   Definitions of political events

According to the Common Principles, the following political events are usually covered by ECAs:

a) Decision of a third country
This is a legislative, administrative or other decision of a state that prevents performance of a commercial or loan contract. This definition distinguishes the third country from the ECA country or the country of the insured exporter or bank, if different from the ECA country.

This definition primarily covers the decision of the foreign buyer's country, the country of import, since such decisions most frequently prevent performance of commercial and loan contracts. A ban on import of specific goods imposed by the foreign buyer's country is a typical example of such a decision

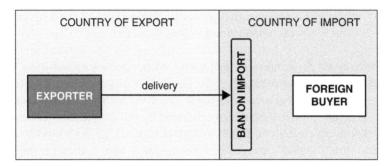

Figure 3.2   Ban on import as political event

(Figure 3.2). The ban on import must be chronologically imposed after the date when the exporter and foreign buyer have entered into the contract. An existing ban on import, imposed before entering into the contract, must be known to the exporter and it cannot be treated as a political event by an ECA.

Export credit transactions usually involve the country of export and the country of import, where the latter is also called the foreign buyer's country. Third countries are not normally involved in such transactions in the way of making decisions that may cause non-performance of a commercial or loan contract. However, such situations may arise when a contract is connected with a third country. An example is a commercial contract for supplying equipment for which an exporter purchases some components from a third country and then assembles them into the final product delivered to a foreign buyer. If the exporter has a contractual obligation to maintain the equipment after its delivery to the foreign buyer, the exporter will be prevented from performing its obligation if the third country bans export of the components necessary for the maintenance. Non-maintenance of the equipment delivered to the foreign buyer constitutes a breach of the commercial contract by the exporter, and the foreign buyer is entitled to withhold payment of the credit to the exporter. In this example, performance of the contract has been prevented by a decision of a third country and, as a consequence, the exporter incurs a loss by non-receiving payment of credit. If non-payment of the credit is covered by an ECA, and the cover includes political risks, the exporter is entitled to claim indemnification from the ECA for the loss incurred in this way.

The above definition excludes decisions of the ECA country and the country of the insured exporter or bank if different from the ECA country. The ECA country and the insured's country are usually the same because ECAs deal mainly with exporters and banks from their countries. However, it is not unusual that a bank that provides a loan to a foreign buyer is from a third country outside of the ECA country and the foreign buyer's country. The insured bank's country may make a decision that prevents performance of the loan contract but such situation is excluded from the definition above.

b) Decision of the ECA country or the insured exporter or bank's country

This definition includes measures of the European Community relating to trade between an EU member state and third countries such as a ban on exports, insofar as its effects are not covered otherwise by the government concerned.

This definition covers two situations excluded from the definition above. In this definition, the performance of a commercial or loan contract is prevented by a decision of the ECA country or the insured exporter or bank's country, if different from the ECA country. Additionally, the definition includes measures of the European Community related to third countries such as a ban on exports, which also may prevent performance of a commercial or loan contract. Measures of the European Community mentioned in the definition above apply to the ECAs from EU member states only.

The wording of this definition is usually extended by various ECAs to include decisions of the United Nations and other decisions made internationally within an international organisation or multilaterally between several states. Such decisions may prevent the performance of a commercial or loan contract and they constitute political risks covered by ECAs. An example of such a decision made by an ECA country is a ban on export (Figure 3.3) or imposing other trade sanctions against the foreign buyer's country.

Some ECAs exclude unilateral decisions made by their countries that are not based on an international agreement from the definition above. If an ECA country's unilateral decision prevents the performance of a commercial or loan contract, the loss caused to the exporter or bank is not covered by these ECAs.

c) Moratorium

In this context, a moratorium can be described as a decision to postpone or suspend a foreign buyer's payment obligation so an exporter or bank cannot

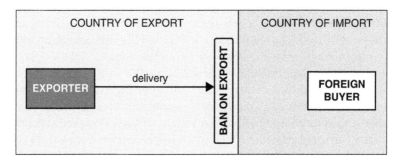

Figure 3.3 Ban on export as political event

enforce the claim for payment of credit against the foreign buyer. A moratorium can be imposed either by the foreign buyer's country or by a third country through which the parties agree to transfer payment in a commercial or loan contract. Historically, moratoriums were imposed by governments in the countries of foreign buyers while a moratorium imposed by a third country rarely affects export credit transactions.

d) Prevention or delay in the transfer of funds
This definition includes legislative or administrative measures, political events or economic difficulties, which are taken or occur out of the ECA's country and which prevent or delay the transfer of payment of credit made by a foreign buyer under a commercial or loan contract. This means that the transfer of payment may be stopped or delayed either in a foreign buyer's country or in a third country.

The usual reason for a foreign buyer's country to take these measures is the lack of foreign currency, when the state uses the available amounts of foreign currency for prioritised purposes. In addition, the transfer of a foreign buyer's payment can be prevented or delayed due to amended foreign exchange regulations in its country or for other reasons. It is useful to explain that prevention or delay in transfer of payment caused by a decision of a foreign buyer's country is the most important political risk for which exporters and banks seek ECA cover (Figure 3.4).

Transfer of payment may also be prevented or delayed by decisions and measures taken by a third country that is not the ECA country or the foreign buyer's country. The risk of such an event is not insignificant in the globalised world where international payments are made through integrated bank payment systems. The function of these payment systems can be affected by unilateral decisions of third countries to prevent money laundering, impose sanctions or achieve other purposes. ECAs are aware that such events may occur in third countries and these events are usually included in their cover for transferring risks.

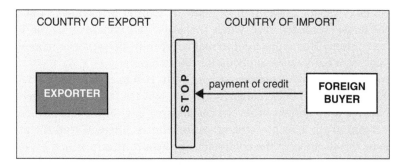

Figure 3.4 Prevention or delay in transfer of payment

The definition above excludes decisions and legislative measures taken by the ECA country that may prevent or delay the transfer of payment made by a foreign buyer. This means that an ECA will not indemnify the insured exporter or bank for a loss caused in this way; this is important to remember. However, many ECAs do not apply this exclusion to decisions and measures taken by the ECA country when they are based on the decisions of the United Nations, the EU or are agreed upon internationally. Therefore, the above exclusion applies only to unilateral decisions and measures taken by the ECA country.

Place of payment

When analysing a political event it is important to determine the place of payment in a commercial or loan contract. The usual place of payment agreed upon in export credit transactions is the country of the insured exporter or bank, which means the foreign buyer's payment obligation is fulfilled when the payment is received by the insured's bank. The payment is not completed when the foreign buyer's bank has attempted to transfer payment to the insured's bank but the transfer has stopped somewhere on the way between the two banks.

ECAs usually cover the risk connected with transfer of payment in the manner agreed in the commercial or loan contract. In other words, non-receipt of payment in the agreed upon place of payment will be treated by ECAs as a loss incurred by the insured exporter or bank. Therefore it is important for the insured exporter or bank to state in the commercial or loan contract that the place of payment is out of the foreign buyer's country in order to include this risk in the ECA cover. The ECA cover usually includes any place of payment out of the foreign buyer's country, whether in the insured's country or a place in a third country.

Some commercial or loan contracts provide that the place of payment is in the foreign buyer's country. In such transactions the risk of preventing or delaying the transfer of payment out of the foreign buyer's country does not exist and it is not included in the ECA cover. However, some ECAs provide additional cover for prevention or delay in transfer of payments out of the foreign buyer's country even when the place of payment is in the foreign buyer's country. This type of additional cover must be expressly requested by an exporter or bank when applying for the ECA cover.

A commercial or loan contract covered by an ECA may provide that a foreign buyer will issue a bill of exchange (draft) for payment of a credit or several bills of exchange for payment of several instalments of a credit. The place of payment stated in the bills of exchange is sometimes different from the place of payment agreed upon in the commercial or loan contract covered by an ECA. Such discrepancy may create confusion regarding the scope of the ECA cover and it needs to be clarified in the commercial or loan contract.

e) Legal provisions adopted in the foreign buyer's country

This definition includes legal provisions declaring payment made by a foreign buyer in local currency to be a valid discharge of the debt, notwithstanding that, as result of fluctuations in exchange rates, such payments, when converted into the currency of the commercial or loan contract, no longer cover the amount of debt at the date of transfer of payment (Figure 3.5).

This particular political event is not unusual in practice and adopting the legislation described above can cause a loss to an exporter or a bank. The loss consists of receiving payment in a local currency far below the real value of the payment in a foreign currency. Some ECA standard terms do not define this particular political event, probably because they consider it covered by a very broad wording of definition (a), analysed above.

f) Force majeure

This political event includes events occurring outside the ECA country, including war, civil war, riot, civil disturbance, natural catastrophes such as cyclone, flood, earthquake, volcanic eruption, tidal wave and nuclear accident insofar as its effects are not insured otherwise.

In the ECA context, all force majeure events are considered political events even though some—natural catastrophes and nuclear accidents—are not of a political nature. Force majeure events, which are beyond control of the contractual parties, may prevent the parties from performing some of their contractual obligations with the effect that the parties are discharged from these obligations. This may cause a loss to an insured exporter or bank, and such losses are usually covered by ECAs. The scope of force majeure clauses used by ECAs may vary regarding the number of events included in these clauses. The interpretation of force majeure clauses may cause some difficulties since some events are not foreseeable and when they occur it can be argued that they are not covered by a particular definition. The definition above sometimes excludes force majeure events that occur in the ECA country. Some ECAs do not make this exclusion and cover all force majeure events wherever they occur.

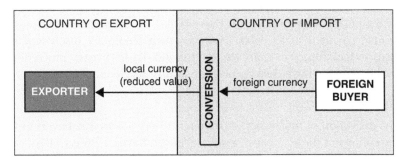

Figure 3.5 Conversion and payment in local currency

3.4   Definitions of commercial events

ECAs use various definitions of commercial events but the differences between these definitions are not significant. The definitions provided in the Common Principles for Export Credit Insurance that constitute the Annex to the EU Directive 98/29/EC from 1998 can be used to illustrate commercial events covered by ECAs. According to the Common Principles the following commercial events are covered by ECAs:

a) Insolvency of a private buyer and, if any, its guarantor, either de jure or de facto
This definition requires a short explanation of the terms 'insolvency de jure', 'insolvency de facto', 'private buyer' and 'insolvency of the guarantor'.

Insolvency

In this context, the term 'insolvency' may be explained as the inability of a foreign buyer to pay its debts as they fall due. This is a general definition but national legislation may contain different definitions of insolvency. For example, one definition of insolvency is the inability of a foreign buyer to pay its debts as they fall due when the inability is not of a temporary character. This definition is less strict than the first, since it gives some time to the foreign buyer to find a solution for its temporary insolvency problems before it is treated as insolvent. Some legislations define insolvency by reference to the minimum amount of debt that is not paid by the foreign buyer when due. Based on different definitions of insolvency, national legislation is sometimes characterised as creditor-friendly or debtor-friendly.

In the context of the ECA cover insolvency de jure is insolvency in which all legislative requirements for classifying a foreign buyer as insolvent are satisfied. Insolvency de facto, on the other hand, is the foreign buyer's inability to pay its debts in spite of demand for payment having been made by a creditor. The de facto insolvency is usually manifested by the foreign buyer's failure to pay a debt when due, but the foreign buyer may admit or declare its inability to pay its debts before they fall due. The de facto insolvency can be temporary when the foreign buyer is able to reorganise its business and resume payment of its debts. However, such temporary insolvency often leads to bankruptcy or filing for another judicial insolvency proceeding by which a foreign buyer seeks protection against its creditors.

Private buyer

The definition of insolvency above refers to private foreign buyers only. In the context of the ECA cover, a private foreign buyer is always a legal entity, usually incorporated as a company. Individuals rarely take part in export credit transactions but if they do they are also treated as private buyers.

When explaining the term 'private buyer', it is useful to mention two categories of foreign buyers called sovereigns and public buyers. A sovereign is a state or a state entity such as a government, ministry, department or other authority that enters into an export credit transaction when purchasing goods or services. Sovereigns are distinguished from private and public buyers because they cannot be liquidated in a bankruptcy proceeding. Therefore this category of foreign buyers is not included in the definition above. The second category of foreign buyers is a company owned or controlled wholly or in majority by a state or government. Such foreign buyers are usually called public foreign buyers but they must be distinguished from sovereigns because they cannot validly bind the state and they can be made bankrupt. Finally, a private buyer is a foreign buyer that is neither sovereign nor public. These three categories of foreign buyers are analysed in Chapter 20.

Insolvency of the guarantor

The above definition includes insolvency of a guarantor as an additional commercial risk in relation to the foreign buyer's insolvency. The insolvency of a guarantor is significant when a guarantee is issued as security for a foreign buyer's obligation to pay a credit. In transactions covered by ECAs, the third party that issues a guarantee is often the parent company of a foreign buyer. Providing a guarantee may positively affect an ECA's assessment of a credit risk and its willingness to provide the ECA cover.

Where a guarantee is provided by a third party and a foreign buyer has defaulted on payment of credit, the insured exporter or bank is obligated to demand payment under the guarantee as a condition for claiming indemnification from the ECA. The insured exporter or bank becomes entitled to claim indemnification from the ECA if the guarantor does not make payment under the guarantee within the time period stipulated in the guarantee. When the guarantor makes payment under the guarantee, the foreign buyer's payment obligation is discharged, the credit has been paid and no indemnification will be paid by the ECA.

In practice, it is not unusual that both the foreign buyer and the guarantor become insolvent, especially in situations where the guarantee is issued by a company that is a parent company of the foreign buyer. Financial difficulties that affect subsidiaries often affect their parent companies and vice versa, and a guarantee issued by a parent company for a payment obligation of a subsidiary can become worthless due to the parent's insolvency.

Some ECAs do not include the insolvency of the guarantor in their standardised definitions of insolvency of the foreign buyer because they state elsewhere in their standard terms that the insured exporter or bank is required to demand payment under a guarantee before claiming indemnification from the ECA. The insolvency of the guarantor is implied by this requirement that must be satisfied before the insured claims indemnification from the ECA.

Insolvency of both the foreign buyer and its guarantor may occur before the credit is due for payment. This may simplify the procedure for demanding payment from the guarantor before claiming indemnification from the ECA because the demand is not necessary when the guarantor has been declared insolvent.

b) Default of the foreign buyer and, if any, its guarantor

The default of a foreign buyer may occur in two forms—payment default and a breach of a non-payment obligation that is stipulated as default in loan agreements and less frequently in commercial contracts. The payment default is failure of a foreign buyer to make payment of a credit that is due according to a commercial or loan contract. The foreign buyer's payment default is almost always caused by financial difficulties but it can also be caused by a mistake or other reasons.

Breach of other contractual obligations such as the breach of a covenant included in a loan agreement may be stipulated in a contract as default. In loan agreements, a covenant is an obligation of the foreign buyer that is different from its obligation to repay the loan. A covenant may provide for the foreign buyer's obligation to maintain financial ratios in its business; this covenant is called a financial covenant. Examples of other covenants include restrictions on disposal of the foreign buyer's assets, negative pledge clause, or a pari passu clause. The foreign buyer's breach of a covenant may occur before payment default and such a breach is seen as an early warning that the foreign buyer is underperforming in its business. This also increases the risk that the foreign buyer might default on repayment of the loan. Due to the seriousness of such a breach, loan agreements provide that the breach of a covenant constitutes a default similar to non-repayment of the loan. When a covenant is breached, this default entitles the bank to use all contractual remedies against the foreign buyer as with a payment default.

Difference between insolvency and payment default

The above analysis of insolvency and payment default gives rise to the question of what the difference is between these two commercial risks. They are very similar and sometimes used synonymously in everyday language.

The most important difference between insolvency and payment default is that they do not necessarily occur simultaneously. It is possible that a foreign buyer declares its insolvency and suspension of payment of its debts before the debts fall due. This means that the foreign buyer has become insolvent but payment default has not yet occurred. When a suspension of payments, also called a standstill, has been declared by the foreign buyer, it is a signal for both the insured and the ECA to try to protect the insured's claim for payment against the foreign buyer. It is also possible that a bankruptcy petition is filed against the foreign buyer before the payment of credit to the insured exporter or bank is due. When a bankruptcy procedure has started, the insured exporter or bank cannot usually do much to protect the claim for payment unless it is secured in some way.

An adverse situation is possible in which the payment default occurs but the foreign buyer is not insolvent. This is a relatively frequent situation that may occur for several reasons. For example, the foreign buyer earns its revenues in local currency and is obligated to pay a credit in a foreign currency. Obtaining foreign currency for payment of credit can take some time and may delay payment of credit. There is no doubt that such a payment delay constitutes payment default according to the commercial or loan contract covered by an ECA, but the foreign buyer is not insolvent. In reality, exporters and banks accept shorter payment delays caused by this event because the default is not caused by the insolvency of a foreign buyer.

c) Arbitrary repudiation or refusal

This is a foreign buyer's decision to interrupt or cancel the commercial contract entered into on credit terms or to refuse to accept goods or services without being entitled to do so.

The term 'repudiation', also called anticipatory breach of contract, comes from English law and applies to situations in which an innocent party to a contract understands from words or conduct of the other contractual party that the other contractual party does not intend to perform its contractual obligation. This must occur before the due date for performance of the contractual obligation of the other party and the innocent party has a right to treat the contract as discharged and claim damages from the other party. Such actions by the innocent party are called repudiation and they are justified in the circumstances described above. There should be no negative consequences for the innocent party to repudiate the contract.

The problem with repudiation is that it may be unjustified. An unjustified or arbitrary repudiation arises when a party, in this case a foreign buyer, mistakenly believes that the exporter does not intend to perform its contractual obligation and repudiates the contract on the grounds of that mistaken belief. An arbitrary repudiation is wrongful because the foreign buyer that treats itself as innocent does not have justification for repudiation.

The definition above applies only when the foreign buyer arbitrarily repudiates a commercial contract. A justified repudiation, when the foreign buyer has the right to repudiate a contract, is not included in the definition above and is not covered by ECAs.

It can be very difficult for an ECA to determine whether a foreign buyer has repudiated the commercial contract arbitrarily or in other words, wrongfully.

If the foreign buyer's repudiation is not obviously wrong, the ECA will instruct the insured exporter to obtain a judgment of court or an arbitration award proving its right to claim payment of the credit from the foreign buyer. ECAs cannot judge in disputes between the insured exporter and the foreign buyer, and this is the only way to determine whether the insured exporter is entitled to be indemnified by the ECA. This issue is analysed in Chapter 19.

Another event included in the definition above is a refusal of the foreign buyer to accept goods or services without being entitled to do so. Such refusal must be distinguished from the arbitrary repudiation described above because the refusal occurs later than the arbitrary repudiation. The general understanding is that a refusal of goods or services is possible only if the goods or services are ready for delivery and the exporter attempted to deliver them to the foreign buyer.

There are many wrongful reasons for rejection of goods or services by foreign buyers, some intentional and some unintentional. An example of an intentional rejection of goods occurs when the foreign buyer has entered into a contract for purchase of goods for resale. If the price of goods decreases substantially before their delivery to the foreign buyer, the resale of the goods at the lower price would result in a loss for the foreign buyer. The foreign buyer may try to escape from this situation by rejecting the goods without being entitled to do so.

An example of an unintentional wrongful rejection of goods by the foreign buyer is a mistaken belief that the goods do not conform to the commercial contract. If it is later found that the goods conformed to the contract, the foreign buyer's refusal of goods constitutes a breach of contract. These are just two examples to illustrate refusal of goods or services by the foreign buyer, but many other situations may arise.

Even in this case it can be difficult for an ECA to determine whether the foreign buyer was entitled to refuse the goods. If refusal is not obviously wrong, the ECA will probably instruct the insured exporter to obtain a court decision or an arbitration award proving its right to claim payment from the foreign buyer. ECAs cannot judge in disputes between the insured and the foreign buyer, and this is the only way to determine whether the insured is entitled to indemnification from the ECA.

3.5   Exclusion of documentation risk

In their standard terms, some ECAs state that their cover does not include documentation risks connected with the commercial or loan contracts they cover. Such risks are usually described as invalidity, illegality or unenforceability of a commercial or loan contract entered into between an exporter or bank and the foreign buyer.

Some ECAs that do not cover the documentation risk do not read the commercial and loan contracts for which they issue the ECA cover, while some do. When requesting information about particular contractual provisions in a commercial or loan contract, some ECAs avoid comments on the wording of these provisions. Despite requesting an insured exporter or bank to structure a commercial or loan contract in a particular way or to include a particular provision in the contract, such ECAs usually refrain from drafting or proposing the wording of any contractual provision. The reason that ECAs deal with commercial or loan contracts in this way is so that they avoid liability for the contractual documentation.

It is not difficult to understand why some ECAs exclude liability for contractual documentation from the ECA cover they provide. Such ECAs deal with a huge number of different international commercial and loan contracts that are governed by various national laws and it is very difficult for an ECA to gather knowledge of each national law that might govern an underlying commercial or loan contract in order to critically review the contractual provisions. Instead, it is more practical and less time consuming to exclude liability for contractual documentation from the ECA cover.

3.6   Distinction between documentation risk and legal risk

Liability for contractual documentation is sometimes called liability for legal risks, but the term 'legal risks' should be used with caution in the context of the ECA cover. This is because the term legal risks can be understood in different ways by the various parties.

In the ECA context, legal risk should not be confused with measures or decisions of a foreign buyer's country or a third country preventing performance of a commercial or loan contract or preventing transfer of payment made by a foreign buyer. Such measures or decisions constitute political events and they are usually made by adopting new legislation in the form of statutes or secondary legislation. Adoption of a new legislation in a third country could be a legal risk but ECAs have classified such events as political risks that are regularly included in the ECA cover. The term 'political risks' has very broad meaning in the ECA context and it is better to say that some ECAs exclude liability for the contractual documentation and avoid using 'legal risks' in this context.

3.7   Risk assessment procedures

Since ECAs provide cover for political and commercial risks, they must assess these risks before issuing an ECA policy. Assessing political and commercial risks is not specific to ECAs because many other participants in international financial and commercial transactions make similar assessments and projections. Therefore the short description that follows is about procedures ECAs apply in the assessment process and not about methods for assessing political and commercial risks.

3.8   Assessment of political risks

When assessing political risks connected with an individual export credit transaction, ECAs analyse whether future political developments could have a negative impact on a foreign buyer's ability to pay a credit. The starting point of this assessment is an ECA country credit policy for covering credit risks in the country of a foreign buyer. ECAs study political risks for the majority of countries in the world and establish country credit policies that are updated periodically. Depending on what is provided in a current country credit policy an ECA may decide whether to issue the ECA cover for a particular credit risk. Many ECAs publish their country policies on their websites making them available to potential applicants for the ECA cover. It is possible that the political situation in the country of a potential foreign buyer has suddenly and unexpectedly deteriorated and the ECA credit policy for that country has not been updated. In this situation, the ECA will not apply the outdated country credit policy and it may decide to await political developments or decide not to issue cover for the credit.

Assessment of a political risk and adopting a country credit policy includes analysis of several factors such as transferability of foreign currency out of the foreign buyer's country, political decisions affecting import into the country, risk of war, riots or commotions, international or bilateral decisions on embargo, sanctions against the country, etc. An ECA country credit policy adopted for a particular foreign country expresses the individual perception of an individual ECA; such a policy may differ from other ECA country credit policies adopted for the same country. Variations in the ECA country credit policies arise because the various ECAs may analyse different elements in their assessments, or the same elements in different ways.

An ECA country credit policy may differ from the OECD country classification used for calculating the minimum premium rates as explained in Chapter 13. However, a different assessment of a country risk by an ECA cannot affect the calculation of a premium charged for the ECA cover according to the OECD Arrangement. In practice, this means the premium cannot be charged under the minimum premium rate established according to the Arrangement. Otherwise, ECAs are allowed to classify a foreign country in a higher category of risk and charge a higher premium rate than the minimum premium rate.

Assessment of a political risk by an ECA is related to a concrete country and export credit transaction and it should not be confused with the political events covered by ECAs that are analysed in this chapter. The occurrence of these political events may cause non-payment of a credit by the foreign buyer only after issuing the ECA policy. Assessment of the political risks, on the other hand, is made by ECAs before issuing the ECA policy for an export credit risk. Once the ECA policy is issued, the ECA is bound by it and no subsequent amendment of the terms governing the ECA policy can be made.

3.9 Assessment of commercial risks

When assessing a commercial risk, ECAs analyse the probability of non-payment of a credit by a foreign buyer caused by insolvency or bankruptcy. In order to make this assessment, ECAs need detailed information about the foreign buyer company, its financial standing and its business. This information contains details about the company's incorporation, total annual turnover, resources needed to make payments of its current and future debts, information about management, number of employees, etc. Another element of commercial risk assessment is an analysis of the willingness of the foreign buyer to pay its debts, also called a company's credit history.

In order to assess a commercial risk, ECAs require a credit report on a foreign buyer, which should be purchased from an independent credit information provider. The costs for purchasing a credit report are usually paid by the exporter or bank that applied for the ECA cover. The information about a foreign buyer obtained by exporters and banks while analysing and negotiating an export credit transaction is also used by ECAs in their assessment of commercial risk. Other sources of information about a foreign buyer include industry reports and analyses available to ECAs.

An exporter or bank's prior experience of dealing with a foreign buyer is important when an ECA assesses a commercial risk. If the experience is good it may positively influence an ECA to issue cover for a credit risk. The experience of an ECA that has previously covered credit risks on the same foreign buyer is also important for the assessment. When a foreign buyer has demonstrated ability to pay its debts, an ECA may issue additional cover for credit risks on the same foreign buyer if requested by an exporter or bank. To the contrary, the negative experience of previous credit transactions with a foreign buyer is a signal for caution. In such situations an ECA may require the foreign buyer to provide security for payment of credit, increase the premium, reduce the percentage of cover, or simply decide not to issue the ECA cover for the credit risk on that particular foreign buyer.

ECAs also analyse how long a foreign buyer has conducted its business. If the foreign buyer has been in business for a long time without disturbances and financial difficulties, the probability of covering a credit risk on such a foreign buyer is higher. ECAs are more cautious when assessing commercial risk on a foreign buyer that has been operating for a short period of time or a foreign buyer which is a newly established company. It is possible that ECAs decide not to issue cover for credit risks on companies that cannot provide reliable records for assessing the commercial risk.

Among other things, ECAs analyse whether the working capital of a foreign buyer company is sufficient for paying its debts as they fall due; if it is not sufficient, the company is not an acceptable risk for ECAs. Some exceptions to this rule are possible if the company receives additional funds from its shareholders or from another financer. However, if such funding is promised to the foreign buyer company, ECAs will ask whether it is made in the form of a legally binding and enforceable undertaking or in another form that is not legally binding. Another important element in the analysis of the foreign buyer is the company's profitability and net worth. An analysis of elements such as the position and strength of competitors of the foreign buyer at the market and willingness of the parent company of the foreign buyer to support it financially are also included in the assessment of commercial risks.

The assessment of commercial risks in short-term transactions is less detailed than the assessment of medium- to long-term transactions. When an exporter deals with a huge number of customers and has obtained the framework supplier credit policy, the exporter can be authorised by the ECA to make its own commercial risk assessments by applying the assessment method approved by the ECA. The framework ECA cover is analysed in Chapter 4.

Part II
Types of ECA Cover

4
Short-Term, Medium- to Long-Term and Partial Cover

ECAs classify export credit risks in several ways and the ECA terminology contains terms such as political and commercial risks, short-term risk, medium- to long-term risk, project risk, country risk, sovereign risk, transferring risk, currency risk, manufacturing risk, etc. Some of these terms are generally known but some have special meaning in the context of ECA cover and need further explanation.

4.1 Basic classification of risks

The basic classification of export credit risks is based on the duration of a credit. According to this classification there are two main types of credit risks—short-term and the medium- to long-term risks. Another type of risk, project finance risk, is sometimes mentioned as a third type in this classification, but it is a sub-type of the medium- to long-term risk instead of a special type of risk. Distinguishing between the short-term, medium- to long-term and project risks is significant for applying the international legal framework that regulates issuing the ECA cover for export credit risks. In addition, these types of credit risks are not assessed in the same way and ECAs process the applications for issuing the ECA cover for these risks in different ways. Finally, the ECA policies for covering short-term, medium- to long-term and project risks may contain different standard and special terms imposing obligations on an insured exporter or bank.

According to the OECD Arrangement, the short-term credit period is less than two years, while the medium- to long term credit period is two years or more. In international trade in general, and out of the ECA context, the sale of goods or services on a credit term shorter than one year is classified as short-term credit. All credits longer than one year are classified as medium- to long-term credits without making a strict distinction between the two.

ECAs may issue credit cover for both short-term and medium- to long-term transactions. ECAs from the EU member states cannot provide cover for short-term credit risks, as explained below and in Chapter 21.

4.2   Characteristics of short-term credit transactions

Short-term credit transactions are the dominant type of export credit transactions in global trade along with transactions where payment is made on delivery. The ECA cover for short-term export credits is also the major type of cover provided by ECAs.

Short-term credit is usually agreed on in transactions with specific types of goods or services, countries of import, foreign buyers and the export companies of specific size. Examples of trade with 180 days' credit include trade with raw materials, machine parts, consumer goods, semi products, tools and similar goods. Even when these goods are sold to a foreign buyer acting as a distributor, the payment is usually agreed as a short-term credit of 180 days or less. The characteristics of a country of import affect the duration of a short-term export credit because foreign buyers from developing countries are usually allowed longer credit payment terms, within the limit of two years. Foreign buyers from industrial countries usually accept shorter credit periods within the same limit. The cash flow of a foreign buyer's business and the size of an export company are also important for the duration of a short-term export credit. Small and medium-sized export companies usually allow shorter export credit terms while large exporters can allow longer credit terms to their foreign buyers, within the short-term credit limit of two years.

ECAs may cover all short-term export credits with durations of less than two years, provided that other ECA requirements are satisfied. However, the ECAs from the EU member states are limited in covering the short-term credits as explained below.

4.3   Characteristics of the short-term cover

The short-term ECA cover is distinguished from the medium- to long-term cover in several ways. The first distinction is the way in which ECAs process applications for issuing the short-term cover. This procedure is less comprehensive and less sophisticated than processing applications for issuing cover in medium- to long-term transactions because of the relatively small value of individual short-term transactions and the large volume of applications for this type of cover with which ECAs deal.

In order to simplify the work with applications for the short-term cover, ECAs may issue a framework cover that includes credit risks in all short-term export credit transactions of an exporter. This type of cover is usually called the whole turnover cover, but other types of the framework cover may be issued by ECAs as well. An ECA framework cover may include all short-term transactions of an exporter with a particular foreign buyer or transactions with all foreign buyers in a particular country of import, for example. The ECA framework cover is used mainly by exporters, but can also be issued to banks. Each ECA framework policy sets a limit of the highest amount of cover the insured exporter or bank cannot exceed without prior approval of the ECA. The ECA framework cover is sometimes called the comprehensive or line of credit cover (Figure 4.1).

By providing framework policies to cover a large number of short-term credit risks, ECAs save the time needed for processing individual short-term transactions and minimise their administrative costs. An insured exporter that has obtained the ECA framework policy for short-term transactions is obligated to provide the ECA with periodic reports on covered transactions, recovered amounts in transactions where indemnification was paid by the ECA and provide other information the ECA may request.

Issuing the framework policies is not the only way for ECAs to cover the short-term export credit risks. Many exporters and banks request cover for individual short-term credit risks and ECAs provide cover for a significant number of individual short-term credit transactions.

Short-term ECA cover is distinguished from medium- to long-term cover by the way the premiums are calculated by the ECAs. In general, the premium rates charged for issuing short-term cover are relatively low compared to the contract value of a commercial or loan contract. Unlike the premium rates charged for issuing the ECA cover in a medium- to long-term transaction, the

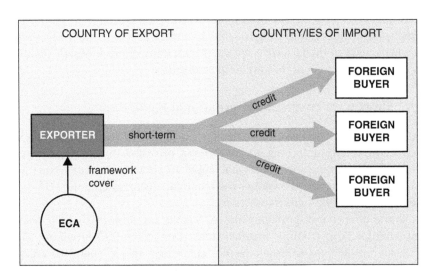

Figure 4.1   ECA framework cover for several short-term credit risks

premium rates for providing the short-term ECA cover are not regulated internationally.

The next difference between short-term and medium- to long-term ECA cover is the way they deal with foreign content in exported goods or services. The foreign content is value added to exported goods or services that are manufactured, assembled or supplied from another country. While the majority of ECAs strictly apply their rules limiting the percentage of foreign content in exported goods or services when providing cover for medium- to long-term transactions, they can be flexible when applying these rules to short-term cover. Some ECAs may issue short-term cover for export of goods with a very high percentage of foreign content or for export of goods that are completely manufactured out of the country of export.

The majority of users of short-term ECA cover are exporters; banks use this type of cover less frequently. Therefore, short-term ECA cover is usually issued as a supplier credit cover. The supplier is another name for an exporter that sells goods or services to a foreign buyer on credit terms. However, if an exporter needs financing from a bank in a short-term transaction covered by an ECA, the exporter may sell its claim for payment of a credit to a bank at a discount and assign its rights to the bank under the ECA policy. ECAs are aware of such dealings between exporters and banks and they accept that the bank, to which the rights under the policy are assigned, assumes the right to claim indemnification from the ECA if the foreign buyer defaults on payment of the credit. This issue and other related issues are analysed in Chapter 6.

Short-term cover is usually issued to cover political and commercial risks, but some exporters may be interested in obtaining this type of cover for political risks only. This depends on the situation in the foreign buyer's country and possible difficulties transferring the foreign buyer's payment out of its country. The percentage of the ECA cover for short-term transactions is usually the same as the cover for medium- to long-term credit risks.

4.4   Short-term cover and international regulations

Credits with the maximum duration of less than two years are classified as short-term credits according to the criteria provided in the Arrangement. However, the Arrangement does not apply to short-term credits and these transactions do not need to satisfy the requirements for issuing the ECA cover for medium- to long-term transactions.

On the other hand, providing the ECA cover for short-term credit risks is restricted for ECAs from EU member states. Due to the EU restrictions, these ECAs are not allowed to issue cover for credit risks shorter than two years in export credit transactions where a foreign buyer is from an EU country or from one of the following OECD countries: Australia, Canada, Japan, New Zealand,

Norway, Switzerland and the USA (Figure 4.2). This restriction does not apply to ECAs from countries outside the EU (Figure 4.3).

The reason for imposing the EU restrictions on issuing the ECA cover for short-term credit risks is that the EU treats such risks as marketable risks because private insurance companies have enough capacity to insure such risks without involving the officially supported ECAs. This is the general rule that applies within the EU but some exceptions are allowed when private insurers lack the capacity to insure the short-term export credit risks.

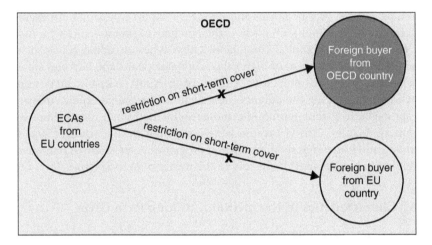

Figure 4.2 Restriction on ECAs from EU member states to issue short-term cover

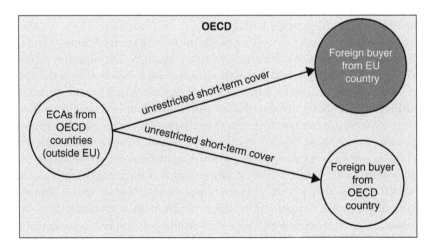

Figure 4.3 Rights of ECAs from non-EU OECD countries to issue short-term cover

4.5   Characteristics of medium- to long-term credit transactions

The Arrangement classifies credits with a duration of two to five years as medium-term credits, while credits longer than five years are considered long-term credits. In the ECA context there is no distinction between medium-term and long-term transactions and they are usually seen as one group of risks, medium- to long-term credit risks. In international commercial contracts in general, out of the ECA context, the duration of a credit between one to five years is classified medium-term while a credit longer than five years is classified as long-term.

Medium- to long-term credit transactions are typical for trade with specific goods or services, specific buyers and the size of export companies. An example of a trade with medium-term credit is the purchase of motor vehicles for industry or some types of capital equipment. Other types of capital goods such as machinery and equipment of high value, complete plants and factories are usually purchased on long-term credit. The size of an export company can be important when negotiating the duration of a credit because large export companies accept medium- to long-term credits more readily than small and medium-sized export companies. This is because large companies have a stronger financial standing and sometimes their production programmes are oriented to manufacturing capital equipment that is sold in the medium- to long-term.

4.6   Characteristics of the medium- to long-term cover

Medium- to long-term ECA cover is distinguished from short-term ECA cover in several ways. The first distinction is that the majority of applications for covering medium- to long-term credits are processed by ECAs individually. Therefore medium- to long-term credit risks are covered by ECAs by issuing a single ECA policy for a single transaction.

Another characteristic of covering medium- to long-term credit risks by ECAs is that such risks are not attractive for private insurers. The duration of insurance policies issued by private insurance companies is nearly always limited to one year and the insurance business is traditionally based on the concept of insuring the risks with the duration of no longer than one year. This is why private insurers are interested in insuring short-term credit risks but they traditionally do not show interest in insuring medium- to long-term credit risks.

The amount of work needed to process applications for covering medium- to long-term credit risks by ECAs is substantial and it may take from a couple of months to a half a year to obtain an ECA policy. This is due to a complex negotiating process between the parties involved in a commercial or loan transaction, comprehensive and time-consuming political and commercial risk assessment, structuring of transactions in which a bank is involved and the decision-making process within ECAs.

An additional characteristic of medium- to long-term ECA cover is that banks play an important role in this type of transaction covered by ECAs. These transactions are often structured as a buyer credit transaction in which a bank provides a loan to a foreign buyer to purchase goods or services from an exporter. In such transactions the exporter receives payment on delivery and does not assume the credit risk, which is assumed by the lending bank to which the foreign buyer will repay the loan. The ECA cover provided in buyer credit transactions is analysed in Chapter 8. The credit risk in a buyer credit transaction may be covered by the ECA from the country of export, while the lending bank may be from the exporter's country or from a third country (Figure 4.4).

Banks may be involved in medium- to long-term export credits in another way. When an exporter has applied for the ECA cover for a medium- to long-term transaction and obtained the ECA policy for a supplier credit risk, the exporter may sell its claim for payment of credit to a bank at a discount. When purchasing such a claim the bank will ask the exporter to assign the rights under the ECA policy to the bank. ECAs are aware of this requirement and they usually accept this type of assignment, provided that the bank is acceptable as a beneficiary under the ECA policy. The effect of assigning the rights under the ECA policy is that the bank becomes the beneficiary of the ECA policy and assumes the right to claim indemnification from the ECA if the foreign buyer defaults on payment of the credit. Many ECAs require the exporter to remain in the capacity of insured even after assigning its rights under the ECA policy to a bank. Assignment of rights under ECA policies is analysed in Chapter 6.

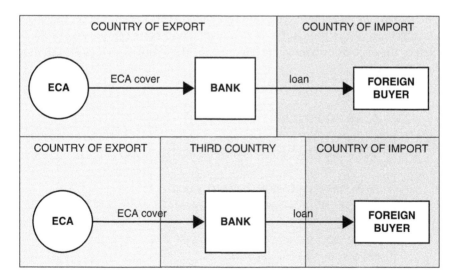

Figure 4.4   Nationality of bank in buyer credit transactions

4.7   Medium- to long-term cover and international regulations

Issuing medium- to long-term ECA cover is regulated internationally by the Arrangement. The Arrangement for Officially Supported Export Credits is applied by ECAs from countries that represent a substantial part of the global export and it affects numerous exporters and banks seeking the ECA cover for their export credit transactions. The Arrangement also affects foreign buyers that purchase goods or services from participating OECD countries since it applies to ECAs from these countries in all export credit transactions, with all foreign buyers from any country in the world. The Arrangement determines the minimum premium rates, maximum repayment terms, minimum cash payments to be made at or before starting point of credit and several other contractual provisions in commercial or loan contracts for which the ECA cover is requested.

The basic Arrangement requirements are analysed separately in this book but it is useful to mention some here. The basic requirement regarding payment of the contractual price in medium- to long-term transactions is that the foreign buyer must make a down payment of at least 15 per cent of the export contract value at or before the starting point of the credit. The down payment is a part of the total contractual price paid by the foreign buyer to the exporter in advance in order to demonstrate the foreign buyer's commitment to the contract. The foreign buyer is obligated to pay the credit in equal instalments at regular intervals of no longer than six months. The contractual interest is calculated on the outstanding amount at the time of payment. The first payment is to be made no later than six months after the starting point of credit. The maximum repayment terms are five to ten years depending on the OECD classification of the foreign buyer's country. Local costs cannot exceed 30 per cent of the export contract value (Figure 4.5). These issues are analysed in more detail in Chapter 21.

- *DOWN PAYMENT 15%*

- *MAXIMUM REPAYMENT TERMS FIVE TO TEN YEARS*

- *REPAYMENT OF CREDIT IN EQUAL AMOUNTS*
  AT REGULAR INTERVALS OF NO LONGER THAN SIX MONTHS

- *LOCAL COSTS CANNOT EXCEED 30% OF THE*
  EXPORT CONTRACT VALUE

Figure 4.5   Arrangement requirements for medium- to long-term transactions

4.8   Characteristics of project finance transactions

The duration of project finance transactions is usually longer than five years, which means they are classified as long-term transactions. However, these transactions are distinguished from other medium- to long-term transactions in several ways. The most important characteristic of a project finance transaction is that the foreign buyer is a specially incorporated project company that has never existed before. Therefore the assessment of risk of non-payment of a credit by such a company is based on projections of the company's future cash flow. This assessment method is different from the method applied when assessing the foreign buyers that have conducted their businesses at least a couple of years before entering into an export credit transaction with an exporter or bank. It is possible for ECAs to assess the foreign buyer's ability to pay a credit by examining its previous business activity and the company's financial results. This is not the case with project companies where the assessment of future cash flow and ability of a project company to pay a credit is based on projections only.

The project financing structure usually involves several investors, called sponsors, and several banks that provide loans to the project company acting as a borrower. Sponsors are not liable for repayment of the bank loans provided to the project company because these loans will be repaid from the project company's future cash flow. Repayment of loans is usually secured by providing security over the assets purchased by the project company (Figure 4.6).

The majority of project finance transactions are agreed upon as long-term credit transactions with duration of credit longer than five years. The project finance model is used to finance infrastructure and industrial projects in areas

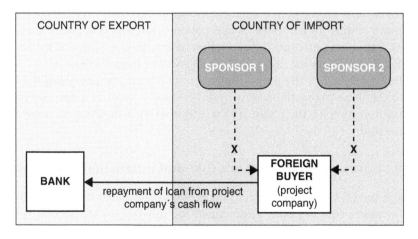

Figure 4.6   Repayment of loan by the project company

such as oil and gas fields, mines, power stations, pipelines, bridges, highways and public utility businesses, for example.

4.9   Characteristics of cover for project finance risks

Project financing is generally more complicated than other forms of financing because there are several risks associated with projects that must be identified and assessed. These are: the risk of a project being cancelled or otherwise not completed, operating risk, price risk and political risk. When analysing whether to issue cover for the risk of non-repayment of a loan by a project company, ECAs have to assess all these risks.

An ECA may be requested by several parties involved in a project to issue various types of the ECA cover. Manufacturers of capital equipment may apply for the ECA cover for the risk of cancelling the project in the manufacturing stage, for example. This risk can be covered by the majority of ECAs by a separate type of ECA cover for manufacturing loss, which is analysed in Chapter 9. The banks involved in the project may apply for the ECA cover for non-repayment of the loans provided to the project company for purchasing the capital equipment. The duration of the ECA cover issued to the banks is usually long-term and the amounts of loans covered by ECAs are substantial.

Processing applications for covering credit risks in project finance transactions can be timely and demanding. ECAs need several months and sometimes a year to process an individual application. The extensive work of an ECA does not always result in providing the ECA cover because the project can be cancelled or prolonged. It is also possible that the application for the ECA cover for a project finance transaction is withdrawn when the project has reached the final stage because another type of credit risk protection became more attractive or cheaper for the project creditors. An applicant for any type of ECA cover is always entitled to withdraw its application before the ECA policy is issued. An ECA that has processed the application is usually not compensated for the work and costs incurred in analysing and assessing the project risks.

The complexity of the project finance transactions and providing the ECA cover for these transactions are why ECAs classify them as a special type of transaction, despite their primary classification as a medium- to long-term transaction.

4.10   Cover for project finance risks and international regulations

Issuing the ECA cover for project finance risks is regulated internationally by the Arrangement. The basic requirement for this type of transaction is that the maximum period for payment of credit is 14 years, which is considerably longer than the maximum duration of credit agreed on in the medium- to long-term transactions. The Arrangement also regulates that payment of the principal may be made in unequal instalments and the principal and interest may be paid in instalments less frequent than semi-annually. It contains other detailed provisions for providing the ECA cover in project finance transactions, but these provisions are not analysed in this book.

The terms used in the Arrangement's provisions on project finance transactions are slightly different from the terms used in this book. Instead of the term 'project company' acting as a foreign buyer, the Arrangement uses the term 'economic unit' whose cash flows and earnings will be used as the funds from which a loan will be repaid and whose assets will be used as collateral for the loan. The term 'collateral' can have various meanings in various contexts, and in financial transactions it is often synonymous with the word 'security'. The term used in this book is security for payment of export credits; it is analysed in Chapter 17.

4.11   Partial cover and different percentages of cover

In practice, ECAs frequently issue a comprehensive ECA cover that includes both political and commercial risks. The comprehensive cover includes nearly all events that may cause non-payment of a credit by a foreign buyer; such a broad scope of cover makes it attractive to exporters and banks. However, some exporters and banks are not interested in obtaining the ECA cover for all political and commercial risks analysed in Chapter 3. In addition, ECAs are not always willing to cover political and commercial risks with the same percentage of cover, which is important when applying for the ECA cover. Below is a short analysis of the possibility of obtaining a partial cover from ECAs and the effect of obtaining cover only for political or commercial events.

4.12   Partial cover

When negotiating and structuring an individual export credit transaction, an exporter or bank may wish to obtain a partial ECA cover for political or commercial risks only, because the exporter or bank has assessed that they only need cover for selected risks while other risks need not be covered. Another reason for requesting a partial ECA cover can be to pay a lower premium to an ECA. For example, an exporter or bank may approach an ECA with a request for the ECA cover for a single political risk without covering any other political or commercial risk. It could be the risk of prevention or delay in transfer of payment of credit out of the foreign buyer's country, a ban on import or another political risk connected to a particular country of import.

ECAs deal with requests for issuing a partial cover in various ways and their practice is not uniform in this respect. Some ECAs provide the partial cover for political risks regularly while other ECAs are either reluctant to issue partial cover or do it exceptionally. The reason for their reluctance is that separating single risks from the comprehensive ECA cover and issuing a partial cover for single risks is not sufficiently tested in practice. As explained in Chapter 3, single risks are defined in the ECA standard terms with general wording and it is difficult sometimes to distinguish them from each other. Uncertainty in interpreting the definitions of political and commercial risks may result in a disagreement between an ECA and the insured when establishing whether an event is covered by a partial ECA cover or not. In order to avoid such situations some ECAs provide only comprehensive cover that includes political and commercial risks.

4.13   Different percentages of ECA cover for political and commercial risks

In practice the majority of ECAs are willing to cover both political and commercial risks, but some ECAs apply different percentages of cover to these two types of risks. The percentage of cover is normally higher for political risks, usually up to 100 per cent, while the percentage of cover for commercial risks rarely exceeds 90 per cent because insured exporters and banks must have an incentive to engage in avoiding or minimising the loss caused by commercial events. This can be achieved if exporters and banks retain a small portion of commercial risks covered by ECAs, usually called the residual risk. This principle is based on the assumption that an insured exporter has a close customer relationship with the foreign buyer, which enables the exporter to engage in finding solutions for payment of credit when the foreign buyer is experiencing financial difficulty. It is also assumed that the active engagement of an exporter may result in minimising a loss for the ECA, reducing the indemnification amount paid to the exporter.

Some ECAs apply the principle above to both exporters and banks, expecting them to actively engage in avoiding or minimising a loss for the ECA. Other ECAs apply this principle to exporters only while banks may obtain 100 per cent of cover for political and commercial risks.

The percentage of the ECA cover for commercial events can be reduced by ECAs as a result of risk assessment of the foreign buyer's business and financial standing. When assessment of the foreign buyer's financial standing and its ability to pay a credit shows a high risk of payment default, it is likely that an ECA will reduce the percentage of cover for commercial risks. An ECA may issue cover for 80 per cent of the credit risk, for example, which means the insured exporter or bank will retain 20 per cent of the risk.

When considering the percentage of cover for political risks, the general view is that it would be unrealistic to expect exporters and banks to influence political events in foreign countries in order to avoid or minimise losses. Therefore ECAs usually cover political risks with 100 per cent of the highest amount of loss stated in an ECA policy. Theoretically, the percentage of the ECA cover for political risks may be reduced by ECAs when the political situation in a foreign buyer's country is rapidly deteriorating and the risk for loss is very high. However, it is more likely that an ECA will decide not to issue cover for any type of risk.

4.14   Consequences of classification of risks as political or commercial

Various political and economic developments in the world mean the border-line between political and commercial events can be unclear. This is important when an ECA cover is issued with different percentages for political and commercial risks or when it is issued for political or commercial risks only. Political and commercial events are defined in the ECA standard terms but the wording of these definitions is usually very general and sometimes difficult to apply to an individual event. This may result in different interpretations of the definitions of political and commercial events and a disagreement between an ECA and an insured exporter or bank when classifying an event that caused a loss. This is important because the classification of an event as political or commercial often determines the percentage of indemnification payable by an ECA to an insured exporter or bank. It also determines whether the insured has a right to claim any indemnification when the ECA cover is issued for political or commercial events only.

An example where the cover for political events is 100 per cent and the cover for commercial events is 90 per cent can be used to illustrate the consequences of the disagreement described above. When a loss caused to the insured by non-payment of a credit is USD 50 million, the ECA will indemnify the entire amount of loss if it is caused by a political event. If the loss is caused by a commercial event, the ECA will indemnify the insured by paying 90 per cent of USD 50 million, which is USD 45 million. The difference is USD 5 million, which is a huge amount of money for any insured exporter or bank to lose if the event is classified as commercial when the insured believes it was political. If the ECA cover is issued for political events only and the event is classified as commercial, the insured will not receive any indemnification. Many exporters and banks are aware of the risk connected to obtaining partial cover and they usually obtain the comprehensive ECA cover, including political and commercial risks.

It is important to explain that disagreements between ECAs and insured exporters or banks regarding classification of an event as political or commercial are rare. This is a result of efforts made by ECAs to update and clarify their definitions of political and commercial events in accordance with the world's current political and economic developments.

In order to avoid disagreements regarding classification of risks as political or commercial, some ECAs offer to issue the ECA cover for political and commercial events with the same percentage of cover, for example 95 per cent. When the percentage of cover is the same for both types of risks, the amount of indemnification payable by an ECA will be the same and no classification of the event that caused the loss is needed.

5
Supplier Credit Cover

A supplier credit is an agreement in a commercial contract under which an exporter will supply goods or services to a foreign buyer on credit terms. Since the exporter is also called a supplier, the agreement is called the supplier credit in the ECA terminology. Payment on credit terms means the foreign buyer will pay either a single amount at a later date or make payments in several instalments on several future dates agreed between the parties. Since the foreign buyer is from another country this type of commercial contract includes export of goods or services from the exporter's country and their import into the foreign buyer's country. The export element in this contract is of significance for obtaining the ECA cover for the risk of non-payment of the credit by the foreign buyer. In the ECA context, the supplier in the supplier credit transaction is called the exporter, which could be a manufacturer of goods, a provider of services, or a trader or agent.

An exporter in a supplier credit transaction is aware that many unforeseen events may prevent the foreign buyer from making payment of the credit according to the terms of the contract. Such events include insolvency of the foreign buyer, political decisions preventing transfer of payments from the foreign buyer's country to the exporter's country, or any other commercial or political event covered by ECAs. In order to protect itself from the loss caused by non-payment of the credit by the foreign buyer, the exporter may obtain the ECA cover for this credit risk. The ECA from which the exporter should request cover is the ECA from the country of export. If the ECA agrees to provide cover for the credit risk in the transaction, it will issue an ECA policy and the exporter will be required to pay the premium to the ECA. The agreement by which the foreign buyer will pay the contractual price on credit terms is called the supplier credit and the ECA cover for this type of risk is called the supplier credit cover.

5.1   Classification of transactions as supplier credit contracts

The simplest form of the supplier credit contract is a sale of goods by an exporter to a foreign buyer on credit terms. However, this term is much broader and includes any other type of contract where one contractual party supplies goods or services to another party. ECAs will generally classify a contract as a supplier contract if the exporter's performance under the contract is different from payment of money. Such performance is either delivery of goods or providing services to a foreign buyer. In exchange for the exporter's performance, the foreign buyer is obligated to pay the contractual price to the exporter on credit terms. All these transactions could be described as 'performance for money' transactions. As explained in Chapter 8, the buyer credit transaction is the 'money for money' transaction where a bank or other financier lends money to a foreign buyer who will repay it at a later date. In the ECA context the supplier credit contracts are often called commercial contracts to distinguish them from loan contracts. In the ECA context the classification of a contract as a supplier or buyer credit contract is significant for determining which type of ECA cover will be issued for the credit risk in the contract.

However, all ECAs do not classify supplier credit contracts in the same way. An example is a lease contract that is classified by some ECAs as a supplier credit contract both when the exporter, typically the manufacturer of the lease object, acts as a lessor and when a bank or another financier acts in the same capacity. Other ECAs apply different criteria and classify the lease contract as a supplier contract only when the exporter acts as a lessor, while a lease contract where a bank acts in the capacity of lessor is classified as a buyer credit contract. Some ECAs have created a special policy to cover the credit risks in lease contracts.

In addition, some ECAs provide special types of policies for large and complex supplier contracts where several types of risks are covered in a combination. An example is the special ECA policy for construction works where the supplier credit risk and the risk connected with a contract bond or guarantee are covered. Other examples of the special ECA policies where several types of risks are covered are transactions for supply of aircrafts and ships, which are separately regulated in the OECD Arrangement. These transactions are not analysed in this book.

For the purpose of this book the supplier credit contracts are the 'performance for money' transactions as described above. Some types of the combined ECA cover, where the supplier credit cover is included, are analysed in Chapter 9.

5.2   Limitations of supplier credit cover

The supplier credit cover provided by ECAs is usually limited to the amount of the contractual price payable on credit terms by the foreign buyer. The contractual price payable normally consists of the principal and contractual interest. Besides the payment of contractual price, commercial contracts sometimes contain provisions on payment of damages for breach of contract, late payment interest, etc. These payment obligations are normally not covered by ECAs. This is usually provided in the standard terms applied by ECAs and this particular provision applies equally to commercial and loan contracts.

5.3 Types of supplier credit cover

Based on duration of a credit the two most important types of ECA supplier credit cover are short-term and medium- to long-term cover. Depending on the number of credit risks covered by a single ECA policy, the short-term supplier credit cover may be issued as a single or a framework cover. The medium- to long-term supplier credit cover is usually issued as a single cover which means that a single credit risk is covered by a single ECA policy.

5.4 Cover for short-term supplier credit

The main characteristic of short-term credit is that its duration is less than two years and the Arrangement does not apply to the ECA cover issued for such credit risks. This means that ECAs are not restricted regarding the percentage of cover, minimum premium rates, repayment intervals of credit and other requirements of the Arrangement. ECAs may cover 100 per cent of a short-term credit, which is not possible when covering the medium- to long-term credits where the Arrangement requires a foreign buyer to make a down payment of 15 per cent of the contractual price. This means that in medium- to long-term transactions, ECAs can cover a maximum of 85 per cent of the contractual price, which is payable on credit terms. When analysing the provision of short-term cover, the ECAs from EU member states are partly restricted from providing this type of cover, which is explained in Chapters 4 and 21.

Another characteristic of the short-term supplier credit cover is that ECAs are less concerned with the foreign content in the exported goods when covering this type of risk. This means ECAs may accept a higher percentage of foreign content than in medium- to long-term credits. Even the risk assessment method applied by ECAs when dealing with short-term credit is different from the method applied to medium- to long-term risks.

Due to the large volume of individual short-term supplier credit risks processed by ECAs and relatively small contractual values of such risks, ECAs often issue framework policies to cover all short-term credit risks of an exporter. The framework policy can be construed to include all credit risks related to, for example, a particular foreign buyer, or all foreign buyers from a particular country or a region.

The short-term supplier credit cover may be issued for single credit risks, too, when a single ECA policy is issued. It is not unusual for ECAs to issue a single short-term ECA cover, especially for larger amounts of credit. The characteristics of short-term credits and the ECA cover for these credit risks are explained in more detail in Chapter 4.

5.5   Cover for medium- to long-term supplier credit

According to the Arrangement, medium- to long-term credits have duration of two years or more. This applies to supplier and buyer credits. The duration of medium-term credits is two to five years, while it is five years or more for long-term credits. In practice, both these credits are treated as one group, called medium- to long-term credits.

The main distinction between short-term and medium- to long-term supplier credits is that the latter are regulated by the Arrangement. The basic Arrangement requirements for medium- to long-term supplier credits are analysed in Chapter 21.

Another characteristic of the medium- to long-term supplier credit cover is that applications for this type of cover are usually processed by ECAs individually, not within the framework policies as for short-term supplier credits. This means that single ECA policies will be issued to cover single medium- to long-term supplier credit risks.

6
Supplier Credit Cover with the Involvement of Banks

An exporter that has agreed on payment of the contractual price on credit terms in a commercial contract with a foreign buyer often needs money earlier than the date the foreign buyer's payment becomes due. In such a situation, the exporter can contact a bank and offer to sell its claim against the foreign buyer to the bank at a discount. If the bank purchases the claim for payment, the exporter would receive the future payment immediately while the bank waits for the payment of credit to be made by the foreign buyer. The bank may decide to buy the claim from the exporter if it is satisfied the commercial transaction between the exporter and the foreign buyer meets its requirements. Before deciding, the bank assesses the foreign buyer's ability to pay the credit and the exporter's ability to perform its obligations under the commercial contract.

Terminology

> *Selling a claim for payment by a supplier to a third party is sometimes called refinancing. Since the term 'refinancing' is used in other contexts and in various meanings, this book avoids it. The term 'selling of claim' is used instead.*

Because purchasing the claim for payment from the exporter includes taking over the credit risk, the bank may want to obtain the ECA cover for loss caused by non-payment of the credit by the foreign buyer. ECAs provide cover for this type of credit risk, but that cover depends on the way in which the bank purchases the claim from the exporter. Some ECAs cover the credit risks in these transactions by applying a single type of the ECA cover, while other ECAs apply different types of cover for various transactions. All these types of ECA cover include cover for political and commercial risks. Sometimes the cover may be issued for political or commercial risks only, which depends on the circumstances of a particular transaction and the willingness of an ECA to issue a partial cover. Below is an analysis of several types of transactions through which banks purchase claims from exporters and the various types of ECA cover provided for credit risks in such transactions.

6.1   The exporter's assignment of claim for payment and rights under ECA policy

Transferring a claim for payment against the foreign buyer from the exporter to a bank is called assignment. Generally, assignment of a claim for payment to a third party is permitted in many jurisdictions so the consent of the contractual debtor is not required. This principle applies to all contracts between creditors and debtors unless the debtor's consent is required by the contract.

The assignment of a claim for payment under a contract is distinguished from the assignment of a contract as a whole, where one contractual party is replaced by a third party. The assignment of a claim for payment is a minor variation of a contract compared to the assignment of a contract as a whole. This means that an exporter will remain in its capacity of the contractual party to the commercial contract with the foreign buyer even after assigning its claim for payment to the bank. In such a capacity the exporter retains all rights and obligations provided in the commercial contract except the right to claim payment of the credit from the foreign buyer (Figure 6.1).

Terminology

The selling of a claim for payment of credit by a supplier to a bank or another financier, also called selling of receivables, can be made in forms such as using the supplier's existing bank credit limits, export factoring, forfaiting, invoice discounting, etc. These forms are not analysed in this book and the terms selling or assigning a claim for payment are used for simplicity.

The assignment of a claim for payment from the exporter to a bank requires variation of the ECA cover for supplier credit where such a cover has been issued to the exporter. Since the risk of non-payment of the credit by the foreign buyer has been taken over by the bank, the bank will ask the exporter to amend the terms of the ECA cover to make the bank the beneficiary of the ECA policy. Therefore the right to claim indemnification from the ECA in case of non-payment of the credit by the foreign buyer and other rights under the ECA policy are transferred from the exporter to the bank. The transfer of rights from the exporter to the bank is also called assignment (Figure 6.2). The right to assign the rights under the ECA policy is usually provided in the standard terms of ECA policies and many exporters exercise this right when selling claims for payment to banks. However this right is usually limited to certain banks while the assignment to other parties is subject to ECA consent.

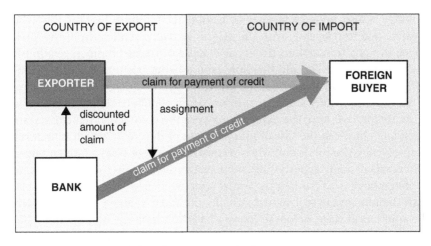

Figure 6.1   Assignment of claim by exporter to bank

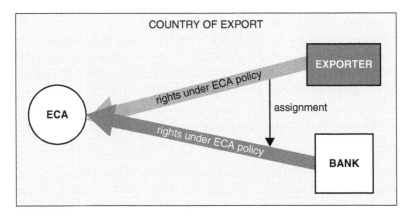

Figure 6.2   Assignment of rights under ECA policy by exporter to bank

Among the rights assigned by the exporter to a bank, the right to claim indemnification from the ECA is the most important one. Other rights assigned to the bank are the right to request instructions from the ECA on how to proceed if the foreign buyer requests rescheduling of a credit, what recovery actions should be taken, etc.

After assigning its rights under an ECA policy to a bank, the exporter remains in the capacity of the insured in relation to the ECA, with all obligations provided under the ECA policy. These obligations are substantial and they include the obligation to pay a premium to the ECA and to disclose information about the covered credit risk and other information of significance for the ECA. The exporter is also under a general obligation to minimise loss for the ECA if possible and to cooperate with the ECA in recovery of a loss from the foreign buyer. In some transactions the exporter has a continued business relationship with the foreign buyer and therefore is in a better position than the bank to obtain information about financial difficulties of the foreign buyer. If disclosed to an ECA in an early stage, such information could enable the ECA to avoid or minimise loss. Also, the exporter may use the contractual remedies against the foreign buyer in the case of non-payment of the credit, which is important in insolvency situations and when recovering the debt from a foreign buyer.

In practice, many exporters intend to assign their claims for payment against a foreign buyer to a bank in the initial stage while negotiating the transaction with the foreign buyer. Exporters usually notify ECAs about such intention in the application stage, before selecting a bank to which the future claim against the foreign buyer will be assigned. ECAs usually accept assignment of the claim for indemnification to a bank at any time before or after issuing the ECA policy. Exporters are also aware that in many transactions banks would not purchase a claim for payment against a foreign buyer without obtaining the ECA cover and assigning the claim for indemnification to a bank.

Purchasing claims for payment against foreign buyers and assignment of the rights under the ECA supplier credit policies is frequently used by exporters and banks. However, from the banks' point of view, the assignment of rights under the ECA supplier credit policies is not completely free of risk.

6.2 The position of the bank after assuming rights under an ECA policy

Banks are concerned with two risks when purchasing a claim for payment against a foreign buyer and becoming a beneficiary under the ECA policy for supplier credit cover. The first is the risk of the exporter's breach of the commercial contract with the foreign buyer that may result in the foreign buyer's refusal to pay the credit. This is important because the foreign buyer may be entitled to withhold or refuse payment of the credit as a contractual remedy for the exporter's breach of contract. If such a situation occurs, the bank to which the claim for payment has been assigned will not receive payment of credit from the foreign buyer. Additionally, the bank will not be entitled to claim indemnification from the ECA for the non-paid amount because the ECA does not cover disputed claims for payment. ECAs exclude disputed claims from the ECA cover for supplier credits.

The foreign buyer's allegation that the exporter has breached the commercial contract is sometimes unjustified and made just as an excuse for the foreign buyer's inability to make payment. In such a situation, an ECA may decide to indemnify the exporter or bank to which the rights under an ECA policy have been assigned. However, ECAs are strict in judging such situations and they rarely indemnify disputed claims. In doubtful situations an ECA will instruct the exporter or bank to obtain a judgment of court or an arbitration award proving the exporter's right to claim payment from the foreign buyer. Obtaining a judgment or award is often a long and burdensome process that delays payment of indemnification to banks, and they do not want to be involved in such situations.

The second risk a bank may see in becoming a beneficiary under an ECA policy is the risk of the exporter's breach of its obligations under the ECA policy. The exporter remains in the capacity of the insured even after assigning the rights under the ECA policy to the bank. If the exporter breaches any of its obligations under the ECA policy, the ECA has the right to several contractual remedies against the exporter. The ECA may reduce the indemnification payable in the case of non-payment of the credit by the foreign buyer and, if the exporter's breach is serious, the ECA may terminate the policy. Termination of the ECA policy means that no indemnification can be claimed either by the exporter or the bank. This would negatively affect the bank to which the rights under the ECA policy have been assigned, since the bank has no better right in relation to the ECA than the exporter. In addition, the bank cannot do much to cure the exporter's breach of obligation under the ECA policy.

When purchasing a claim against the foreign buyer from the exporter, the bank may request the right of recourse against the exporter in the case of non-receipt of payment of credit or indemnification caused by the exporter's breaches of its obligations described above. This is required in many transactions between exporters and banks, and exporters agree to repay the amount the bank does not receive from the foreign buyer or the ECA. However, the exporter's agreement to repay the non-paid amounts to the bank is connected with the risk that the exporter may be insolvent when the bank claims for repayment of the money. Some exporters are reluctant to accept the bank's right of recourse because they see the risk in their breach of the commercial contract or an obligation under an ECA policy as insignificant.

Situations in which an exporter is in breach of a commercial contract or an obligation under an ECA policy rarely occur. In practice, when an exporter has issues with the foreign buyer regarding its performance under a commercial contract, such issues are usually resolved without affecting the right of the bank to which the claim for payment against the foreign buyer is assigned. The same can be said about the contractual relationship between insured exporters and ECAs. In addition, both ECAs and banks assess the exporter's ability to perform its obligations under the commercial contract before issuing the ECA cover or purchasing the claim against the foreign buyer. If an ECA believes a particular exporter does not have the capacity to perform its obligations under the commercial contract with the foreign buyer, it will not issue the ECA cover to the exporter. Consequently, the bank will not purchase the claim for payment against the foreign buyer if the credit risk is not covered by the ECA.

6.3   The exporter's transfer of bill of exchange and assignment of rights under ECA policy

In many transactions where an exporter sells its contractual claim for payment against a foreign buyer to a bank, the future payment obligation of the foreign buyer is documented by one or several bills of exchange (drafts). A bill of exchange is a separate document containing an unconditional obligation to pay a sum of money on a future date. Since bills of exchange are negotiable instruments that are transferable to third parties, the exporter may sell the bills of exchange to a bank at a discount. In this way, the bank purchases the claim for future payment represented by the bill of exchange and the exporter receives an immediate payment of credit at a lesser value instead of waiting for the payment of the full amount of credit on the due date. Discounts may be made at any time before presenting a bill of exchange for payment on the due date and it may be agreed upon with or without the bank's recourse to the exporter in case of non-payment under the bill of exchange. In this context, recourse is the bank's right to claim repayment from the exporter of the amount the bank paid when purchasing the bill of exchange.

When a bill of exchange is issued, the foreign buyer's payment obligation is separated from the underlying commercial contract and contained in the bills as separate documents. Due to this separation and the legal nature of the bill of exchange as an unconditional payment obligation, the foreign buyer is prevented from disputing or refusing payment under a bill of exchange by alleging the breach of the commercial contract by the exporter.

From the bank's point of view, purchasing a bill of exchange is a better solution than purchasing the contractual claim for payment against the foreign buyer. Preventing the foreign buyer from disputing or refusing payment under a bill of exchange by alleging a breach of the commercial contract by the exporter eliminates an important risk with which the banks are concerned. Consequently, purchasing bills of exchange provides banks with more certainty regarding payment of the credit than purchasing a contractual claim for payment in the form of assignment. This solution is frequently used by exporters when selling claims for payment against foreign buyers to banks. However, issuing bills is not mandatory in commercial contracts between exporters and foreign buyers. A foreign buyer may reject issuing the bills of exchange; therefore the solution described above cannot be used.

6.4   Insufficiency of the bank's position under ECA policy

When an exporter sells bills of exchange to a bank, the bank requires the exporter to assign its rights under the ECA policy to it. Such assignment is accepted by ECAs as explained previously in this chapter. The bank's position after becoming a beneficiary under the ECA supplier credit policy is no better than the exporter's position. The bank does not acquire a better right against the ECA despite its holding of bills of exchange. The ECA policy for supplier credit, issued to an exporter, covers only non-payment of the exporter's contractual claim for payment against the foreign buyer. It does not cover non-payment under the bills of exchange separately from the commercial contract. In other words, the pure ECA supplier credit cover is not created specifically for bills of exchange but for the exporter's contractual claim for payment against the foreign buyer.

The consequence of the bank's position described above is that the risk of the exporter's breach of contract resulting in the foreign buyer's refusal to pay the credit is not covered by the ECA. This may negatively affect the bank since it is not eligible to claim indemnification from the ECA for non-payment under the bills of exchange when the foreign buyer alleges the exporter's breach of contract.

This situation is exceptional in practice since foreign buyers are aware the payment under the bills of exchange is unconditional and separated from commercial contracts. They are also aware that they cannot involve banks in their disputes with exporters and that refusal to make payment under a bill of exchange because of a dispute with an exporter constitutes violation of legislation regulating the bills of exchange. In practice, the payment discipline of foreign buyers is better when making payment to banks under bills of exchange than when making payment of credits to exporters. Therefore, the risk of a foreign buyer's unlawful refusal to make payment under a bill of exchange by alleging the exporter's breach of the commercial contract is low. However, banks dealing with this type of transaction are interested in eliminating all types of risks, which is why some ECAs have created a separate type of ECA cover for non-payment under the bills of exchange.

6.5 Cover for bills of exchange (drafts)

This type of cover is issued by ECAs directly to banks for the risk of non-payment under a bill of exchange. This is the same transaction as described above where an exporter sells a bill of exchange to a bank at a discount, but the difference is that the bank acts in the capacity of the insured in relation to the ECA. By acting in the capacity of the insured, the bank assumes all rights and obligations under the ECA policy (Figure 6.3). Therefore the bank can claim indemnification from the ECA in case of non-payment under a bill of exchange and this right is independent of the exporter's possible breach of the commercial contract. This type of cover gives the bank control over the ECA policy and a stronger position in relation to the ECA compared to the situation described above where the exporter acts as the insured and the bank acts as the beneficiary.

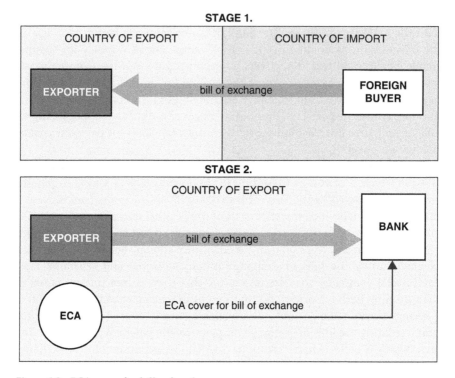

Figure 6.3   ECA cover for bills of exchange

Purchasing bills of exchange and obtaining the direct ECA cover is a better solution for a bank than purchasing bills of exchange where the ordinary ECA supplier credit cover is issued to the exporter. By obtaining the direct ECA cover, the bank eliminates the risk of disputing the claim for payment by the foreign buyer and the risk of breach of the exporter's obligations under the ECA policy. This is because the ECA covers the risk of non-payment under the bills of exchange and not the risk of non-payment of the credit under the commercial contract between the exporter and foreign buyer.

ECAs that provide this type of cover to banks rely on the legal nature of a bill of exchange as a document containing an unconditional obligation to pay a sum of money on a future date. These ECAs estimate the risk of a foreign buyer's unlawful refusal to make payment under a bill of exchange as low. They also rely on the enforceability of a claim for payment in a bill of exchange independently of possible disputes between the exporter and foreign buyer.

When issuing the cover for bills of exchange, ECAs normally require the exporter to issue a document confirming the bills of exchange are issued in connection to an export credit contract between an exporter and a foreign buyer. Although this type of cover is issued to improve the position of the banks when obtaining the ECA cover for bills of exchange, its main purpose is supporting export and enabling exporters to sell their claims for payment against foreign buyers. The bills of exchange that are not issued in connection with export credit contracts are not eligible for the ECA cover. The exporter is not involved in issuing this type of ECA cover except for issuing the document mentioned above.

The ECA cover for bills of exchange is practical for banks, but it cannot be used in all supplier credit transactions where a bank is interested in purchasing a claim for payment against the foreign buyer because the foreign buyer's future payments established in commercial contracts with exporters are not always documented with the bills of exchange. In addition, not all ECAs provide cover for bills of exchange.

In addition, some practical difficulties may arise when dealing with bills of exchange. The bills of exchange must be presented for payment on the due date. If the payment is not made, the holder of the bills is, in many jurisdictions, required to make an official protest, usually at the notary public. This requirement depends on whether the bill is an 'inland' or a 'foreign' bill and whether a clause 'without protest' is included in it. The protest procedure is relatively strict and deadlines are short, usually two days after the due date for payment under the bill. The problem with such a short deadline is that it is easy for banks that have obtained the ECA cover for a bill of exchange to miss. This may negatively affect the enforcement of payment under the non-paid bill of exchange, in turn negatively affecting the bank's right to claim indemnification from the ECA.

6.6   Cover for promissory notes

This type of cover is similar to the ECA cover for bills of exchange described above. The ECA cover for promissory notes is issued by some ECAs directly to a bank for the risk of non-payment under a promissory note purchased from an exporter. A promissory note is a written and unconditional promise from the issuer, in this case the foreign buyer, to pay a specific amount at a future date. The promissory notes used in such transactions are transferable to third persons and banks are willing to discount promissory notes if they satisfy their requirements. When discounting a promissory note, the bank pays the exporter the nominal value of the promissory note less the discount fee. This gives the exporter an immediate payment of a lesser amount instead of waiting for the future payment of a full amount on the due date. Discounting promissory notes may be agreed upon with or without the bank's recourse to the exporter, similar to when a bank discounts bills of exchange.

By purchasing the promissory notes from the exporter, the bank takes over the risk of non-payment under the notes and is interested in obtaining the ECA cover for this risk. This type of cover can be obtained from some ECAs, but not from all of them.

Since a promissory note is a document that separates the claim for payment against the foreign buyer from the commercial contract like a bill of exchange, obtaining this type of ECA cover is favourable for banks. By obtaining the ECA cover for promissory notes, banks eliminate the risk of the exporter's breach of the commercial contract and the risk of the exporter's breach of its obligations under the ECA policy. In this type of cover, the bank acts as the insured and assumes all rights and obligations under the ECA policy (Figure 6.4). The exporter is not involved in this type of ECA cover.

Since the main purpose of this type of the ECA cover is to support national export, the ECAs that provide the cover for promissory notes normally require the exporter to confirm in writing that the promissory notes are issued in connection with an export credit contract between an exporter and a foreign buyer. The promissory notes issued in connection with other commercial contracts that do not include export of goods or services are not eligible for this type of ECA cover.

The ECA cover for promissory notes cannot be used in all supplier credit cover transactions when a bank is interested in purchasing a claim for payment

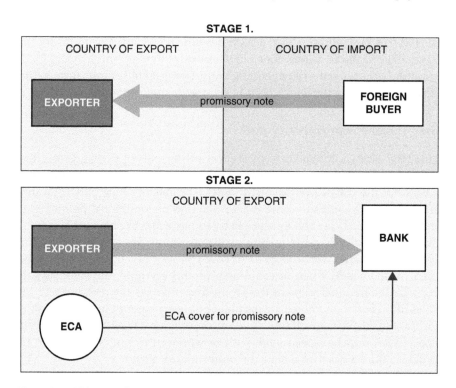

Figure 6.4   ECA cover for promissory notes

against the foreign buyer because the foreign buyer's future payments are not always documented with promissory notes. In addition, the ECA cover for promissory notes is not provided by all ECAs.

It is possible that an exporter, when selling identical goods under identical terms to two buyers in two countries, agrees on issuing of bills of exchange with a foreign buyer in one country of import and issuing of promissory notes with a foreign buyer in another country of import. This is not unusual since using one or another instrument depends on tradition and trade customs in a country of import.

6.7   Cover for account receivables

This type of cover is issued by a few ECAs for the same transaction described previously in this chapter in which an exporter assigns its claim for future payment against the foreign buyer to a bank at a discount. At the same time, the exporter assigns its rights under the ECA policy to the bank, which becomes a beneficiary entitled to claim indemnification from the ECA in the case of non-payment of the credit by the foreign buyer. The exporter remains in the capacity of the insured under the ECA policy.

When purchasing a claim for payment against a foreign buyer, the banks involved in such transactions are aware of the risk of the exporter's breach of the commercial contract with the foreign buyer and the risk of the exporter's breach of its obligations under the ECA policy. Due to these two risks, some banks prefer obtaining the ECA policy directly from the ECA without involving the exporter in that transaction. If the ECA policy is issued directly to a bank, in the capacity of the insured, the terms of that policy would be more favourable than if the bank acts as a beneficiary under the ECA supplier credit policy. This type of ECA cover, provided by few ECAs, is sometimes called the account receivables cover (Figure 6.5). This name is confusing because several other types of ECA cover also can be called the account receivables cover. In this type of cover the bank is in a similar position as under the ECA cover for bills of exchange. The main difference between these two types of cover is that no bills of exchange are required for issuing the ECA cover for account receivables.

From the bank's point of view, the advantage of the ECA cover for account receivables is the elimination of the risk of the exporter's breach of contract with the foreign buyer and the risk of the exporter's breach of its obligations under the ECA policy. As explained earlier in this chapter, these two risks are not covered by ECAs.

From the ECA's point of view, the structure above is weak and the majority of ECAs do not provide this type of cover to banks because banks would expect ECAs to indemnify them even in situations where the non-payment of a credit by a foreign buyer is caused by the exporter's breach of the commercial

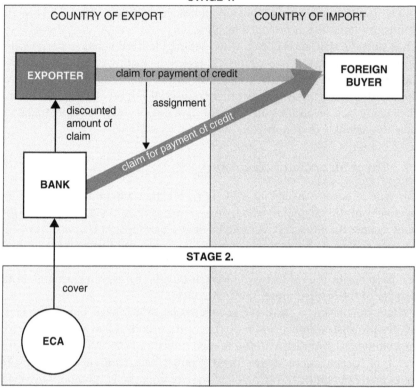

Figure 6.5   ECA cover for account receivables issued directly to bank

contract. This risk is expressly excluded from nearly all ECA policies, and this exclusion is one of the basic principles of the ECA business. In addition, ECAs would be prevented from recovering any amount from a foreign buyer that was entitled to withhold or refuse payment of credit under the commercial contract because of the exporter's breach of contract.

Another reason for the reluctance of ECAs to provide the account receivables cover is that they see several advantages of having the exporter in the capacity of insured in a supplier credit transaction. This is because the exporter is a party to the commercial contract with the foreign buyer and may use the contractual remedies against the foreign buyer to minimise or avoid loss for the ECA. In addition, some exporters have continuous business relations with the foreign buyer that enable them to monitor the financial standing of the foreign buyer and inform the ECA if that standing is deteriorating. An early warning about increase of a credit risk can sometimes enable the ECA to act immediately to mitigate or prevent the loss caused by non-payment of the credit.

7
Supplier Credit Cover in Complex Transactions

As explained in Chapter 5, a supplier credit contract is a commercial contract where an exporter supplies goods or services to a foreign buyer on credit terms. In contracts for export of goods the exporter is usually a company incorporated in the country where the goods are manufactured, while in contracts for export of services the exporter is a company that performs its services either in the foreign buyer's country, a third country or the country of its incorporation.

In its simplest form the supplier credit contract is entered into by a single exporter and a foreign buyer, but this type of contract may be more complex. An example of a complex supplier credit contract is a construction contract between several construction firms acting in the capacity of exporters and a foreign buyer. Another example is an export credit transaction where a third party acts as an intermediary or an agent; therefore the exporter and foreign buyer do not have a direct contractual relationship. A transaction where a multinational company involves its subsidiary from another country in selling goods or services to a foreign buyer is also an example of a complex supplier credit contract. Foreign subsidiaries of multinational companies often act as their agents, distributors or intermediaries when selling goods or services to foreign buyers in countries of import.

The structure of export transactions where several exporters are involved or where third parties act between an exporter and a foreign buyer makes the work of ECAs more complex when providing cover for credit risks in such transactions. The higher complexity of an export transaction may negatively affect a company's eligibility for ECA cover for a credit risk when acting as a supplier. When difficulties obtaining the ECA cover for a complex export credit transaction arise, the parties should consider whether the transaction might be restructured to satisfy the ECA requirements. This and other issues connected with providing the ECA cover in complex supplier credit transactions are analysed below.

7.1   Cover where several parties are involved on the exporter's side

A supplier credit contract may be structured so that several exporters enter into an export credit contract with a single foreign buyer. When it is agreed that each exporter in such a contract has a separate claim and will receive a separate payment from the foreign buyer, the ECA supplier credit cover can be provided by issuing separate ECA policies to each exporter. Each ECA policy issued in this way covers the non-payment of a separate amount payable to an individual exporter. Instead of several ECA policies, the ECA may issue a single policy to all exporters by stating the separate amounts of cover provided to each exporter.

Where several exporters act in a consortium in a single supplier credit contract and it is agreed that the foreign buyer will make payment of the credit to one exporter only, usually called the consortium leader, the ECA supplier credit cover may be issued to each exporter in the consortium as described above. The consortium leader represents other exporters in relation to the ECA by applying for the ECA cover, paying the premium, claiming indemnification, etc. This type of supplier credit cover is typically issued for the risk of non-payment of the credit by the foreign buyer caused by commercial and political events. The consortium leader's payment obligation to other exporters, which arises after receiving payment from the foreign buyer, is usually not covered by this type of ECA cover.

However, some ECAs cover the political risk for prevention or delay in transfer of payment from the consortium leader to other exporters. This situation may occur when political events prevent the consortium leader from transferring payment out of the foreign buyer's country after receiving payment from the foreign buyer. Similarly, some ECAs cover political events that prevent the transfer of payment from the consortium leader's country to the countries of other exporters. Preventing or delaying the transfer of money is an important political risk that is usually covered by ECAs, but the scope of this type of cover depends on the place of payment agreed between the exporter and foreign buyer. The importance of the agreed place of payment for determining the scope of the ECA cover is analysed in Chapter 3.

7.2   Cover where the contract is between the exporter and its sub-supplier

Exporters often purchase various components for manufacturing a final product that will be supplied to a foreign buyer. These components are purchased from sub-suppliers and the payment in these transactions is often agreed on credit terms. In some transactions the value of components supplied by a sub-supplier on credit terms is substantial and the exporter's ability to pay the credit to the sub-supplier directly depends on the exporter's transaction with the foreign buyer. Therefore, in the case of non-payment of a credit by the foreign buyer, the exporter will not be able to make payment of the credit to the sub-supplier. In this structure, the sub-supplier is indirectly affected by the credit risk assumed by the exporter in the supplier credit contract with the foreign buyer. For this reason some sub-suppliers approach ECAs requesting the ECA cover for their credit risks agreed upon in their sub-supplier contracts with exporters.

The problem with transactions between sub-suppliers and exporters is that such transactions are not export transactions, which means the ECAs cannot cover the credit risks sub-suppliers have on exporters. In addition, sub-suppliers do not have any contractual claim for payment against a foreign buyer. Under exceptional circumstances, some ECAs may provide the ECA cover to a sub-supplier for the risk of non-payment by the exporter, but only when the sub-supplier is from the same country as the exporter. The risk covered by this type of cover is purely commercial and the ECA covers the exporter's insolvency, making it unable to make payment to the sub-supplier.

7.3 Cover issued to the exporter when acting through an intermediary in a country of import

Exporters sometimes enter into transactions where an intermediary from a country of import takes part in selling the exporter's goods or services in the intermediary's country. Such an intermediary is a legal entity, incorporated in the country of import, where it resells goods to local buyers on credit terms. In this structure the exporter does not have any control over the intermediary and its business in the country of import. The exporter does not sell the goods directly to local buyers, also called end buyers, and does not have any claim for payment against them.

The payment between the intermediary and exporter in this type of transaction is contingent, sometimes called the 'if and when' payment. The exporter sells goods or services to the intermediary in the country of import and the intermediary resells them to an end buyer in the same country on credit terms. Both the intermediary and exporter must wait for payment of the credit from the end buyer, which will be made to the intermediary, not the exporter. The intermediary's obligation to pay the exporter arises when the intermediary receives payment of the credit from the end buyer.

In a transaction entered on 'if and when' terms, the credit risk is assumed by the exporter because the exporter and not the intermediary will incur a loss if the end buyer does not pay the credit to the intermediary. Therefore exporters are interested in obtaining ECA cover for such credit risks and some ECAs provide this type of cover. The ECA cover is issued to the exporter for the risk of non-payment by the end buyer to the intermediary since the contract between the intermediary and end buyer provides payment on credit terms (Figure 7.1).

This type of the ECA cover does not always include all risks connected with this transaction. Often ECAs will not cover the risk of non-payment by the intermediary to the exporter since that payment is not agreed on credit terms. An intermediary that has received the payment from the end buyer may become insolvent and unable to convey the payment to the exporter. This particular risk, which is of a commercial nature, is usually not covered by ECAs.

In some situations, when non-payment by the intermediary to the exporter is caused by a political event, such a loss may be covered by some ECAs. Political events are out of the control of the contractual parties and therefore some ECAs are willing to cover political risks preventing payment from the intermediary to the exporter. However, this cover does not include commercial risks such as insolvency or payment default of the foreign intermediary.

The position of an ECA that provided cover for a credit risk in the transaction described above is weakened regarding recovery of the claim against the end buyer. The exporter to which the ECA cover is issued does not have any con-tractual relationship with the end buyer and cannot assign the claim against the end buyer to the ECA when claiming indemnification for the loss caused by non-payment of the credit. Such assignment is requested by ECAs in other transactions where an exporter has a direct contractual relationship with a for-eign buyer. The chances the ECA can recover any payment from the end buyer depend on a recovery action taken by the foreign intermediary because only the intermediary has a direct claim for payment against the end buyer. When

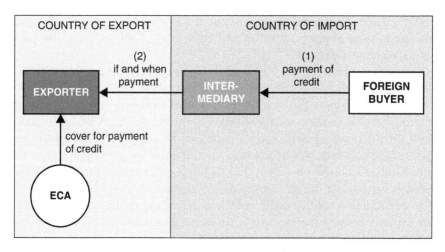

Figure 7.1   Cover issued to exporter when acting through foreign intermediary

taking a recovery action, the intermediary does not have any contractual obligation to follow instructions issued by the ECA. In addition, the intermediary is not obligated to try to avoid or minimise a loss for the ECA, like an insured exporter in a transaction in which an intermediary is not involved. To improve its position, the ECA may require the exporter to include specific provisions in its contract with the intermediary under which the intermediary must engage in recovery of the claim from the end buyer.

7.4   Cover issued to the exporter when acting through an intermediary in a third country

In the transaction above, the intermediary can be from a country other than the country of export or the country of import. Even in this transaction, the intermediary's obligation to make payment to the exporter is established in 'if and when' terms. Therefore, the intermediary is obligated to pay the exporter first when it receives payment from the end buyer in the country of import. Since this transaction is very similar to the transaction where the intermediary is from the country of import, it could be argued that this transaction is eligible for ECA cover from an ECA in the country of export because the credit risk is assumed by the exporter.

The ECA from the country of export may object to this structure and argue that this transaction consists of two international export transactions, the first between the exporter and the intermediary and the second between the intermediary acting as an exporter from its country and the foreign buyer in the country of import. Since the payment in the second transaction is agreed on credit terms it can be argued that the intermediary should obtain the ECA cover from the ECA in its country. This would not change the exporter's position significantly compared to a transaction where the ECA cover is issued by the ECA in the exporter's country.

However, obtaining the ECA cover from the ECA in intermediary's country is not always possible. The ECA in the intermediary's country may be reluctant to issue cover to the intermediary due to the lack of local content in the goods supplied to the end buyer. Also, it is possible there is no officially supported ECA in the intermediary's country.

When an intermediary from a third country cannot obtain cover from the ECA in its country, the only remaining solution is for the ECA from the exporter's country to issue the cover. The main argument for providing such cover is that the credit risk in the transaction is assumed by the exporter instead of the intermediary. As in the previous example, the ECA cover is limited to the risk of non-payment of the credit by the end buyer to the intermediary. The risk of non-payment by the intermediary to the exporter is not covered, except when it is caused by political events.

7.5   Cover issued to the exporter when acting through its subsidiary in a country of import

Today, numerous multinational companies have incorporated their subsidiaries in countries of import with the purpose of involving them in export transactions. Subsidiaries often purchase and import goods supplied by a parent company and resell them in the country of import to local buyers on credit terms.

There are several reasons for structuring export transactions in this way. The most important reason is to reduce the transaction costs by avoiding payment of high agent fees to local agents, and approaching potential local buyers with the goods ready for delivery, imported and cleared through customs. Also, structuring export transactions like this can be financially beneficial according to the local regulation in a country of import.

An export transaction structured as described above consists of two transactions. In the first transaction, the exporter sells the goods to the foreign buyer, the exporter's subsidiary incorporated in the country of import. This transaction is structured as a supplier contract where the importer is obligated to pay the exporter for the goods. The supplier contract between the exporter and its subsidiary acting as the importer is an export transaction traditionally covered by ECAs.

The second supplier contract is entered into within the country of import, between the subsidiary and the end buyer. This is a domestic contract between two domestic parties, the subsidiary acting in the capacity of a seller and the end buyer. This transaction does not contain any element of export and import because the goods have already been exported by the exporter and imported by its subsidiary into the country of import within the first transaction. While the first contract is an international contract between two contractual parties from various countries, the second one, between the importing subsidiary and the end buyer is purely domestic contract and agreed on credit terms (Figure 7.2).

The question is which payment risk the exporter wants the ECA to cover from the country of export. Is it the risk that its subsidiary in the country of import will not pay the purchase price for the goods delivered to it, or the

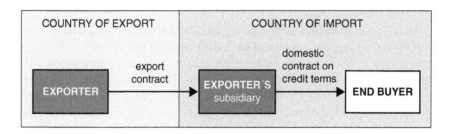

Figure 7.2   Export transactions with subsidiaries acting as importers

risk that the end buyer will not pay the subsidiary for the goods purchased on credit terms? Obviously the credit risk on the end buyer needs to be covered by the ECA, not the risk on the exporter's subsidiary. The exporter owns and controls its foreign subsidiary and may instruct it to pay the exporter. On the other hand, the end buyer may become insolvent or unable to pay the credit due to a political or commercial event. Non-payment of the credit by the end buyer to the subsidiary usually results in non-payment by the subsidiary to the exporter, causing a loss for the exporter. Therefore the exporter is interested in obtaining the ECA cover for the credit risk on the end buyer. However, providing this type of cover can be connected with difficulties that are described below.

7.6 Difficulties covering credit risks in domestic transactions

The first difficulty is that the exporter is not eligible to obtain ECA cover from the ECA in the country of export for a loss caused by non-payment of the credit by an end buyer to its subsidiary in the country of import. This is because the exporter does not have any direct contractual relationship with the end buyer and does not assume any formal credit risk on the end buyer. The second difficulty is that the exporter cannot claim payment from the end buyer and cannot assign the claim for payment against the end buyer to the ECA when claiming indemnification from the ECA. It is only the exporter's subsidiary from the country of import that has a direct contractual relationship with the end buyer and has right to claim payment of the credit from the end buyer. The credit risk on the end buyer is assumed by the subsidiary, not the exporter.

The solution to the problem above would be to issue the ECA cover to the exporter's subsidiary in the country of import for the loss caused by non-payment of the credit by the end buyer. The subsidiary is a separate legal entity incorporated in the country of import and it has legal capacity to enter into transactions with the ECA from the country of export. However, it is not always possible to issue the ECA cover to the foreign subsidiary for covering the credit risk in a purely domestic transaction.

The local law regulating the insurance business may prevent issuing the ECA cover to a foreign subsidiary for credit risk in a domestic transaction with the end buyer. The insurance business is strictly regulated in many countries and only properly licensed insurance companies are allowed to operate. Insurance companies are controlled by a supervising authority that can investigate and initiate proceedings against a legal entity or individual that conducts insurance business without licence. Additionally, some countries hold the directors of a company that has breached the insurance law criminally liable.

That restriction affects ECAs in the same way as any other insurer that does not hold a licence to conduct the insurance business in a foreign country. The fact that ECAs provide cover for credit risks with official support of their states

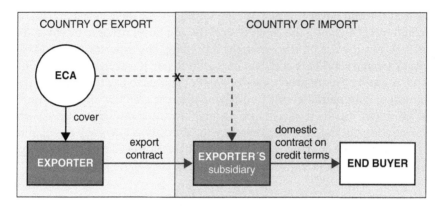

Figure 7.3 Restriction on carrying on insurance business in foreign country

does not change anything in this respect. Foreign insurers are not allowed to enter into a domestic market in a country of import and insure credit risks in domestic transactions (Figure 7.3).

It is likely the restriction above affects even ECAs that provide cover in the form of guarantees. Providing ECA cover in the form of guarantee is classified in some jurisdictions as conducting insurance business because the two basic characteristics of the ECA guarantees—covering a loss caused by non-payment of a credit and charging a premium for issuing a guarantee—are identical to insurance policies issued by ECAs. If an ECA guarantee issued to cover a domestic credit risk is classified in a foreign jurisdiction as an insurance policy, then issuing a guarantee can be classified as conducting insurance business without licence.

7.7 Solutions for covering credit risks in domestic transactions by foreign ECAs

The difficulty with issuing the ECA cover for credit risks in domestic transactions in foreign countries can be resolved by shifting the credit risk from the country of import to the country of export. This can be arranged by providing payment on 'if and when' terms in the contract between the exporter and its foreign subsidiary or by the issuing of a guarantee or a similar undertaking by the exporter to its foreign subsidiary.

When the foreign subsidiary's payment to the exporter is agreed on 'if and when' terms, the exporter will receive payment for the exported goods if and when its foreign subsidiary receives payment from the end buyer. The foreign subsidiary's obligation to pay the exporter is contingent and it arises first when the foreign subsidiary receives payment of the credit from the end buyer (Figure 7.4).

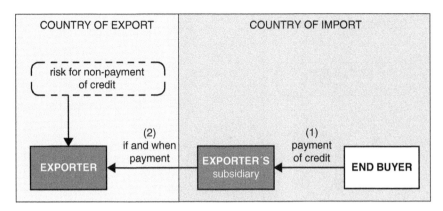

Figure 7.4 Shifting of credit risk by including 'if and when' payment terms

When the exporter and its foreign subsidiary have agreed on 'if and when' payment terms, the exporter assumes the risk of non-payment by the end buyer. When the exporter assumes the credit risk, it becomes eligible for ECA cover from the ECA in the country of export. The transaction between the exporter and its foreign subsidiary is international, not domestic, and many ECAs will issue the supplier credit cover to the exporter for this credit risk. By providing ECA cover in an international transaction between two entities from two countries the ECA cannot violate the law regulating the insurance business in the country of import.

Another way to shift the credit risk is issuing a guarantee by the exporter to its foreign subsidiary for non-payment of the credit by the end buyer. In this transaction the exporter receives payment for the exported goods from its foreign subsidiary upon delivery of the goods to the subsidiary. The foreign subsidiary then resells the goods to the end buyer in the country of import on credit terms. The foreign subsidiary assumes the risk of non-payment of the credit in this transaction, but it can be shifted to the exporter if the exporter issues a guarantee or similar undertaking to its foreign subsidiary. With this guarantee the exporter agrees to repay the purchase price to the foreign subsidiary if the end buyer does not pay the credit to the foreign subsidiary (Figure 7.5).

The ECA from the exporter's country may issue the ECA cover to the exporter for the credit risk included in the guarantee issued by the exporter to its foreign subsidiary. A guarantee issued by the exporter to its foreign subsidiary is an international transaction eligible for the credit risk cover by the ECA in the country of export. Providing the ECA cover for an international transaction cannot violate the law regulating the insurance business in the country of import.

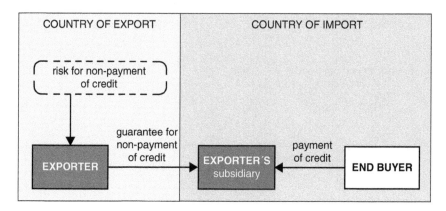

Figure 7.5   Shifting of credit risk by issuing a guarantee

From an exporter's point of view, the two ways to shift the credit risk are not always the most effective, because exporters treat their foreign subsidiaries as separate entities, incorporated in the country of import and managed according to local legislation. Foreign subsidiaries have their own balance sheets and financial results and their credit risks should stay on their books. However, when ECAs are prevented from covering credit risks in domestic transactions in the countries of import, the 'if and when' structure and the exporter's guarantee structure for shifting the credit risk to the exporter are the appropriate ways for obtaining ECA cover for such risks.

The position of ECAs that provide the ECA cover in the two solutions described above is weakened regarding recovery of a claim from the end buyer. The exporter in such a transaction cannot assign the claim for payment against the end buyer to the ECA because the exporter does not have a contractual relationship with the end buyer in the country of import. The ECA may require the exporter to arrange assignment of the claim for payment of credit by the foreign subsidiary to the ECA, but it is uncertain whether such assignment is valid and enforceable under the law of the country of import.

Where the claim for payment against the end buyer can be assigned by the subsidiary to the ECA, the claim can be denominated in a local currency, which may cause more difficulty for the ECA. In some countries of import the ECA may not be entitled to convert the recovered amount into a foreign currency and transfer it out of the country. Therefore the ECAs that provide this type of cover depend on the exporter's foreign subsidiary and its engagement in recovery of the claim from the end buyer. ECAs are aware of insufficiencies of this type of supplier credit cover and they try to construe the terms of their policies issued to exporters in a way that makes exporters liable for obligating their subsidiaries to engage in recovery of a claim from an end buyer.

7.8   Reinsuring of a domestic insurer by a foreign ECA

Another way to cover the credit risks in domestic transactions in a foreign country by an ECA from the country of export is the reinsuring of a domestic insurance company. In this type of ECA cover a domestic insurance company in the country of import insures the credit risk of the exporter's subsidiary in its domestic transaction with the end buyer. The credit risk in this transaction may be insured by a domestic insurance company that is properly licensed for conducting insurance business in the country of import.

The next step in this transaction is reinsuring the domestic insurer by the ECA from the country of export. The ECA takes over the major part of the credit risk by reinsuring the domestic insurer, which retains a small percentage of the credit risk on its books. The domestic insurer charges the insurance premium to the foreign subsidiary and pays the reinsurance premium to the ECA. The domestic insurer retains a percentage of the premium that is proportional to the retained percentage of the credit risk, and it may charge the ECA an additional amount for administrative costs.

It is unclear whether this structure is applicable in all countries of import and an investigation should be made before entering into the insurance and reinsurance transactions. The investigation, usually made in the form of obtaining a legal opinion, makes this type of transaction more expensive and may delay a transaction between the exporter's foreign subsidiary and the end buyer. Another problem in this structure could be the discrepancy between the terms of the ECA policy and the policy of the domestic insurer. Such discrepancy is difficult to eliminate through the reinsurance contract. Generally, this solution is not frequently applied because it is relatively complicated, expensive and time-consuming.

7.9   Global cover

Multinational exporters sometimes propose that ECAs issue cover for all credit risks that arise in their global trade from any country of export to any country of import. If a policy for global cover is issued to a parent company by the ECA in the country of the parent's incorporation, the policy probably would not violate the law regulating the insurance business in foreign countries. The global policy would cover credit losses of all companies in a group, both the parent and its subsidiaries, wherever they are incorporated and for any loss they may incur with non-payment of credits by their buyers.

The problem with the global credit risk cover is that it is not in line with the purpose of the ECA cover. This purpose is supporting national export, which does not include export from countries where the parent company has placed its subsidiaries. The foreign subsidiaries may apply for the ECA cover in their countries of incorporation when exporting and selling goods or services to foreign buyers. The ECAs in the countries where the parent companies are incorporated are reluctant to issue such global policies and engage their capacity in supporting exports from other countries.

7.10   Cover for political risks in transactions between exporters and their foreign subsidiaries

ECAs do not cover the credit risk in a transaction between an exporter and its foreign subsidiary because the exporter controls its foreign subsidiary and it may instruct the subsidiary to pay for the goods or services received from the exporter. ECAs apply various definitions of the term 'control of a subsidiary' based on the percentage of the exporter's shareholding in the foreign subsidiary. The general understanding is that an exporter controls a foreign subsidiary if it holds more than 50 per cent of shares in the subsidiary.

However, sometimes the payment made by a foreign subsidiary to an exporter is not received by the exporter due to events that are out of the control of the parties in the transaction. These are political events usually covered by ECAs and described in Chapter 3. Therefore some ECAs issue the ECA cover for political risks in transactions between an exporter and its foreign subsidiary. This cover does not include commercial risks such as insolvency and the foreign subsidiary's payment default.

8
Buyer Credit Cover

In the context of the ECA cover, buyer credit is a loan granted by a bank or another lender to a foreign buyer for the purchase of goods or services from an exporter. Unlike the supplier credit, where an exporter and foreign buyer agree on payment of the contractual price on credit terms, the buyer credit means that the foreign buyer borrows money from the bank to pay the exporter on delivery. The term 'buyer credit' is different from 'supplier credit' because the exporter (supplier) is not a party to the loan contract between the bank and the foreign buyer.

When entering into a loan contract, usually called a loan agreement, the foreign buyer acts as borrower. However, this book uses 'foreign buyer' instead of 'borrower' for two reasons. First, the foreign buyer is a special category of borrower because its connection with the export transaction makes the lending bank eligible for the ECA cover. The second reason is the purpose of the loan provided by a bank to the foreign buyer, which is payment of the price agreed in the commercial contract between the exporter and the foreign buyer. The foreign buyer acts in two capacities that are connected to each other, the capacity of buyer in the commercial contract with the exporter and the capacity of borrower in the loan agreement with the bank.

The bank that provides a loan to a foreign buyer knows that various political and commercial events may prevent the foreign buyer from repaying the loan and therefore is interested in obtaining the buyer credit cover from the ECA in the country of export (Figure 8.1). The bank pays a premium to the ECA that issues the policy to the bank, covering the bank's loss caused by non-repayment of the loan by the foreign buyer.

Terminology

The terms 'buyer credit cover' and 'supplier credit cover' are among the very few internationally accepted ECA terms that have the same meaning when used by the majority of ECAs and numerous users of the ECA cover. When dealing with other

> *types of the ECA cover described in this book, it is important to remember that a single type of the ECA cover can be provided by ECAs under different names. Therefore it is necessary to understand the concept of a particular type of the ECA cover and the risk covered instead of relying on a short heading under which a particular type of the ECA cover is provided.*

Numerous loan transactions covered by ECAs are medium- to long-term transactions with repayment periods of two years or more. In addition, the buyer credit cover for medium- to long-term risks is often issued by ECAs for the risks in single transactions. However, this type of cover also can be provided for short-term credit risks, which are loans with repayment periods of less than two years. The short-term buyer credit cover may be issued for single risks and for several risks included in a framework cover. The framework cover is described in Chapter 4.

8.1 Purpose of the loan and payment of the loan amount

The foreign buyer is party to two contracts, the commercial contract with the exporter and the loan contract with the lending bank. The purpose of borrowing money from the bank is to pay the contractual price to the exporter for goods or services purchased by the foreign buyer. Therefore, the commercial contract and the loan contract are connected and the bank must take into account certain provisions of the commercial contract when paying out the loan amount. For this reason, the bank contractually limits using the loan amount for paying the contractual price to the exporter. The foreign buyer is not allowed to use the loan amount for any other purpose and the bank strictly controls this. The bank normally stipulates in the loan agreement that it will make payment of the loan amount directly to the exporter after presentation of the required documents signed by the foreign buyer. These documents, called acceptance certificates, contain the foreign buyer's confirmation that the exporter has completed delivery of goods or services in accordance with the commercial contract.

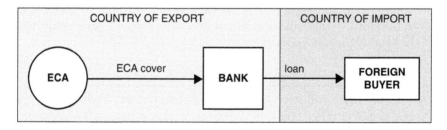

Figure 8.1 ECA buyer credit cover

Since ECAs support their national exports by issuing the buyer credit cover to banks, they require the lending bank to pay the loan amount directly to the exporter as described above. This requirement is provided as a standard term of the ECA policies for the buyer credit cover. Furthermore, some ECAs provide that their policies for the buyer credit cover will become effective when the exporter receives payment from the bank. If a lending bank pays the loan amount to the foreign buyer, contrary to the ECA requirement, and the foreign buyer fails to pay that amount to the exporter, such a risk is not covered by ECAs. This is why banks strictly control the use of the loan amount for the allowed purpose only.

Terminology

Payment of the loan amount by the bank to the exporter is also called disbursement or drawdown.

8.2   Separating the loan agreement from the commercial contract

In spite of the connection between the commercial contract and the loan agreement, lending banks strictly separate the foreign buyer's obligation to repay a loan from a possible dispute regarding performance of the exporter's contractual obligations under the commercial contract. They include a special separation clause in the loan agreement that prevents the foreign buyer from delaying or suspending repayment of the loan due to the breach of the commercial contract by the exporter. Therefore the foreign buyer is obligated to repay the loan to the lending bank even when it later appears the exporter's delivery does not conform to the requirements of the commercial contract.

Terminology

In ECA terminology, the separation clause included in the loan agreement is sometimes called the Isabella Clause.

8.3   Limitations of buyer credit cover

The buyer credit cover is limited to the risk of non-repayment of the loan amount by the foreign buyer. The loan amount covered by ECAs normally consists of the principal and the contractual interest. Other obligations of the foreign buyer, including obligation to pay the late payment interest, damages for breach of the loan agreement and similar payment obligations, normally are not covered by ECAs. This limitation is usually included as a standard term of the ECA policies for the buyer credit cover.

8.4   ECA requirements for issuing cover for medium- to long-term buyer credits

When the buyer credit cover for a medium- to long-term loan is provided by an ECA from a country that participates in the OECD Arrangement, the loan transaction must satisfy several requirements. The basic requirement for this type of cover is that the foreign buyer must pay a minimum of 15 per cent of the export contract value at or before the starting point of credit. The term 'export contract value' is related to the commercial contract between the exporter and the foreign buyer that borrows money from a bank for paying the contractual price to the exporter. Therefore the foreign buyer must make a down payment of 15 per cent of the contractual price to the exporter in order to borrow the remaining 85 per cent from the bank. The 85 per cent of the contractual price is the maximum loan amount that can be covered by the ECAs that apply the Arrangement when issuing the buyer credit cover for medium- to long-term buyer credit transactions.

The Arrangement also regulates that the repayment period of a loan covered by an ECA cannot be longer than five to ten years. The foreign buyer is obligated to repay its credit in equal amounts at regular intervals of no more than six months. The first repayment is to be made no later than six months after the starting point of credit. Interest is calculated on the outstanding amount at the time of payment. ECAs cannot charge a premium for the ECA cover at a lower rate than the minimum premium rate, which the Arrangement also regulates.

Chapter 21 analyses the Arrangement in more detail. When analysing the Arrangement it is important to remember that it applies to medium- to long-term buyer credit transactions only. It does not apply to short-term buyer credit transactions.

8.5   Other ECA requirements for issuing buyer credit cover

When issuing the buyer credit cover to a lending bank, ECAs may require some provisions to be included in the loan agreement. Depending on the risk assessment of a particular loan transaction, an ECA may require various types of security to be provided for repayment of the loan. An ECA may also require the inclusion of various covenants in the loan agreement where financial covenants are of special importance. A financial covenant is a contractual provision in a loan agreement that imposes obligations on the foreign buyer regarding its liquidity, solvency and capital requirements.

Other covenants that a bank may be required to include in loan agreements are: a negative pledge preventing the foreign buyer from creating or permitting security over its assets without consent of the lending bank; pari passu providing that the foreign buyer's payment obligation under the loan

```
┌─────────────────────────────────────────────────────────┐
│                                                         │
│   BASIC OECD ARRANGEMENT REQUIREMENTS                   │
│                                                         │
│   • DOWN PAYMENT 15%                                    │
│                                                         │
│   • MAXIMUM REPAYMENT TERMS FIVE TO TEN YEARS           │
│                                                         │
│   • REPAYMENT OF CREDIT IN EQUAL AMOUNTS                │
│     ATT REGULAR INTERVALS OF NO LONGER THAN SIX MONTHS  │
│                                                         │
│   ECA SPECIFIC REQUIREMENTS                             │
│                                                         │
│   • SECURITY                                            │
│                                                         │
│   • FINANCIAL AND OTHER COVENANTS                       │
│                                                         │
└─────────────────────────────────────────────────────────┘
```

Figure 8.2   Requirements for issuing ECA cover in medium- to long-term transactions

agreement will rank equally with its other payment obligations; restriction on disposals preventing or limiting the foreign buyer to dispose over all or some of its assets, etc. The number and scope of covenants an ECA may require in a loan agreement depends on the ECA's assessment of the risk that the foreign buyer will default on repayment of the loan (Figure 8.2).

By requiring the inclusion of certain provisions into loan agreements, ECAs may interfere in loan transactions more than they interfere in commercial contracts when issuing the supplier credit cover. This depends partly on the nature of international loan agreements that give the bank more control over the foreign buyer's business than exporters have in relation to foreign buyers under various commercial contracts.

8.6   Buyer credit cover for bank-to-bank loans

Issuing the ECA cover is possible even when two banks are involved in providing a loan to a foreign buyer. This transaction consists of two loan agreements, one when a foreign bank provides a loan to a local bank and the second when the local bank provides a loan to a local buyer for purchasing goods or services from an exporter.

The buyer credit cover is issued by an ECA to the foreign bank for the risk of non-repayment of the loan by the local bank (Figure 8.3). This particular loan agreement is separated from the loan agreement between the local bank and the local buyer in terms of repayment of the loan. Therefore the local bank must repay the loan to the foreign bank even if the local buyer defaults on repayment of its loan to the local bank. Since the ECA cover is provided to the foreign bank only, it does not include the risk of non-repayment of the loan by the local buyer to the local bank.

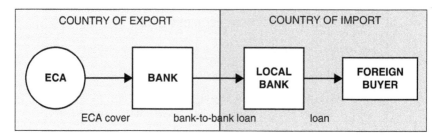

Figure 8.3   ECA buyer credit cover for bank-to-bank loans

The bank-to-bank loan structure described above may be used for various reasons. The local bank may borrow foreign currency from a foreign bank at a lower interest rate because of the underlying export transaction. In such a situation the local bank and the local buyer may choose to reduce transaction costs by involving the foreign bank in this type of transaction.

The foreign bank may be unable to assess the foreign buyer's ability to repay the loan and is willing to lend money to the local bank but not to the foreign buyer. The local bank often has a good local knowledge and relationship with the local buyer, and is willing to enter into the loan transaction structured as a bank-to-bank loan. This structure can be used for other reasons as well.

8.7   Buyer credit cover issued to several banks in syndicate

ECAs deal with the banks from the countries of export and with multinational banks when issuing cover for non-repayment of a loan provided to a foreign buyer. The classic loan structure where a single bank acts as a lender and the foreign buyer acts as a borrower is still frequently applied in export credit trans-actions, but the loan transactions can be structured in another way.

The financial amounts involved in export credit transactions increase all the time, and banks are not always willing to lend the entire loan amount to a foreign buyer, even when the risk of non-repayment of the loan is covered by an ECA. This is especially the case where the loan amount is large and a single bank does not want to take the entire residual risk. As explained in Chapter 4, the residual risk is the percentage of a credit risk that is not covered by an ECA. This percentage is usually five or ten per cent of a loan amount, but even such a low percentage may represent a large amount. When a single bank is prevented from acting as a single lender it may invite other banks to participate in a loan, usually in the form of a syndicated loan. In a syndicated loan transaction two or more banks provide a loan to a foreign buyer on common terms. Each syndi-cated bank acts as a lender for a specified portion of the loan amount. The syndi-cated loan transaction is documented and governed by a single loan agreement between all parties involved. The number of banks in a syndicate depends on the total amount of the loan and complexity of the transaction. One bank in a bank syndicate is appointed as an agent or lead bank. The agent bank usually applies for the ECA cover for the entire credit risk in a syndicated loan (Figure 8.4).

Issuing the buyer credit cover to several banks in a syndicated loan transaction is acceptable for ECAs as long as all banks satisfy the criteria of a particular ECA regarding their reputation and ability to perform their obligations under the loan agreement and ECA policy. ECAs usually deal with the agent bank because it is more practical than dealing with several banks involved in the same transaction.

ECAs require the agent bank to provide a power of attorney giving it the right to act for and on behalf of all syndicated banks in relation to the ECA. In the case of non-repayment of the loan by the foreign buyer, the agent bank claims payment of the entire amount of indemnification from the ECA. After receiving the indemnification the agent will transfer the proportionate shares of the indemnified amount to each bank in the syndicate.

8.8 Buyer credit cover and loan participation

Participation of other banks in an existing loan transaction is also possible. Such participation may be in the form of assigning of a portion of the loan by the lending bank to a new bank or banks with the foreign buyer's consent. After completing the assignment the new bank that joins the loan agreement becomes a lender along with the original lending bank, each bank for its portion of the loan. The result of loan participation is a contractual structure

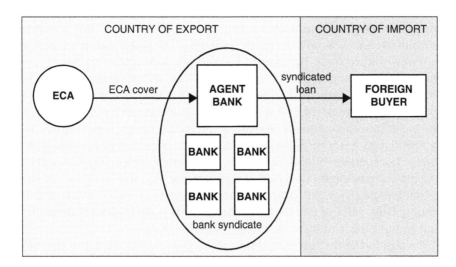

Figure 8.4   ECA buyer credit cover for syndicated loan

similar to the syndicated loan described above. Where the ECA cover is issued to the original lending bank, the intended participation of another bank must be approved by the ECA. If the ECA approves this transaction, the new bank will become the co-insured bank under the existing ECA policy.

Terminology

> *The terms 'loan participation' and 'loan sub-participation' have no commonly accepted legal meaning and they can be confused with each other. The term 'loan participation' is also used for a transaction described below as a loan sub-participation, which is important to remember when dealing with these transactions.*

8.9   Buyer credit cover and funded loan sub-participation

In a loan sub-participation transaction a sub-participant agrees to pay a portion of the loan amount to a lending bank without becoming a lender under the existing loan agreement between the lending bank and the foreign buyer. The sub-participant shares repayments of the loan proportionally with the lending bank, including the contractual interest, and it assumes the risk of non-repayment of the loan by the foreign buyer. The sub-participant is not a contractual party to the loan agreement and it does not have any contractual relationship with the foreign buyer. Therefore the sub-participant cannot claim repayment of the loan or exercise other contractual rights against the foreign buyer.

Since the sub-participant is not a party to the loan agreement it cannot assume the capacity of a co-insured under the ECA policy issued to cover the risk of non-repayment of the loan in which it sub-participates. This is a disadvantage of sub-participation because only the insured lending bank is entitled to claim indemnification from the ECA in case of the foreign buyer's default on repayment of the loan. The insured bank will be indemnified by the ECA for the entire amount non-paid by the foreign buyer, including the proportional share of the sub-participant. The sub-participant has no right to claim any indemnification from the ECA if the insured bank does not transfer its share of the indemnification amount received by the ECA to the sub-participant. The sub-participant takes three risks, the risk of non-repayment of the loan by the foreign buyer under the loan agreement, the risk that the lending bank will not pay the sub-participant its repaid amounts of the loan that are regularly paid by the foreign buyer and received by the lending bank, and the risk that the lending bank will not pay the sub-participant its portion of the indemnification amount the lending bank received from the ECA.

The position of the sub-participant can be improved in relation to the ECA if the lending bank partly assigns its rights under the ECA policy to the sub-participant proportional to the sub-participant's participation in the loan. As a result, the ECA would cover the sub-participant's loss caused by non-repayment of the loan by the foreign buyer and the sub-participant would be eligible to claim indemnification directly from the ECA. This would eliminate the risk that the lending bank would not pay the sub-participant its portion of indemnification received from the ECA. This solution requires the lending bank to assign the entire non-paid amount of credit to the ECA in case of indemnification because the sub-participant does not own any claim against the foreign buyer and cannot assign a claim to the ECA. This sub-participation is called funded sub-participation because the sub-participant pays a portion of the loan amount to the lending bank when entering into the sub-participating contract.

8.10   Buyer credit cover and unfunded loan sub-participation

Another form of sub-participation in a loan transaction is called unfunded sub-participation. In this transaction the sub-participant does not pay any portion of the loan amount to the lending bank when entering into the sub-participating agreement. This transaction is usually structured and documented in the form of guarantee issued by the sub-participant to the lending bank for non-repayment of a portion of the loan amount by the foreign buyer. In return for issuing such a guarantee, the sub-participant receives fees from the lending bank or shares the contractual interest paid by the foreign buyer under the loan agreement with the lending bank. However, the sub-participant does not share repayment of the principal of the loan amount with the lending bank because the sub-participant has not funded any part of it.

The sub-participant's main obligation is to pay the lending bank a proportional amount of the loan amount in the event of the foreign buyer's default. As with funded loan participation, the sub-participant does not have any contractual relationship with the foreign buyer and cannot exercise contractual rights against it. When a non-funded sub-participation in the loan agreement is documented as a guarantee and the ECA cover is obtained for the risk of non-repayment of the loan by the foreign buyer, three issues must be observed. First, the sub-participant is not a party to the loan agreement and consequently cannot become the co-insured under the ECA policy. Second, an ECA may understand the sub-participant's undertaking in the form of guarantee as security for repayment of the loan, which may affect the lending bank's right to claim indemnification from the ECA because the majority of ECAs require an insured bank or exporter to demand payment under the guarantee before claiming indemnification for a loss caused by non-repayment of a loan. If the insured bank makes such a demand and the sub-participant pays the lending bank its portion of the non-repaid amount of the loan, under its sub-participating guarantee, an ECA may understand that the sub-participant has acted as guarantor for the loan repayment. As a consequence, the ECA may reduce its indemnification paid to the lending bank for the amount paid by the sub-participant. In order to avoid such confusion, the lending bank should disclose the existence of sub-participation to the ECA when applying for ECA cover and explain the distinction between sub-participation and guarantee. Third, the sub-participant does not have any rights against the ECA, as with funded sub-participation as explained above. However, even in this transaction, the position of the sub-participant can be improved in relation to the ECA by a partial assignment of rights under the ECA policy as with funded sub-participation.

8.11   Buyer credit cover issued to a multinational bank acting through a local branch

Multinational banks sometimes provide their loans to foreign buyers by negotiating a loan through a branch registered in a foreign buyer's country. When applying for the buyer credit cover for a loan transaction negotiated in this way, some multinational banks ask ECAs to include the name of the lending bank and the name of its local branch registered in the foreign buyer's country in their policy document. Involving a multinational bank's local branch in providing the ECA cover raises the question of whether such a loan transaction can be viewed as a domestic transaction that takes place in the foreign buyer's country and whether providing the ECA cover in a domestic transaction violates the legislation regulating the insurance business in the foreign buyer's country. As explained in Chapter 7, if a foreign ECA insures credit risks in domestic transactions between a foreign buyer and another party from its country, it can be characterised in some jurisdictions as conducting insurance business in the foreign buyer's country without license.

It is typically argued that a branch registered in the foreign buyer's country is not an independent legal entity but instead an organisational part or extension of the multinational bank. The contractual parties to the loan agreement are the multinational bank and foreign buyer and, since the multinational bank is incorporated in a country other than the foreign buyer's country, it is an international agreement, not domestic. Consequently, the credit risk in an international loan agreement can be covered by the ECA from the country of export without violating the legislation on insurance business in the foreign buyer's country. The appearance of the name of the bank's local branch in an ECA policy does not change anything in the international character of the loan agreement. This argument is based on the general principles of the law of contract and the legislation governing the incorporation of banks and registration of their foreign branches.

However, the legal status of a local branch of a foreign bank changes over time and today such a branch is treated as an independent legal entity for specific purposes in some jurisdictions. A local branch can be treated in a foreign buyer's country as an independent legal entity for the purpose of implementing local legislation on insolvency, bankruptcy, tax, issuing securities, etc. The varying legal status of a local branch of a foreign bank, when it is treated as a legal entity for selected purposes and as a dependent extension of the foreign bank for other purposes, is sometimes called the hybrid status. This status of a local branch may complicate the analysis of the problem above and result in uncertainty regarding the question of whether a loan agreement containing the name of a local branch in addition to the name of the multinational bank will be viewed as a domestic contract in some jurisdictions. Consequently, it may create uncertainty regarding the question of whether the provision of ECA cover by a foreign ECA for the credit risk agreed in a domestic contract violates the legislation on insurance business in the foreign buyer's country.

Additionally, many developed financial markets are in the process of strengthening their regulations that govern financial services, and this should be considered when analysing this problem. This process may establish completely different criteria for determining where a financial service takes place by disregarding the country of incorporation of a multinational bank. Providing the ECA cover is also a financial service and it is important to follow regulatory changes in this area to determine whether a foreign ECA is allowed to provide cover for a loan agreement negotiated by a local branch of a multinational bank.

The best way to deal with this issue and avoid uncertainty is to exclude the name of a local branch of multinational bank from the ECA documentation. In reality, ECAs deal with banks that are incorporated and have their principal place of business out of the foreign buyer's country and the ECA policies should mirror this factual relationship. Including the name of a local branch in the ECA policy adds nothing to the policy in terms of its validity or the scope of the ECA cover provided to a multinational bank acting as the insured. This way of construing ECA policies does not affect the right of multinational banks to book their transactions internally in a way they find appropriate.

9
Other Types of ECA Cover

The most important types of the ECA cover are the supplier credit and buyer credit cover, both of which cover the risk of non-payment of a credit by a foreign buyer. However, exporters and banks deal with other types of risks connected to export transactions for which they need cover from ECAs. These risks may arise in an early stage of an export transaction, before the date for delivery of goods or services to a foreign buyer, and after completing the delivery. In order to support their national exports, numerous ECAs provide cover for several types of risks that differ from the risk of non-payment of credit by a foreign buyer. In addition, ECAs follow development in the international trade and facilitate the needs of exporters and banks by issuing specially tailored policies for complex export transactions. These special policies include several types of risks.

Below is an analysis of the ECA cover for manufacturing loss issued to exporters, pre-shipment cover issued to banks, cover for contract bonds and guarantees, interconnected bonds and guarantees issued to banks, the counter-indemnity cover issued to exporters and cover for confirmed letters of credit. These are examples of the ECA cover issued to exporters and banks in connection to export transactions but other types of cover may be provided for specific risks in export transactions.

Terminology

Different ECAs use various names for the same or very similar types of cover. Therefore it is necessary to understand the concept of a particular type of the ECA cover and the risk covered instead of relying on a short heading under which a particular type of ECA cover is provided.

9.1   Cover for manufacturing loss

ECAs provide this type of cover to exporters for a loss they may incur between the date of signing a commercial contract and the date for delivery of goods or services to a foreign buyer. This period, also called the manufacturing period, can be relatively long depending on the nature of goods or services to be manufactured and delivered to the foreign buyer.

As with other export transactions analysed in this book, various political or commercial events may interrupt or suspend the exporter's work during the manufacturing period. ECAs cover a loss caused to the exporter by an interruption or suspension of its manufacturing process that lasts more than six months. These are two basic requirements for covering manufacturing loss, but some ECAs have additional requirements regarding the suspension or interruption of a commercial contract. Normally ECAs do not cover manufacturing loss when a commercial contract is interrupted or suspended because of the exporter's breach of contract.

The manufacturing loss cover provided by ECAs is useful for exporters when investing substantial amounts of money in labour and material during the manufacturing process. When the performance of a commercial contract and delivery of the goods is delayed or becomes impossible, the exporter may incur a loss that is difficult to recover from the foreign buyer. Some commercial contracts state that a foreign buyer will provide partial payments of the contractual price during the manufacturing period to cover manufacturing costs and minimise the exporter's possible manufacturing loss. However, not all foreign buyers are willing to accept these payment terms and only exporters with a strong bargaining position may protect themselves from a manufacturing loss in this way.

Exporters are in a better position where the OECD Arrangement applies since it requires down payment of 15 per cent of the contractual price. The down payment may be enough to cover manufacturing costs, but the manufacturing costs in some transactions are significantly higher than the amount paid as the down payment. In such situations obtaining the ECA cover for manufacturing loss can be an appropriate protection for exporters against this type of loss. The extent of the ECA cover for manufacturing loss depends on the delivery terms in the commercial contract, which can be quite long for the supply of capital goods or specially manufactured equipment.

9.2   Calculation of manufacturing loss

The calculation of a manufacturing loss is different from the calculation of loss under the ECA cover for supplier credit and buyer credit. The manufacturing loss includes only the effective manufacturing costs incurred by the exporter, such as the costs of labour and material. The transaction profit, which exporters include in the contractual price, is usually not included in this type of ECA cover. The highest amount of manufacturing loss is limited by the ECA policy as with other types of losses covered by ECAs.

When covering this type of loss, ECAs do not differentiate between political and commercial events that may interrupt or suspend the exporter's performance during the manufacturing period. In practice, this means this type of loss is covered by the same percentage of cover irrespective of the nature of the event that caused it.

In order to distinguish the cover for manufacturing loss and the supplier credit cover it is important to see these two types of the ECA cover from a time perspective. Manufacturing loss may incur before the date for delivery of goods or services to a foreign buyer while the loss caused by non-payment of a credit by a foreign buyer may incur after the delivery is complete and the foreign buyer's obligation to pay the credit has arisen.

9.3   Cover for manufacturing loss combined with supplier credit or buyer credit cover

The ECA cover for manufacturing loss may be combined with the ECA cover for supplier credit. An example of such combination is a commercial contract for supply of specially manufactured goods where the payment of contractual price is agreed upon on credit terms. Due to the specific characteristics of the goods, the exporter needs time for their manufacturing before delivering the goods to the foreign buyer. The exporter may obtain the ECA cover for the manufacturing loss caused by the interruption or suspension of the contract with the foreign buyer during the manufacturing period.

Once the delivery of goods is completed, a new risk arises—the risk of non-payment of the credit by the foreign buyer. Even this risk can be covered by ECAs in the form of supplier credit cover. By obtaining the manufacturing loss cover and the supplier credit cover for the risks connected with the same foreign buyer and commercial contract, the exporter is protected in all stages of the commercial contract. Both these types of cover are included in a single ECA policy, usually called a combined policy.

It is also possible to combine the manufacturing loss cover issued to an exporter and the buyer credit cover issued to a bank that provides a loan to a foreign buyer for payment of the contractual price to the exporter. An example of this combination is a transaction where the exporter needs time to manufacture goods before delivering them to the foreign buyer that will pay the contractual price on delivery. The exporter may obtain the ECA cover for manufacturing loss caused by interruption or suspension of the commercial contract during the manufacturing period. Since the payment of the entire contractual price is due on delivery, the exporter is not interested in obtaining any other type of the ECA cover. On the other hand, the foreign buyer borrows money from the bank and the risk of non-repayment of the loan may be covered by the same ECA that covers the manufacturing loss. Since the commercial contract and loan agreement are connected, the ECA may cover both in the form of a combined cover. In this example, the ECA policies are issued to the exporter and the bank. Exporters or banks frequently use a combination of the ECA cover for manufacturing loss with the cover for supplier credit or buyer credit, but other types of the ECA cover also may be combined.

9.4   Pre-shipment cover issued to banks

This type of cover is issued to a bank for the risk of non-repayment of a loan provided to an exporter for financing the manufacture of goods or services for export (Figure 9.1). The pre-shipment cover issued to banks is different from other types of the ECA cover because it is issued to cover a credit risk in a loan transaction that takes place in the country of export, without a connection to the country of import. The exporter uses the loan amount to purchase the materials, products or services necessary for manufacturing the goods for export.

ECAs provide the pre-shipment cover to banks because banks are not always willing to lend money to an exporter for working capital during the manufacturing period of goods or services for export. However, a bank may change its position if the risk for non-repayment of such a loan is covered by an ECA. Numerous ECAs support their national exports by providing this type of cover which is of special importance for small and medium-sized companies when manufacturing goods or services for export.

This type of ECA cover has nothing to do with the foreign buyer and its obligation to pay the contractual price for the exported goods. The pre-shipment cover is related to an early stage of an export transaction and its purpose is to enable the exporter to manufacture the goods or services for export. If the exporter does not repay the loan and the ECA indemnifies the lending bank for the loss, the ECA will try to recover the loss from the exporter. This recovery takes place in the country of export and the foreign buyer is not involved. The distinction between political and commercial risks is not significant for this type of ECA cover since it covers non-repayment of the loan by applying the same percentage of cover.

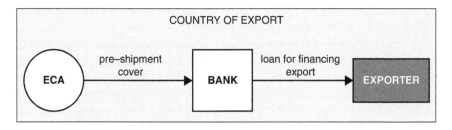

Figure 9.1   ECA pre-shipment cover issued to bank for loan to exporter

9.5   Cover for contract bonds and guarantees

ECAs issue this type of cover to banks for a loss caused by making payment under a contract bond or guarantee issued by a bank to a foreign buyer as a beneficiary. ECAs require that a contract bond or guarantee must be issued by a bank at the request of an exporter in connection with its commercial contract with a foreign buyer. When issuing this type of bond or guarantee, the bank requires the exporter to indemnify the bank for a payment made to the foreign buyer under the bond or guarantee. The exporter's undertaking to indemnify the bank is often called the counter-indemnity or counter-guarantee.

The exporter that issued the counter-indemnity to the bank may become insolvent and unable to indemnify the bank for the amount the bank has paid to the foreign buyer under a bond or guarantee. ECAs cover this risk by issuing the ECA cover to the bank for the loss caused by not receiving indemnification from the exporter. After paying the foreign buyer, the bank is required to request indemnification from the exporter and, if the exporter does not indemnify the bank, the bank becomes entitled to claim indemnification from the ECA. When claiming indemnification from the ECA, the bank is required to assign to the ECA its right to claim indemnification from the exporter. After indemnifying the bank the ECA will try to recover the indemnified amount from the exporter.

9.6   Cover for justified and unfair calling of contract bonds and guarantees

The purpose of contractual bonds and guarantees, usually unconditional and payable on first demand, is to protect a foreign buyer against a breach of a commercial contract by an exporter. As long as the exporter is not in breach of the commercial contract, the foreign buyer is not supposed to call a bond or a guarantee or demand payment from the bank that issued a guarantee. However, due to the legal nature of unconditional bonds and guarantees, the foreign buyer can call a bond or a guarantee when the exporter is in breach of the commercial contract and when no breach has occurred. Calling a bond or guarantee caused by the exporter's breach of the commercial contract is called justified calling, while a calling that is not caused by the exporter's breach is called unfair, unjustified or abusive calling.

The distinction between the justified and unfair calling of an unconditional and on demand guarantee is not significant for the bank since it must pay the foreign buyer regardless of the reason for calling. When issuing bonds and guarantees at an exporter's request, banks are interested in obtaining an ECA policy to cover losses caused by both justified and unfair calling. Numerous ECAs provide this type of the ECA cover, covering any payment made by the

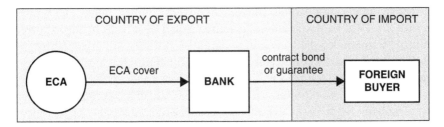

Figure 9.2   ECA cover issued to bank for contract bond or guarantee

bank under a bond or guarantee that is not indemnified by the exporter. Some ECAs provide this type of cover for unfair calling only.

The percentage of cover typically provided in this type of ECA policy ranges from 80 to 90 per cent of the bank's loss, but it can be even lower because ECAs want banks to pressure the exporter to solve issues with the foreign buyer that may arise in performing the commercial contract and avoid calling of a bond or guarantee. The risk of justified or unfair calling of a bond or a guarantee is neither political nor commercial in the meaning described in Chapter 3. It is a risk of a possible breach of the commercial contract by the exporter that results in calling a bond or guarantee or a foreign buyer's breach of the commercial contract when calling a bond or a guarantee without being entitled to do so under the commercial contract (Figure 9.2).

Types of contract bonds

> *Some usual types of contract bonds or guarantees issued to a foreign buyer as a beneficiary are:*
>
> *Performance bond or guarantee that guarantees payment of an amount to a foreign buyer if the exporter fails to make delivery or complete contractual works in accordance with the terms and conditions of the commercial contract;*
>
> *Advance payment guarantee that guarantees that any advance payment made by the foreign buyer to the exporter will be repaid if the exporter fails to deliver goods or services for which the foreign buyer has made the advance payment;*
>
> *Bid bond or guarantee that guarantees payment of an amount to a foreign buyer if the exporter fails to enter into the commercial contract with the foreign buyer when its bid has been accepted by the foreign buyer.*

9.7   Cover for interconnected bonds and guarantees

Contract bonds and guarantees are sometimes issued as several interconnected guarantees. An example of such a structure is a bond or a guarantee issued to the foreign buyer by a bank in the foreign buyer's country, called a local bank. In turn the local bank receives a guarantee issued by a bank in the exporter's country, sometimes called a counter-guarantee. With a counter-guarantee, the bank in the exporter's country undertakes to indemnify the local bank for the amount the local bank paid to the foreign buyer under the bond or guarantee. The bank in the exporter's country that has issued a counter-guarantee to the local bank requires the exporter to issue another guarantee, often called a counter-indemnity. With a counter-indemnity, the exporter agrees to pay the bank in the exporter's country the amount this bank paid the local bank in the foreign buyer's country.

The ECA cover for contract bonds or guarantees is issued to the bank in the exporter's country for the risk of calling the counter-guarantee by the local bank in the foreign buyer's country (Figure 9.3). The indemnification under the ECA policy issued to the bank in the exporter's country will be paid by the ECA only if the exporter does not indemnify the bank when requested.

9.8   Cover for counter indemnity issued to exporters

This type of cover is issued by ECAs to exporters for the risk of indemnifying a bank in case of unfair calling of a bond or guarantee issued by the bank to a foreign buyer. When issuing a bond or a guarantee to a foreign buyer at the exporter's request, the bank requires the exporter to indemnify the bank in case of calling the bond or guarantee. The exporter's undertaking to indemnify the bank is called the counter-indemnity and it includes both the justified and unfair calling of the bond or guarantee.

Since the exporter will take the final loss caused by the foreign buyer's calling of a bond or guarantee, the exporter may obtain the ECA cover but only for the loss caused by indemnifying the bank for unfair calling of the bond or guarantee. When the foreign buyer has made a justified calling of the bond or guarantee and the exporter has indemnified the bank for this payment, the

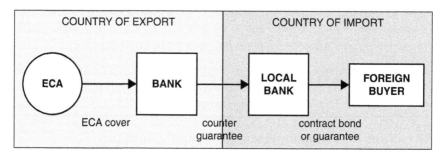

Figure 9.3   ECA cover issued to bank for counter guarantee

exporter's loss is not included in this type of ECA cover because the calling of a bond or guarantee is caused by the exporter's breach of commercial contract with the foreign buyer.

Paying of indemnification under this type of the ECA cover requires assessing whether the foreign buyer's calling of the bond or guarantee was justified. ECAs do not make such an assessment since it is difficult to assess all facts, contractual provisions of the commercial contract between the exporter and the foreign buyer and arguments of the contractual parties. Instead of making such an assessment, ECAs require the exporter to obtain a judgment of a court or an arbitration award against the foreign buyer proving that the foreign buyer's calling of the bond or guarantee was unfair. Obtaining such a judgment or award can be a burdensome procedure with an uncertain outcome. In some exceptional cases, ECAs may assess the foreign buyer's calling of a bond or guarantee themselves, but they do this in special situations only.

It is important to observe the difference in the scope of the ECA cover for contract bonds and guarantees issued to banks and the ECA cover for counter-indemnity issued to exporters. The cover issued to banks normally includes justified and unfair calling while the cover issued to exporters includes unfair calling only.

9.9 Cover for confirmed letters of credit

In the ECA context, the letter of credit is a method of payment against presented documents often agreed upon between an exporter and a foreign buyer. The letter of credit transaction involves two banks—the bank of the foreign buyer which issues a letter of credit and a bank in the exporter's country. The bank in the exporter's country advises the letter of credit to the exporter, but it may also confirm it. By confirming the letter of credit, the bank in the exporter's country assumes the same obligations as the issuing bank, including the obligation to make payment to the exporter against presented documents if they satisfy all terms of the letter of credit.

When the confirming bank receives the documents required under the letter of credit, it examines them and makes payment to the exporter if it is satisfied the documents comply with the terms in the letter of credit. After that, the confirming bank conveys the documents to the issuing bank and requests payment from the issuing bank of the amount already paid to the exporter. In this transaction, the confirming bank takes the risk that the issuing bank does not pay under the confirmed letter of credit. The non-payment by the issuing bank may be caused by political and commercial events and confirming banks are interested in obtaining the ECA cover for this risk before they confirm a letter of credit. Many ECAs provide ECA cover to confirming banks for the risk of

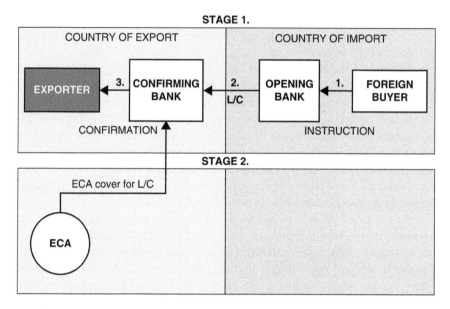

Figure 9.4   ECA cover for confirmed letter of credit (L/C)

non-payment by an issuing bank under a confirmed letter of credit (Figure 9.4). The percentage of the ECA cover is often lower in this type of cover than the percentage of the ECA cover in the supplier credit and buyer credit transactions. Some ECAs will indemnify the confirming bank with only 50 per cent of the loss caused by the non-payment of the issuing bank.

The exporter is not involved in this type of ECA cover that is issued to the confirming bank because the exporter has already received payment from the confirming bank and may not incur a loss if the issuing bank does not make payment to the confirming bank. By providing the cover for the confirmed letters of credit, ECAs indirectly support their national exports. The political and commercial risks connected with a foreign issuing bank can be such that the bank in the exporter's country simply does not want to confirm the letter of credit if the risk of non-payment by the issuing bank is not covered by an ECA. ECAs are aware that it is easier for an exporter to deal with the bank in its country than with the issuing bank in the foreign buyer's country; therefore they provide this type of cover.

9.10   Applicability of OECD and EU regulations

The OECD and EU regulation analysed in Chapter 21 applies to ECA cover for manufacturing loss only. It is not applicable to the ECA cover for contract bonds and guarantees, interconnected bonds and guarantees, counter-indemnity cover issued to exporters, cover for confirmed letters of credit and pre-shipment cover issued to banks. In the EU, these five types of cover are regulated by the Commission Notice on the application of Articles 87 and 88 of the EC Treaty to State Aid in the form of guarantees (2008/C 155/02), which states the maximum percentage of cover ECAs from EU member states can provide is 80 per cent.

10
Foreign Investment Cover

The ECA cover for foreign investments is insurance or a guarantee provided to an investor for a loss of investment made in a foreign country, resulting from expropriation, nationalisation, war, riots, civil disturbances, restrictions on transfer of funds and other political events. The contractual parties in an investment contract are the investor and the recipient of the investment. The recipient is called the investment project and it can be a company, enterprise or other form of business activity. The country where the investment is made and where the investment project is located is called the host country and it is different from the investor's country. The ECA cover for foreign investments is limited to losses caused by political events only and commercial events such as insolvency, bankruptcy or underperformance of the investment project are not included in this type of cover.

The ECA cover for foreign investments is different from the ECA cover for export credits because the risks associated with foreign investments are different from the risks associated with export credit transactions. Export credits are easier to define because the losses covered by ECAs appear in the form of non-payment of a specific amount of credit under a commercial or loan contract. Foreign investments are more complex transactions where a loss incurred by an investor may take various forms because investors expect different returns of investment or benefits from their foreign investments; these benefits may take forms such as shareholding, repayment of an investment loan, profit from a business activity, ownership of assets, etc.

Providing the ECA cover for a loss that investors may incur in foreign investment transactions is not regulated internationally, which means the scope of this type of cover varies among ECAs. The same can be said for premiums charged by ECAs, duration of cover and other terms for covering a loss of investment. The ECA cover for foreign investments is a complex subject to be analysed in a separate book; for the purpose of this book the analysis is limited to this chapter only.

Similarity of political events

> *Political events covered by ECAs when providing foreign investment cover are similar but not identical to political events covered by ECAs in export credit transactions.*

10.1 Political events that may cause loss of investment

ECAs that provide this type of cover define political events that may cause losses in foreign investment transactions in various ways. Below is a short summary of select political events that are frequently covered by ECAs. However, this list is not exhaustive and ECAs may apply different definitions of the same political events or include additional political events in their cover. The definitions of political events included in the standard terms of various ECAs are usually comprehensive and contain many details not analysed in this summary.

a) Expropriation, nationalisation and similar measures
ECAs cover a loss caused to an insured investor by expropriation, nationalisation, confiscation or other action or measure of a host country's government that results in a reduction or elimination of ownership, control or rights to the foreign investment. The host country is where an investment is made, which differs from the investor's country.

Because it is impossible to foresee and define all political events that may occur in the future, the wording of definitions ECAs apply to political events for this type of cover are very general. Therefore it can be difficult to establish whether an individual measure taken by a host government has caused a loss to an investor by reducing or eliminating ownership of an investment. Today, host governments rarely nationalise or expropriate foreign investments because they may achieve similar effects by taking other measures that are not openly directed against foreign investments. When analysing a measure taken by a host government, it is important to determine whether it is equally applicable to domestic investments without discriminating against foreign investments. A measure that is applied equally to foreign and domestic investments such as fiscal or tax regulation cannot be classified as expropriation or a similar political event.

ECAs usually include in this type of cover a loss caused by a special type of political event called the creeping expropriation, which consists of a series of actions or measures taken over time by a host government that reduce or eliminate ownership, control or rights to the foreign investment. These measures may take forms such as a gradual increase in tax rates on profits that make an investment unprofitable, imposing increasing barriers for transferring profits or dividends out of the host country, gradual increase of property tax rates for foreign companies or changing the percentage of ownership which must be held by local shareholders.

b) Currency inconvertibility and preventing or delaying of transfer of funds

An investor expects that its foreign investment will be returned and the amounts representing the return will be freely transferred from the host country to the investor's country. In addition, foreign investments often generate revenues in a local currency that must be converted into a hard currency before transferring the funds out of the host country. Both currency conversion and their transfer out of the host country may be prevented or delayed by legislative or administrative measures taken by a host country's government. A loss for an investor caused by these events is usually covered by ECAs. Some ECAs cover only prevention or delay of funds transfer while other ECAs cover both the inconvertibility and transferring risks.

When covering the risk of preventing or delaying of funds transfer, ECAs require that the transfer is attempted and the non-transferred amount is deposited in a separate bank account and kept apart from the investment project's account. ECAs may require the application of the same procedure when covering the inconvertibility of a local currency into a hard currency.

c) War, civil disturbance and terrorist acts

A loss, damage, destruction or disappearance of a foreign investment caused by events such as war, civil disturbance, terrorist acts and similar acts of violence are also covered by ECAs. These events may result in a temporary interruption of the investment project's business or the project's permanent inability to conduct operations without causing any physical damage to the investment project's assets. Nearly all ECAs cover losses caused by war, civil disturbance and terrorist acts, but the standard terms of some ECAs require that these events must be politically motivated.

d) Breach of contract by a government

An investor may enter into contracts such as concession contracts, power purchase contracts, etc., with a government or public authority in a host country. If the government or public authority breaches or repudiates the contract, that breach may result in a loss in the form of depriving the investor of the right to, or control over, the investment, loss of value of the investment, or obstacles or delay of repayment of the investment. Some ECAs cover this type of loss only if a contract is breached by a government, while other ECAs will also cover a loss caused by a breach of contract by a state-owned company in a host country.

In the event of breach or repudiation of a contract by a host government, some ECAs require the insured investor to start the dispute resolution mechanism agreed upon in the contract with the host government. This mechanism usually operates in the form of an arbitration proceeding and the insured investor will be indemnified by the ECA only if the arbitration award proves the investor's right against the host government. After obtaining an arbitration award in its favour, the insured investor is not required to attempt enforcement of the award as a condition for receiving indemnification from the ECA. Some ECAs will pay indemnification for a loss if obtaining an arbitration award or a dispute resolution process is delayed due to the interference of the host government.

e) Breach of government's unconditional payment obligation
Governments in host countries sometimes agree to pay a foreign investor in the form of an unconditional payment obligation by issuing an on-demand guarantee, for example. Because of the unconditional nature of such an undertaking, a host government is prevented from disputing its payment obligation when the foreign investor demands payment. ECAs usually cover the risk of the government's breach of an unconditional payment obligation that has caused a loss to an investor.

This political event is different than when a host government breaches a contract with an investor. In the previous situation the government may dispute its payment obligation by claiming the investor breached the contract first and the government's action is just a contractual remedy for the investor's breach. This is why an ECA may require an insured investor to obtain an arbitration award proving its right against the host government. When a host government breaches an unconditional payment obligation, it is easier for an ECA to assess the investor's right against the government and indemnify the investor. Therefore ECAs do not require the insured investor to obtain an arbitration award proving its right to claim payment under the government's unconditional payment obligation.

f) Instability or deterioration of functions of society
Instability or deterioration of societal functions in a host country may prevent an investor from using its investment, which may result in losses similar to those caused by war, civil disturbance and terrorist acts. Such events may prevent repayment of the investment, causing a loss to the investor. A loss caused to an investor by this event is included in the ECA cover for foreign investments provided by some ECAs.

10.2   Investments eligible for obtaining cover

Among the foreign investments that are eligible for ECA cover, two types are covered by ECAs most frequently: investments in equity and investment loans. An investment in equity—in other words in the share capital—can be in cash or in kind in the form of equipment, machinery, services, etc. When investing in equity, foreign investors receive shares in a company or enterprise acting in the capacity of the investment project.

Another type of investment frequently covered by ECAs is an investment loan provided by a foreign investor to an investment project. The purpose of this loan is not necessarily related to the export of goods or services from an ECA country and it does not result in shareholding in the investment project. An investment loan can be provided to an investment project by a shareholding or by a non-shareholding investor and both loans are eligible for the ECA cover. In addition, ECAs may cover a loss caused by making payment under a shareholder guarantee issued by a foreign investor in the capacity of shareholder in an investment project. Such a guarantee is issued for a payment obligation of the investment project.

Other types of investments such as technical assistance and management contracts, asset securitisations, capital market bond issues, leasing, services, and franchising and licensing agreements also may be covered by some ECAs. An investor may make foreign investments in several countries at the same time as a part of a larger cross-border investment transaction. Even this kind of investment may be eligible for ECA cover.

A foreign investment can be made in the form of a new investment project or in the form of expansion, modernisation, improvement, or enhancement of an existing investment project. Acquisitions of foreign enterprises, including privatisation of state-owned enterprises, may be covered by some ECAs.

10.3   Legal status of investment projects

An investment project can be a local subsidiary of an investor incorporated in a host country or a company or enterprise that is not controlled by the investor. Sometimes an investment project is an organisational part or a unit within the investor's company that conducts or runs business in a host country. Although such a part or unit does not have the legal status of a company or an enterprise according to the legislation of the host country, the investment made by the investor company for carrying out such works or running a business can be covered by ECAs as a foreign investment.

10.4   Eligible investors

Since ECAs support their national economies, they provide the ECA cover for foreign investments to investors from their countries only. Normally other investors are not eligible for this type of ECA cover. When an insured investor intends to assign the ECA policy to a third person, the ECA's consent is required for such assignment. Investors that seek the ECA cover for their foreign investments are typically incorporated as companies but most ECAs do not have any requirements regarding the form of incorporation and legal status of an investor.

The eligibility of an investor to obtain the ECA cover for a foreign investment depends on the ECA's assessment of the investor's ability to carry out the investment transaction and to conduct business in a host country in the way presented to the ECA.

10.5　Highest amount of cover

The highest amount of loss covered by an ECA is always stated in an ECA policy covering a loss of foreign investment. This amount represents the value of the investment made by the insured investor. ECAs usually cover 90 to 95 per cent of the highest amount of loss stated in an ECA policy, but this percentage may be lower.

An ECA cover may be structured so the highest amount of loss of investment is covered separately from the cover for a loss of revenues attributable to the investment project. In such transactions the loss of revenues could be covered by the same policy and limited by stating a separate highest amount for this type of loss. Otherwise, where the ECA cover includes both risks, the highest amount of the ECA cover comprises all losses without classifying them into separate categories.

10.6　Percentage of cover and partial cover

As with the export credit insurance and guarantees, most ECAs do not cover 100 per cent of the highest amount of loss stated in an ECA policy for foreign investments. The insured investor is required to retain a small percentage of risk, called the retained risk or the residual risk, which is 5 to 10 per cent of the highest amount covered by an ECA.

Covering less than 100 per cent of a loss of foreign investment is different from the ECA cover for export credit risks, where 100 per cent of political risks are usually covered. This is because ECAs expect the insured investors to be more active in avoiding losses than exporters or banks in export credit transactions. This expectation is based on the assumption that foreign investors usually have closer business relationships with investment projects and have better local knowledge about host countries than exporters and banks when entering into export credit transactions. This should enable an investor to minimise or avoid a loss of investment in an early stage.

Some ECAs are willing to provide a partial foreign investment cover limited to selected political events or to a single event requested by an investor. However, the practice of ECAs differs in this respect; some ECAs provide only complete cover that includes all political events defined in their standard terms because the political events that may cause a loss of investment are sometimes difficult to distinguish from each other, resulting in a disagreement between an insured investor and an ECA when establishing whether a particular event is covered by the ECA. The risk that a single definition of a political event is interpreted in different ways by an insured investor and an ECA is considerable due to the general wording of definitions of political events applied by ECAs. In order to avoid disputes with the insured investors, some ECAs provide only cover for all political events defined in their standard terms for foreign investments. These ECAs are not willing to issue a partial cover for selected events only.

10.7   Duration of cover for foreign investments

The duration of the ECA cover for foreign investments can differ. This type of cover is usually issued on a yearly basis for one or several years and some ECAs may provide a long-term cover with duration of up to ten years. If the insured investor and ECA agree, the ECA cover issued for one year can be automatically renewed for a new period with the same duration.

10.8   Premium

Unlike premiums for the ECA cover for export credits, the premium rates charged by ECAs for providing the ECA cover for foreign investments are not internationally regulated. This means that premiums are calculated on a case-by-case basis, taking into consideration the risks connected with a host country, industry sector, terms of transaction and type of foreign investment. The premium charged by an ECA is payable in advance for one year. If an investor does not pay the premium, the ECA policy will not be issued or, where it is issued, it will not come into effect and will not be binding for the ECA.

10.9   Waiting period

A waiting period is applied by ECAs to establish whether a loss of investment or obstacles to transferring funds out of the host country is temporary or permanent. Waiting periods applied by various ECAs vary between three to six months. The waiting period is not applied where it is obvious that the investment was damaged or destroyed in war or a similar event.

10.10   Assignment of claim

An insured investor is required to assign its claim against the host country to the ECA as a condition for receiving indemnification for the loss of investment.

This includes assignment of security where it is provided to the insured investor and assignment of claim for damages.

10.11   Indemnification

Indemnification is compensation paid by an ECA to an insured investor for a loss of investment caused by a political event covered by the ECA. ECAs apply various methods for calculating the losses of various types of investments. Calculation methods are more complex when an investment is made in the form of equity than when it is made as an investment loan. Below is a short description of indemnification methods applied by some ECAs when calculating indemnification for a loss of various types of investments.

When calculating indemnification for a loss of investment made in the form of equity, the amount that represents a nominal value or net book value of an investment is reduced for amounts defined by ECAs in their standard terms as deductible. An example of a deductible is an amount received by the investor by enforcing security. Another example is a residual value of an investment that must be deducted when the investment is not completely lost. In this case, the methods for calculating the residual value of an investment may differ among ECAs. Sometimes a government in a host country agrees to compensate the insured investor for a loss of investment, but such compensation does not amount to the investor's total loss. An amount paid by a host government as compensation for the insured's loss is deductible when an ECA calculates indemnification. The list of possible deductibles applied by various ECAs is not exhausted by the examples above.

In the case of war, civil disturbance and terrorist acts resulting in physical destruction of or damage to an asset belonging to an investment project, the indemnification usually covers the cost of replacement of the asset or the cost of its reparation. When an asset is not replaced or repaired the indemnification is calculated as a nominal or net book value of the asset.

When a loss is caused by currency inconvertibility, or preventing or delaying transfer of funds, the indemnification covers the non-converted or the non-transferred principal amount and the accrued interest. The late payment interest is not included in this type of ECA cover. The insured investor is indemnified in a hard currency if not otherwise agreed with the ECA.

The same calculation method is applied when a loss results from a breach of contract by a host government. Even in this case the insured investor will be indemnified for the non-paid principal amount and the accrued interest. Where the host government has disputed the insured's claim for payment and the insured has obtained an arbitration award or a judgment of a court proving its right, the indemnification will be paid by the ECA according to the arbitration award or judgment.

The indemnification covering the non-paid principal amount and accrued interest will be paid to the insured investor even when the loss of investment is caused by a breach of a government's unconditional payment obligation. The same calculation method is applied to non-repayment of an investment loan by the investment project.

10.12   Obligations of the insured investor

When covering a loss of a foreign investment, ECAs apply various standard terms for regulating an insured investor's obligations under an ECA policy. It is not possible to consider these terms in detail in this short analysis, but it should be explained that some basic principles governing the ECA cover for export credits are also applied to ECA cover for foreign investments.

Among the obligations of the insured investor the most important one is the obligation to notify the ECA about any occurrence of an event that may cause a loss and about an increase of the risk covered by the ECA. An early warning about these circumstances may enable an ECA to act to avoid or limit a loss. An insured investor is under a general obligation to avoid or limit a loss and consult the ECA regarding the appropriateness of the actions taken for this purpose.

The insured investor cannot assign an ECA policy to third parties without the ECA's consent. Consent is also required to amend the terms of the foreign investment contract and to waive the insured's rights under the contract.

Bilateral investment treaties

Numerous countries bilaterally agree on terms under which companies and individuals from one country may invest in the other. Such agreements are made in the form of a bilateral investment treaty (BIT), an international contract entered into by two states. Among other issues, a BIT may regulate the right of a foreign investor to transfer funds related to investment out of the host country; oblige a host country to apply international law in case of expropriation or nationalisation of assets belonging to an investment project, require acceptance of international arbitration in case of a dispute between an investor and a host country, etc.

The ECA cover for foreign investments is not connected or dependent on a BIT between an ECA country and a host country. The ECA cover is a separate transaction between an ECA and investor, and it can be provided for a foreign investment made in any foreign country, regardless of the existence of a BIT between the ECA country and a host country.

11
ECA Direct Loans

ECA direct loans are specific transactions that are different from the ECA cover. An ECA direct loan is a loan provided by an ECA to a foreign buyer for purchasing goods or services from the ECA country. When providing a direct loan, the ECA acts as lender while the foreign buyer acts as borrower. The loan transaction between the ECA and the foreign buyer is similar to a loan transaction between a bank and a foreign buyer, described in Chapter 8. ECA direct loans are not the main subject of this book and the short analysis of the main characteristics of ECA direct loans is limited to this chapter only.

Due to the variety of organisational forms of the ECAs, in some countries direct loans are provided by the same ECA that provides the ECA cover, while in other countries two separate ECAs are established for providing the cover and direct loans.

11.1 Purpose of direct loans

The main purpose of ECA direct lending is to support national export. ECA direct loans are an important supplemental source of finance when commercial banks are not willing or cannot provide loans to foreign buyers. ECAs are not substitutes for private sources of finance and do not compete with commercial banks.

Another important purpose of ECA direct lending is to neutralise the effect of export credit subsidies provided by some exporting countries to support their national exports. These subsidies take the form of favourable interest rates and long repayment terms between ECAs and foreign buyers in direct loan agreements. Such favourable borrowing terms make the goods or services from the subsidising country more attractive to foreign buyers than the same goods or services from exporting countries without subsidies. ECAs from the countries that participate in the OECD Arrangement and the ECAs from other exporting countries that voluntarily apply the Arrangement do not compete with each other by subsidising their exports. When the ECAs from these countries provide direct loans to foreign buyers, they are allowed to match the terms of loans provided by the ECAs from the subsidising countries to some extent.

Some ECAs provide loans to national exporters for working capital purposes during the manufacturing of goods or services for export. This type of loan, which is usually provided by banks and covered by ECAs, is described separately in Chapter 9.

11.2　Misconceptions about direct loans

Since the ECA business is relatively unknown to many participants in international trade, there are misconceptions about the terms under which ECAs provide their direct loans to foreign buyers. One misconception is that all ECAs subsidise their national exports by lending at low interest rates. This cannot be said for the ECAs from the countries that participate in the Arrangement since they apply interest rates that cannot fall below the minimum levels.

Another misconception is that repayment terms of all ECA direct loans are very long and favourable for foreign buyers. As a matter of fact, even this aspect of the ECA direct lending is regulated internationally and the ECAs that apply the Arrangement are not free to agree on longer repayment terms than regulated.

11.3　International regulations for direct loans

The ECAs from the countries that participate in the Arrangement have to adhere to the Arrangement's regulations on the terms of direct loans they provide to foreign buyers. Therefore these ECAs cannot agree on repayment terms and interest rates that do not comply with the Arrangement. Below is a short description of the main Arrangement provisions that also apply when issuing the ECA cover; they are described in more detail in Chapter 21:

a) The Arrangement applies to ECA direct loans with repayment terms of two years or more.
b) The basic Arrangement requirement for providing an ECA direct loan is that a foreign buyer must make a down payment of minimum 15 per cent of the export contract value at or before the starting point of the credit. The down payment is a part of the total contractual price paid by a foreign buyer to an exporter in advance to demonstrate its commitment to the contract. Since the Arrangement requires the down payment to be at least 15 per cent, the rest of the export contract value, 85 per cent, may be financed by an ECA direct loan.

　　An ECA direct loan of maximum 85 per cent of the export contract value includes third country supplies but excludes local costs. Chapter 21 provides more explanation of the terms 'export contract value', 'local costs' and the 'starting point of credit'.

c) The Arrangement provides that the maximum repayment terms of the ECA direct loans are limited to either five or ten years. Which alternative will be applied depends on the classification of the foreign buyer's country, either in Category I or Category II. The countries classified in Category I are those from the World Bank's graduation list, while all other countries are classified in Category II. If a foreign buyer is from a Category I country, the maximum repayment term of an ECA direct loan is five years and if it is from a Category II country, the maximum repayment term is ten years.

d) The principal sum of the ECA direct loans must be repaid in equal instalments that fall due for payment no less frequently than every six months. The first instalment of principal and interest must be paid no later than six months after the starting point of credit.

The list above is a short description of some basic terms used in the Arrangement, which contains numerous provisions that are not analysed in this book. The special parts of the Arrangement, called 'sector understandings', contain provisions on official support for export of ships, nuclear power plants, civil aircraft and renewable energies and water projects. None of these sector understandings are analysed in this book.

When acting as direct lenders or providers of the ECA cover, ECAs from countries that participate in the Arrangement are obligated to apply the international convention on combating bribery of foreign officials, environmental and social impact regulation and other international documents. These documents are described in Chapter 22.

11.4 Minimum interest rates for direct loans

When ECAs act as direct lenders by providing loans with fixed interest rates to foreign buyers, the interest rates cannot fall below the minimum provided in the Arrangement. These are commercial interest reference rates (CIRRs), a set of currency-specific interest rates for major OECD countries. The majority of CIRRs are based on the five-year government bond yields or on three-, five- and seven-year bond yields according to the length of the repayment period. The CIRRs are adjusted monthly and are intended to reflect commercial rates.

An advantage of applying a CIRR is that an ECA may offer applicants a specific interest rate that will be applied to an ECA direct loan. An offer is open for acceptance for a period of 120 days. After receiving the ECA offer the applicant for the ECA direct loan knows the specific interest rate that will be applied to the ECA direct loan if the transaction is concluded within the time period left for acceptance of the ECA offer.

An application for an ECA direct loan with a CIRR should be submitted to an ECA before signing the commercial contract. Banks and exporters may apply for ECA direct loans with CIRR.

CIRR is not always the best solution for an exporter, bank or a foreign buyer. A CIRR may be higher than the market interest rate, which depends on various market factors. Therefore it is necessary to analyse which solution is the best for an applicant and other participants in a transaction that is intended to be financed by an ECA direct loan. Instead of a CIRR, an ECA may agree to provide a direct loan to a foreign buyer with the market interest rate.

11.5   Application and offer for direct loans

The process of arranging an ECA direct loan follows negotiating and finalising an underlying commercial transaction. The process is usually divided into three stages—application, offer and entering into a loan agreement. Structuring the procedure in three stages is necessary because some commercial transactions for which the ECA direct loan is requested may take a long time to negotiate and finalise.

ECAs usually provide application forms for ECA direct loans. The applications contain questions about the commercial transaction and other issues necessary to assess whether a direct ECA loan can be provided to an applicant. The application for an ECA direct loan must be submitted to an ECA before signing the commercial contract.

If an ECA is willing to provide a direct loan, it will issue an offer to the applicant. An offer for a direct loan issued by an ECA may contain requirements for providing security for repayment of the loan, inclusion of other specific provisions in the loan agreement and other requirements. The offer always states the time period for acceptance. During this period the offer is binding for the ECA, which allows the applicant to conclude negotiations, sign the contract with the foreign buyer and accept the ECA offer.

Once the offer has been accepted, some ECAs provide a direct loan without further involvement of a bank or exporter. In such transactions the ECA negotiates the terms and enters into the loan agreement with the foreign buyer directly.

11.6   Arranging direct loans by banks

When the applicant for an ECA direct loan is a bank, the transaction consists of several stages. In the first stage the bank negotiates the provision of a loan to a foreign buyer to purchase goods or services from an ECA country and applies to the ECA for a direct loan. The ECA issues an offer to the bank, which allows the bank to enter into the loan agreement with the foreign buyer. The bank provides contractual documentation and all other documents necessary for the loan transaction with the intention of assigning the loan agreement to the ECA in a later stage. When the loan agreement is signed the bank accepts the ECA offer for a direct loan.

When the bank receives the ECA loan amount, the bank, still acting as a lender, pays that amount according to the loan agreement. As explained in Chapter 8, banks state in their loan agreements that the loan amount will be paid to the exporter from which the foreign buyer purchases goods or services. Such payment is made against a certificate issued by a foreign buyer certifying that the exporter has completed delivery according to the commercial contract. The banks and ECAs apply this way of disbursement of the loan amount to ensure it will be used for the intended purpose of the loan.

After disbursement of the loan amount, the bank assigns the loan agreement to the ECA and the ECA replaces the bank in the capacity of lender in relation to the foreign buyer. After completing the assignment, the bank sometimes continues to act as an agent on behalf of the ECA and administers the loan. Since the ECA becomes the lender in relation to the foreign buyer, the foreign buyer is obligated to repay the loan to the ECA. When arranging this kind of transaction, some ECAs ask banks to take the documentation risk for the loan agreement and other loan documentation. Chapter 3 explains exclusion of documentation risk.

ECA direct loans are often drafted by banks and subsequently assigned to ECAs. Therefore the ECA direct loans are documented with the standardised documentation for international loan agreements that banks usually apply. This documentation contains provisions such as representations and warranties, financial and other covenants, events of default, governing law and jurisdiction clauses, etc. However, when issuing an offer for an ECA direct loan, an ECA may instruct a bank to include specific contractual provisions in the loan agreement or require security for repayment of the loan.

11.7   Arranging direct loans by exporters

When an ECA direct loan is arranged by an exporter, the procedure is similar but not exactly the same as when the loan is arranged by a bank. In this kind of transaction an exporter applies for the ECA direct loan while negotiating a commercial contract with a foreign buyer, in which the payment on credit terms is agreed. If the ECA issues an offer for providing the loan, the exporter may sign the commercial contract with the foreign buyer.

After signing the commercial contract, the ECA may enter directly into a loan agreement with the foreign buyer or the exporter may assign its claim for payment of credit against the foreign buyer to the ECA. Most ECAs do not replace exporters as contractual parties in commercial contracts because they cannot perform the obligations an exporter may have under a commercial contract such as maintenance of the delivered equipment, providing spare parts, etc. After entering into a direct loan agreement between the ECA and the foreign buyer or assigning the claim for payment of credit to the ECA, the exporter receives payment of the discounted amount of credit from the ECA.

When the transaction is complete, the ECA becomes a creditor in relation to the foreign buyer whose credit will be paid to the ECA. The exporter ceases to be the creditor in relation to the foreign buyer after receiving the discounted amount of credit from the ECA in advance. The documentation used for this transaction is either a loan agreement between the ECA and the foreign buyer or an assignment document by which the exporter's claim for payment of credit is assigned to the ECA.

Sometimes the payment obligation of the foreign buyer is documented by promissory notes or bills of exchange (drafts) and the transfer of the claim for payment is completed by transferring such instruments from the exporter to the ECA. This transaction is described in more detail in Chapter 6.

11.8   The ECA's recourse against a bank or an exporter

When entering into transactions in which a bank or an exporter assigns a loan agreement or a claim for payment of credit to an ECA, ECAs require the right of recourse against the bank or exporter. The right of recourse can be agreed for situations when the loan agreement between the bank and the foreign buyer, drafted by the bank and assigned to the ECA, turns out to be illegal, void or unenforceable. This might result in non-payment of the loan by the foreign buyer caused by the bank's failure to provide proper loan documentation. In this case, the bank will be liable to the ECA for the loss incurred by the ECA. A similar right of recourse is usually agreed between the ECA and an exporter in case the foreign buyer refuses payment of a credit by alleging a breach of the commercial contract by the exporter. The same right is also agreed when a commercial contract, negotiated and drafted by the exporter, turns out to be illegal, void or unenforceable.

11.9   Charging a premium for credit risk

Another issue that arises when ECAs provide direct loans is charging a premium for the credit risk. The premium is charged by ECAs when covering credit risk by issuing the ECA cover, but it can be charged even when an ECA acts as the direct lender because the ECA will take the final loss caused by non-payment of the credit by the foreign buyer. In countries where two ECAs separately provide direct loans and the ECA cover, the ECA that acts as a direct lender will require the bank or exporter to obtain the ECA cover from the other ECA before entering into direct a loan transaction. In connection to assignment of the loan agreement, a new policy may be issued to the lending ECA or the rights under the ECA policy issued to the bank can be assigned to the lending ECA. It is also possible that the ECA acting as a direct lender will obtain the ECA cover direct from the other ECA when providing a loan directly without involving a commercial bank.

11.10   Tied aid

The idea of tied aid is important in this context, even though it is not the subject matter of this book. The term 'tied aid' is used to describe arrangements where a donor government provides aid to a foreign government that is explicitly tied to purchasing goods or services from exporters in the donor's country. Tied aid is also regulated internationally by the Arrangement. It is a special arrangement that usually involves assistance agencies in donor countries. However, tied aid is not among the most frequently used types of export transactions and therefore it is not included in this book.

Part III
Procedures

12
Application, Offer, and Policy

The process of issuing the ECA cover follows the negotiation of and entering into a commercial or loan contract for which the ECA cover is requested. Providing the ECA cover in individual transactions is divided into three stages—application, making an ECA offer and issuing the ECA policy. Other terms for these stages used by various ECAs are the proposal, preliminary commitment and final commitment. Providing the framework cover, described in Chapter 4, is different from issuing the ECA cover for individual transactions described below.

Terminology

Some ECAs call the ECA policy the guarantee, final commitment or cover. All these terms are good for use and the terms used in this book are chosen for the reason of simplicity only.

Some ECAs use an initial procedure that includes issuing a document called a letter of interest. The letter of interest is issued by an ECA to an exporter or bank when starting negotiations with a potential foreign buyer. Such a letter is a brief, preliminary and informal statement that indicates the possibility of covering a credit risk in a transaction with a particular foreign buyer. The letter of interest sometimes indicates the amount of premium payable to the ECA, calculated according to short information provided by the exporter or bank. The letter of interest is not legally binding, which means the ECA is not obligated to issue cover for a transaction for which the letter is issued.

The amount of work and time needed to process an application by an ECA depends on the complexity of the transaction for which the ECA cover is requested and the progress an exporter or bank makes in closing the deal with a potential foreign buyer. It is important for an exporter or bank involved in negotiations with a potential foreign buyer to know whether the ECA from the country of export is willing to cover the credit risk in the transaction. It is necessary to inform the exporter or bank about this while the transaction is still in the negotiating stage, before a commercial or loan contract with the foreign buyer is signed. Applying for ECA cover after signing the contract might result in difficulties for the exporter or bank if the ECA decides not to cover the credit risk in the contract. By issuing an offer, the ECA assures the exporter or bank that the cover will be issued if the deal with the foreign buyer is closed and the commercial or loan contract is signed. An ECA offer states the terms for covering the credit risk in the transaction, including the premium the ECA will charge.

When the commercial or loan contract is signed, the exporter or bank may request the issuing of the ECA policy. The ECA policy is effective from the date stated in the policy document, provided that the premium is paid to the ECA. After issuing the ECA policy the exporter or bank is usually called the insured.

In practice, it is not unusual that the transaction for which an offer has been issued by an ECA cannot be concluded for some reason. In such situations the offer issued by the ECA will simply expire or be cancelled by the exporter or bank.

12.1   Application for issuing cover

This is the initial stage of the procedure in which an exporter or bank submits a written request for ECA cover. In order to make this procedure easier for exporters and banks, numerous ECAs provide application forms on their websites. By answering the questions contained in an application form, the applicant provides the ECA with detailed information about the transaction for which the ECA cover is requested. It is practical for ECAs to use application forms because they receive complete information about the underlying commercial or loan transaction in an early stage of their work. Some ECAs provide an online function for applying for the ECA cover on their websites.

ECA application forms contain questions about the intended commercial or loan contract and the foreign buyer. ECAs request information about the date or expected date for signing a commercial or loan contract, the currency in which the contract is denominated, payment terms, possible security for payment of the credit, date or dates for performance of the exporter's contractual obligations such as commencement of work, shipping of goods, installation and commissioning of equipment or other obligations in a commercial contract. ECAs also request information about the foreign content in the goods or services to be exported and about the relationship between the exporter company and the foreign buyer company in terms of ownership.

ECAs expect the applicant to submit its application during the negotiating stage of a transaction before the goods are shipped or services performed and before the commercial or loan contract is signed. Application forms usually contain a statement that the applicant has truly stated all material facts in the application form, which the applicant certifies with the signature of the authorised signatory for the applicant company.

In addition to the application form, the applicant is usually required to submit other documents to the ECA such as the foreign buyer's company's audited financial statements for the past two or three years and sometimes the interim financial statement for the year in which the cover is requested. ECAs use these documents to assess the foreign buyer's ability to pay the credit.

If the applicant is unknown to the ECA to which it has applied for ECA cover, the ECA may ask the applicant to provide documents and information about its incorporation and registration, financial standing, experience of the applicant's business, experience of the company's management, etc. These documents are necessary for assessing the applicant's ability to perform its obligations under the commercial contract with the foreign buyer.

When issuing cover to banks, ECAs often require a document called the exporter's certificate. By issuing this document, an exporter certifies the foreign buyer will purchase goods or services from the exporter, for which the foreign buyer will pay with the proceeds of the loan. The exporter's certificate is required because ECAs will cover a loan transaction between a bank and a foreign buyer only if the loan is provided for purchasing of goods or services from the ECA country. Otherwise, the loan transaction would not be eligible for the ECA cover.

Many ECAs require the applicant to sign a separate declaration regarding bribery and money laundering and attach it to the application. This declaration contains a statement certifying that neither the applicant nor its employees are involved in any corrupt activity and the underlying commercial or loan transaction will not be used for money laundering. This declaration is especially important for ECAs from the countries that have ratified the OECD Convention on Combating Bribery of Foreign Public Officials in International Business Transactions. This convention is described in Chapter 22.

ECAs provide different application forms for various types of the ECA cover such as the framework cover for short-term transactions, individual short-term transactions, medium- to long-term cover for exporters, medium- to long-term cover for lenders, cover for letters of credit, foreign investment cover, pre-shipment cover, etc. The application forms provided by ECAs are fairly comprehensive, containing questions that applicants are required to answer and several statements they are required to sign.

ECAs often need additional information from the applicant about the transaction for which the ECA cover is requested. Generally, after submitting the formal application, the procedure requires continuous communication between the applicant and the ECA to adjust the underlying transaction to the ECA's standard terms and international regulations applied by a particular ECA. During this stage, the applicant will ask about the amount and terms for payment of premium that will be charged by the ECA for issuing the policy. ECAs can indicate the amount of premium, but it is only an estimate that can be changed depending on the ECA's credit risk assessment and on amending the transaction terms as a result of continuing negotiations between the applicant and the foreign buyer.

An application submitted to an ECA is not binding and the applicant can withdraw it. ECAs know that closing a deal with a foreign buyer can be a demanding process in which an applicant may amend the terms of a transaction several times and inform the ECA about the amendments. This must be noted by the ECA and considered when processing the application.

When the ECA receives the necessary information, it will assess the credit risk in the underlying commercial or loan transaction, calculate the premium and decide whether to cover a particular credit risk and under which terms. Some ECAs charge a fee for handling the application but the fees are not high and in some situations the fee is refundable.

12.2   Offer for issuing the ECA policy

After assessing the credit risk and analysing the terms of a transaction, an ECA will decide whether to cover a particular credit risk. The decision can be made at various levels within an ECA; the decision depends on the amount of credit for which the ECA cover is requested, classification of risk, type of cover requested, etc. The ECA officers who handle applications are often called underwriters and their work with applications is called underwriting. Underwriters may be authorised to decide whether to issue the ECA cover for limited amounts while decisions on issuing cover for higher amounts are made by a board, committee or similar body within an ECA.

When an ECA decides it will cover a particular risk, an offer will be issued to the applicant. The offer contains all terms of the future ECA policy and the amount of premium to be paid to the ECA by the applicant. Some ECAs require the provision of security for payment of the credit by the foreign buyer or inclusion of specific terms in a commercial or loan contract. These requirements are included in the offer as conditions for the ECA cover. Issuing the ECA offer is the most important stage of the process because it enables the applicant to enter into the commercial or loan contract with the foreign buyer. This should be made according to the contractual terms disclosed to the ECA in the application stage. The ECA offer is a unilateral document that is binding for a specific period of time. During that period the ECA cannot withdraw or amend the offer except for the reasons stated in the offer. A reason for withdrawal of an offer by an ECA is substantial increase of the risk for non-payment of a credit. Increase of risk after issuing an offer is described in more detail in Chapter 23.

An ECA offer is usually open for six months provided that the risk assessed by the ECA before issuing the offer remains unchanged. When the applicant needs additional time for concluding its commercial or loan transaction, ECAs may extend the validity period stated in the offer. Many ECAs charge a fee for extending the validity period, but this fee can be refundable if the offer is accepted and the ECA policy is issued. If the validity period expires before the applicant requests issuing of the ECA policy, the offer will expire and it will no longer be binding on the ECA.

Sometimes the applicant asks the ECA to amend an offer that has been issued already because of the amendments of the contract agreed with the foreign buyer after issuing the offer. An applicant may request an amendment of the terms of the offer related to payment of credit, providing security, dates for performance of contractual obligations, commencement of work, shipping of goods, quantity of the goods to be delivered, etc. The terms of a loan agreement may be amended in a similar way. In complex transactions an ECA offer can be amended several times before finalising the contract between the applicant and the foreign buyer.

ECAs are not obligated to issue a new offer when the terms of a commercial or loan contract are amended in a way that is unacceptable for issuing the ECA cover. ECAs may find the amended terms are acceptable but the risk previously assessed has increased, which may result in a higher premium for covering such a risk. The previous premium may increase if, for example, the new period for payment of credit is longer than the original period. The premium amount also may decrease if the repayment period is shortened or if the foreign buyer's country has been re-classified in a lower risk category.

12.3   The ECA policy

After receiving an ECA offer and closing a deal with the foreign buyer by entering into a commercial or loan contract, the applicant may request the ECA to issue the ECA policy. When the ECA policy is issued and the premium charged by the ECA is paid, the policy becomes effective and binding on the ECA. From this moment the applicant becomes the insured and the ECA is obligated to indemnify the insured for the loss caused by non-payment of a credit by the foreign buyer. The ECA policy is sometimes called the final commitment or guarantee. Issuing the ECA policy is the final stage of procedure for providing the ECA cover.

Some ECA policies cover a credit risk from a date earlier than the date of issuance of the offer and the due date for payment of premium. Such a policy is binding on the ECA provided that the premium is paid on a later date, as stated by the ECA.

An ECA policy can be amended only if the ECA and the insured consent to the amendment. In practice, ECA policies are rarely amended, except when the foreign buyer's credit is renegotiated, usually by extending a due date or dates for payment. The insured exporter or bank may accept the new payment schedule and request the ECA to amend the policy covering the risk of non-payment of the credit according to the new due date or dates. If the ECA accepts the proposed amendment, the existing ECA policy will be amended to cover the new payment schedule. In situations where the foreign buyer's credit is rescheduled with the ECA's consent, the insured exporter or bank still has the right to request indemnification from the ECA according to the original payment schedule without requesting an amendment of the ECA policy. Rescheduling the foreign buyer's credit and the insured's right to indemnification is analysed in Chapter 19.

The insured exporter may assign its rights under the policy to a bank and notify the ECA about the assignment. The insured can do this when applying for the ECA cover or later, after issuance of the ECA offer or the ECA policy. As explained in Chapter 6, the assignment of rights under the ECA policy occurs when an exporter assigns its claim for payment against the foreign buyer to a bank and notifies the ECA. If the bank to which the exporter's claim is assigned is acceptable to the ECA, it will include a provision in the ECA policy providing that the bank is beneficiary under the policy. The right to claim indemnification from the ECA in case of non-payment of the credit is the most important right assigned in this way. Assignment of rights under the ECA policy is always required by banks when discounting a an exporter's claim for payment against the foreign buyer.

An important rule applied by the majority of ECAs is that the premium for the ECA cover must be paid up front before issuing the ECA policy. The ECA policy may be issued to cover the risk that arises before paying the premium, but it is provided in the policy document that it will not be effective and binding on the ECA if the premium is not paid.

ECA policies are effective and binding during the period stipulated for payment of credit in the commercial or loan contract. If the foreign buyer makes its payments according to the schedule, the ECA policy will expire when the final credit payment is made. An ECA policy may be cancelled earlier, when the foreign buyer prepays its loan to a bank, for example.

13
Premium

In the ECA context, the premium is a fee charged by ECAs for providing the ECA cover for the risk of non-payment of a credit by a foreign buyer and for other risks covered by ECAs. The term 'premium' comes from the insurance business, which has many similarities with the ECA cover. However, the premium charged by ECAs does not have the same purpose as premiums charged by insurance companies. The purpose of the ECA premium is to create financial reserves for potential losses and cover the operating costs of ECAs. Unlike insurance companies, ECAs are not expected to make profit. Another difference is that insurance companies may become insolvent and bankrupt if their financial reserves are insufficient for paying all claims resulting from the insured risks. ECAs cannot become insolvent when their financial reserves are insufficient for paying all claims because they will receive additional funds from the state.

13.1 Different premium rates for various types of cover

The premium calculation methods that ECAs apply to cover various types of risks are complicated and calculation details are not analysed in this book. Premium calculation methods for providing the ECA cover for export credits with payment terms of two years or more have been agreed upon internationally. These methods are regulated in detail in the OECD Arrangement, which is related to the World Trade Organisation's Agreement on Subsidies and Countervailing Measures that prohibits premiums that do not cover the losses and long-term operating costs of ECAs. Export credits with payment terms of two years or more are also called medium- to long-term credits. The purpose of regulating the minimum premium rates internationally is the same as other aspects of officially supported export credits—providing a level playing field for exporters and encouraging competition based on the quality and price of their goods and services.

Premium rates applied by ECAs when providing other types of the ECA cover, other than the cover for medium- to long-term export credits, are not internationally regulated. Therefore the Arrangement does not apply to the ECA cover for short-term export credits, contractual guarantees, foreign investments, counter-indemnity cover issued to exporters, etc. ECAs apply their own internal premium regulations when calculating premium rates for other types of cover.

13.2   Basic elements for calculating the premium rate

When a credit risk is assessed by an ECA as acceptable for issuing the ECA cover, several basic elements will be considered when calculating the premium rate. The first element is the amount of credit or other risk for which the ECA cover is requested. Other elements can be an amount payable under a contractual guarantee or an amount of foreign investment to which the Arrangement does not apply. It is easy to conclude that a higher premium will be charged for covering a higher amount of credit or other risk. The amount of credit is called the principal value and this term usually includes the principal amount plus interest, but it can be defined in various ways.

The second element for calculating a premium rate is the time at risk or the duration of the ECA cover. This could be the period for payment of a credit, the validity period of a contractual guarantee, etc. The basic rule applied by ECAs is that a longer time at risk will result in a higher premium for the ECA cover. This rule applies whether the Arrangement applies or not.

The third element for calculating a premium rate is percentage of the ECA cover. ECAs may decide to issue cover at various percentages for political and commercial risks. Generally, a lower percentage of cover should result in a lower premium rate, but this is not always the case.

An exporter or bank may request a reduction in the scope of cover to lower the premium. The scope of cover may be reduced by excluding some political events or by obtaining cover for political or commercial risks only. Some ECAs accept this and issue a partial cover for selected political risks or political or commercial risks only. Exclusion of a particular type of risk from the ECA cover should result in a lower premium rate, but this is not a mandatory rule and ECAs may have different policies for this type of cover. Providing partial ECA cover is analysed in Chapter 4.

13.3   Minimum premium rates

The Arrangement contains comprehensive provisions for calculating minimum premium rates applied by ECAs for providing the cover for export credit risks with the duration of two years or more. A minimum premium rate for covering an individual export credit risk is expressed in a percentage of the amount of credit.

The main method of calculating a minimum premium rate for an export credit risk is applying a country risk category for the country in which the foreign buyer company is based. For this purpose all countries are classified according to the likelihood of whether they will service their external debts. Other elements used for the country risk classification include a government's moratorium on payments, political events that prevent or delay transfer of payment made under commercial or loan contracts or decisions of authorities in a country to convert payments denominated in foreign currency into payments in local currency, making payments insufficient for paying the entire amount of debt.

All countries are classified into one of eight categories from nil to seven, with minimum premium rates for categories from one to seven but not for the category nil. The minimum premium rates start at category one and the highest minimum premium rate is applied for countries in category seven. The country risk classification is monitored and reviewed at least once a year, which may result in re-classifying a country in a lower or higher category.

When calculating a minimum premium rate for an individual credit risk, an ECA cannot classify a foreign buyer in a more favourable category than the category of the foreign buyer's country. This is the main rule but the Arrangement provides several exemptions from this rule that are described further in the text.

The countries in the category nil are the high income OECD and euro area countries determined by the World Bank on an annual basis according to per capita gross national income. The level of country risk for countries in the category nil is negligible and the calculation of premium rates for credit risks on foreign buyers from these countries is based on an assessment of the creditworthiness of an individual foreign buyer. Even this calculation method, which is quite complex, is regulated in the Arrangement.

It is important to remember that even in this context the minimum premium rates are applied by the ECAs from the countries that participate in the Arrangement. The ECAs from other countries are not obligated to apply these premium rates.

13.4   Buyer risk categories

The Arrangement provides criteria for classifying foreign buyers in order to calculate premium rates. These criteria include numerous elements such as the status of a foreign buyer, generating revenues, liquidity levels and management abilities. Other criteria are quality of financial and ownership disclosure, likelihood of obtaining financial support from a parent company and major uncertainties in the foreign buyer's business. Based on these criteria, foreign buyers are classified into seven categories to calculate premium rates for the ECA cover.

The highest and most exceptional category is the 'better than sovereign foreign buyer'. The next category is 'sovereign', followed by 'the equivalent to the sovereign' category. The middle categories are 'very good credit quality', 'good to moderately good credit quality' and 'moderate credit quality'. The lower categories are 'moderately weak credit quality' and 'weak credit quality'.

13.5   Reducing minimum premium rate

The Arrangement provides three methods that allow ECAs to charge premium rates below the minimum. Applying these methods is not simple because several strict requirements must be satisfied by a foreign buyer or third party that provides security for payment of credit. Therefore the description of these three methods that follows is just a short illustration of the Arrangement's comprehensive provisions that involve numerous details.

13.6   Third party payment guarantee

Where a third party guarantees payment of a credit covered by an ECA, the premium rate may be calculated according to the third party's country risk classification and its buyer risk category. This is possible when the third party (guarantor) is from a country that is classified in a more favourable country risk category than the foreign buyer's country. The same method is applied when the third party is classified in a more favourable buyer risk category than the foreign buyer.

The Arrangement regulates that the guarantee issued by a third party must cover the entire duration of the foreign buyer's credit, that it must be irrevocable, unconditional, payable on demand and it must satisfy several other detailed requirements. The guarantee can be issued by a multilateral or regional institution that is classified on a case-by-case basis in a country risk category ranging from nil to seven.

13.7   Mitigation techniques

The Arrangement allows the charging of a premium below the minimum premium rate for a particular export credit transaction when security over a specific bank account is provided or when payment of an export credit is established in a local currency. This reduction of the minimum premium rate is called the country risk mitigation technique.

The first type of country risk mitigation technique—the offshore future flow structure combined with offshore escrow account—is a complicated contractual structure with numerous requirements that must be satisfied according to the Arrangement. Simply described, this technique is a contractual assignment of the foreign buyer's foreign currency receivables such that they will be deposited into a bank account at a bank outside the foreign buyer's country. The account, also called the escrow account, and the bank where it is opened should not be controlled by the foreign buyer. This mitigation technique applies when a foreign buyer has long-term contracts with financially strong foreign customers whose payments in foreign currency provide a continual cash flow to the foreign buyer. When this cash flow is directed to an escrow account and applied as payment of the foreign buyer's credit, the risk of non-payment of the credit is reduced. In this situation, the ECA may apply a country risk category that is one level lower than the foreign buyer's country risk category, resulting in a lower premium rate.

The second type of country risk mitigation technique provided in the Arrangement is local currency financing. In this technique, an export credit is denominated and paid in the local currency of the foreign buyer's country. This payment structure eliminates the risk connected with converting the local currency into a hard currency and transferring the hard currency out of the foreign buyer's country. Since the scope of ECA cover is reduced, ECAs may allow a discount of no more than 20 per cent of the minimum premium rate calculated according to the foreign buyer's country risk category.

13.8   Enhancement of credit risk by providing security

The Arrangement allows the charging of a premium below the minimum premium rate when one of four types of security is provided by the foreign buyer. Providing these types of security is called buyer risk credit enhancement. The first type of security, the assignment of contract proceeds or receivables, requires that the foreign buyer's receivables, as agreed in contracts with its strong customers, be assigned to the insured exporter or bank. This type of assignment of receivables should result in preferential treatment of the insured exporter or bank in relation to the foreign buyer's other creditors.

The second credit enhancement type of security is the asset based security created over very mobile and valuable pieces of property or the property that has value in itself. Such security, which must be provided in favour of the insured exporter or bank, should be enforced easily against the foreign buyer in case of non-payment of a credit.

The third credit enhancement type of security provided in the Arrangement is the fixed asset security. This type of security is usually created over equipment in an assembly line used by the foreign buyer. The effect of creating security over this type of asset is an improved negotiating position for the insured exporter or bank in case of non-payment of credit by the foreign buyer.

The fourth credit enhancement security requires opening an escrow account in favour of the insured exporter or bank in the form of a debt service reserve account where a specific amount of money is deposited by the foreign buyer as security for payment of credit. Instead of a specific amount of money, the foreign buyer's receivables may be held in an escrow account for the same purpose.

13.9   Security and reducing the premium rate to the minimum

ECAs may consider other types of security that are not provided in the Arrangement as methods for reducing a minimum premium rate when calculating the premium rate. However, this possibility is limited to credit risks where an ECA has calculated a higher premium rate than the minimum premium rate applicable according to the foreign buyer's country risk category. Providing acceptable security for payment of the foreign buyer's credit may reduce the premium to the level of the minimum premium rate, but not below that. The Arrangement does not regulate charging premium rates above the minimum premium rate and ECAs are free to make these calculations according to their internal policies and criteria.

Providing security does not always result in a reduced premium rate charged by an ECA. This is the case when the premium is already charged at the minimum rate and the security provided by the foreign buyer is not of the kind that may affect the premium rate according to the Arrangement. Another example is an ECA's requirement for providing security as a basic condition for issuing the ECA cover where the premium will be charged at the minimum rate or above that. Providing security for payment of export credits and dealing with security by ECAs is explained in Chapter 17.

13.10   Increased premium rate

Calculating a premium rate for covering an export credit risk does not always result in charging the minimum premium rate. ECAs are free to charge a premium rate above the minimum provided in the Arrangement, which depends on the assessment of credit risk in each individual transaction.

Sometimes charging higher premium rates is connected with the foreign buyer's inability to provide security for payment of credit. A higher premium rate may be charged in a transaction where an ECA has requested security as a basic condition for the ECA cover. If the foreign buyer is unable to provide the requested security the ECA may still decide to cover the credit risk by charging a higher premium rate. Sometimes providing security is a complex procedure that requires registration in a public register that may take a long time to complete. When the insured has requested issuing the ECA policy before the required security is effective, the ECA may charge an additional premium payable until all formalities are satisfied and the procedure for providing security is completed.

An additional premium may be charged if the foreign buyer is unable to provide security due to a negative pledge clause included in its existing loan or commercial contract. This situation arises rarely because the foreign buyer's existing creditors typically consent that the foreign buyer may provide security for the export credit for which the ECA cover is requested. However, when consent cannot be obtained from the existing creditors, the foreign buyer is prevented from providing security for payment of the export credit. In this situation an ECA may charge an additional premium for covering the risk of non-payment of the credit that will be unsecured in relation to the foreign buyer's existing credits.

In exceptional situations a foreign buyer has already created security over its existing and future assets when entering into contracts with its existing creditors. Creating security over future assets, also called after acquired assets, is possible in legal systems based on English law but not in other legal systems. When this type of security is created, the new asset, purchased and financed by a new export credit, will not be used as security for payment of that particular credit. Instead, it will be used as security for payment of the existing credits of the foreign buyer. ECAs are reluctant to issue cover when the credit they cover will be unsecured and the asset financed by this credit will be used to secure payment of the existing credits of the foreign buyer. However, if an individual ECA issues cover under these terms, it is very likely it will charge an increased premium.

13.11   Payment of premium

The premium ECAs charge is expressed as a percentage of the amount of credit for which the cover is issued; ECAs normally request the entire amount of premium to be paid in advance. When an ECA policy is issued before the due date for payment of premium, it usually states that the policy will not come into effect and it will not be binding for the ECA if the premium is not paid. Some ECAs accept payment of premium in arrears under special terms.

The premium can be partially repaid by an ECA to an insured when a foreign buyer prepays a credit before it falls due. This is possible when the foreign buyer has obtained cheaper financing or is capable to prepay the credit from its own revenue. When a credit is prepaid, the insured exporter or bank may request cancellation of the ECA policy and repayment of the premium, prorated to the period during which the ECA policy covered the credit risk. The majority of ECAs accept cancellation of a policy for this reason and they repay the 'unused' portion of the premium. ECAs can regulate repayment of premium in various ways.

13.12   Shifting the premium costs to foreign buyers

In legal terms, the parties that enter into a contractual relationship resulting in issuing the ECA cover are an insured and an ECA. Consequently, only the insured is obligated to pay the premium charged by the ECA when issuing the policy. A foreign buyer is not a party to this contract and therefore it is not liable to pay the premium to the ECA. However, in reality, the insured exporters and banks shift the costs of premiums payable to ECAs to foreign buyers, which is usually stipulated in commercial and loan contracts. Therefore an exporter will claim indemnification from the foreign buyer for the amount of premium paid by the exporter to the ECA. The amount of premium paid by the exporter to the ECA can be included in the amount of credit the foreign buyer will pay to the exporter. Shifting the premium amount from the exporter to the foreign buyer does not mean the foreign buyer enters into a contractual relationship with the ECA. The exporter remains in the capacity of insured under the ECA policy and is obligated to pay the premium to the ECA, regardless of its right to be indemnified by the foreign buyer for this amount.

Banks that provide loans to foreign buyers also shift the costs of the ECA premium to foreign buyers. For example, a bank may claim against a foreign buyer to pay the amount of premium to it directly as an indemnification for the amount paid by the bank to the ECA. Banks also can include the amount of premium in the loan amount the foreign buyer will repay to the bank. Shifting the premium costs to a foreign buyer does not mean the foreign buyer enters into a contractual relationship with the ECA.

The Arrangement allows ECAs to cover the risk of non-repayment of the premium charged for issuing the ECA cover when this amount is included in the total amount of export credit. Therefore an exporter or bank that has paid the premium to an ECA from its own funds and included it in the total amount of export credit will be indemnified by the ECA for this amount in case of non-payment of the credit by the foreign buyer. Financing the premium and its repayment should not affect calculation of export contract value analysed in Chapter 21 because the Arrangement gives the power to ECAs to decide this issue by providing that the amount of premium may or may not be included in the export contract value.

In some transactions an exporter may include the amount of the ECA premium in the contractual price payable on credit terms and shift the premium cost to the foreign buyer without informing the foreign buyer about obtaining the ECA cover and paying the premium. Sometimes, when shifting the premium costs is not possible, the exporter may obtain the ECA cover and pay the premium from its own funds without informing the foreign buyer. This is possible because the insured exporters and banks are not obligated to inform foreign buyers about obtaining the ECA cover.

13.13   Indication of a premium rate

It is important for exporters and banks to obtain information about the approximate amount of premium for issuing the ECA cover when they negotiate their transactions with foreign buyers. The majority of ECAs are willing to provide an indication of a premium rate in a particular export credit transaction before issuing the ECA cover. An indication is not binding for ECAs but this information can be useful to exporters and banks when calculating and negotiating new transactions. Today, many ECAs have a premium calculator function on their websites where Internet users can calculate their premium by providing basic information about an export credit transaction.

14
Foreign Content

In the ECA context, the foreign content is value added to goods or services manufactured, assembled or supplied from another country (Figure 14.1). The foreign content is significant for exporters and banks when obtaining the ECA cover since they have to satisfy the requirements ECAs have in this respect. It is important to distinguish the term 'foreign content' from the term 'local cost' because foreign content is not internationally regulated while local cost is regulated in the OECD Arrangement. Local cost is described in Chapter 21.

Historically, goods for export were manufactured entirely or to a large part in a country of export. Some components of the final product were purchased from other countries and these components were called the foreign content in a final product. Numerous export goods are still manufactured in this manner, but the manufacturing process has changed substantially in the global economy. Today multinational companies from exporting countries have subsidiaries in other countries where they manufacture the majority of components or assemble the final product. Some multinational companies from exporting countries have only research and development activities in the country where their headquarters are located while their entire manufacturing process is placed in other countries (Figure 14.2).

These changes may affect multinational companies' eligibility to obtain the ECA cover from ECAs in the countries where their headquarters are located. The ECAs that previously provided the ECA cover to multinational companies may be reluctant to support export from the foreign countries where the subsidiaries of multinational companies conduct business. In this situation, multinational companies may be advised that their subsidiaries should obtain the ECA cover from the ECAs in the countries where they manufacture the goods for export. However, it can be difficult to obtain the ECA cover in developing countries because some of these countries have not established export credit agencies. Other developing countries have established their ECAs but their

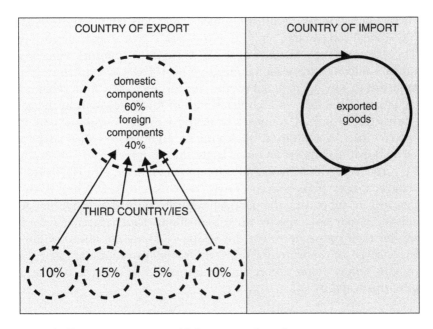

Figure 14.1 Foreign components added to exported goods

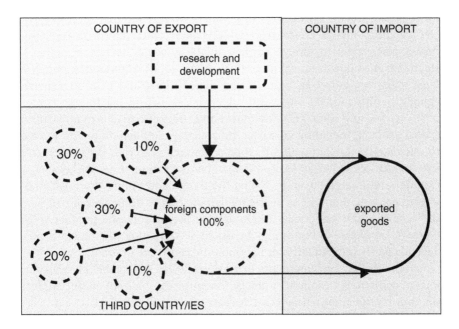

Figure 14.2 Entire manufacturing placed in third countries

capacity to provide cover is often insufficient and does not satisfy the needs of multinational companies.

The reason for the reluctance of the ECAs from the countries where multinational companies are headquartered to provide cover is that these ECAs are established to support national export. Supporting export from other countries, either in the form of high percentage of foreign content in the goods exported from the ECA countries or in the form of covering export from other countries, is contrary to that purpose. Additionally, when supporting their national exports, ECAs often apply their internal limits for exposure on a particular country, economic sector, foreign buyer, etc., which reduces the total capacity of ECAs to cover new credit risks. If an ECA uses its capacity created for supporting the national export to support exports from other countries, it may lack capacity when the national exporters request the ECA cover for their transactions. For this reason ECAs are not always willing to provide cover for export transactions with a high percentage of foreign content, especially for large export transactions that may engage a considerable part of their capacity.

14.1   Determining the foreign content

Foreign content is not internationally regulated and ECAs are free to define it according to their views on supporting national export and domestic employment opportunities. This results in a variety of ECA internal rules and policies regulating foreign content. Some ECAs apply different criteria and accept higher percentages of foreign content in the goods or services exported by small and medium-sized exporters than in the goods or services exported by large exporters. Other ECAs apply the same criteria and treat all exporters equally in this respect. The basic value for calculating the foreign content may vary because some ECAs use direct and indirect costs for manufacturing a final product, including labour and materials, administration, and research to calculate the foreign content, while a transaction's profit is excluded from this calculation. Other ECAs use the total contractual price agreed between an exporter and foreign buyer, including the transaction's profit, to calculate the foreign content. Some ECAs define foreign content as domestic content when the foreign goods or services are integrated into a domestic product so the domestic certificate of origin may be issued. Determining the foreign content depends partly on regulation of the domestic certificate of origin.

Some ECAs have requirements in addition to the acceptable percentage of foreign content. For example, some ECAs require the goods to be shipped from the country of export whose ECA provides the ECA cover.

Foreign content is usually expressed as a percentage of the total contractual value of the exported goods or services, and the majority of ECAs have internal regulations on the acceptable percentage of foreign content for which they may provide cover. The acceptable percentage of foreign content varies from low to very high but this is also changing over time. Some ECAs are flexible regarding a higher percentage of foreign content if the foreign components used to manufacture the export goods or services are produced by a foreign subsidiary of a multinational company headquartered in the ECA country. Some ECAs are willing to provide cover even when the foreign content exceeds the acceptable percentage, but with a higher premium.

14.2 National interest

Due to changes in the global economy the term 'foreign content' has become inadequate when applied to new forms of export transactions for which ECA cover is requested. This is especially the case when national manufacturers have placed their entire manufacturing process abroad, keeping only research and development activities in the countries where their headquarters are located. As a result, these companies do not export goods or services from the countries where they are headquartered. Even though these changes result in a loss of employment opportunities in the ECA countries, these countries still benefit from the business activities of the multinational companies in several ways. Research and development activities provide many employment opportunities in the ECA country and the revenues of a multinational company as a whole, including the revenues of foreign subsidiaries, are partly transferred to the ECA country.

In order to adjust their support to the new forms of business activities where classic terms such as export and foreign content are no longer adequate, some ECAs have amended their requirements for providing the ECA cover. Several ECAs replaced the term 'foreign content' with 'national interest'. This new term is more flexible and can be interpreted more broadly than 'foreign content'. 'National interest' applies to classic export transactions with or without foreign content and to the new transactions where no classic export takes place.

14.3 Determining the national interest

The term 'national interest' is difficult to define and its interpretation varies among the ECAs that apply it in ECA cover. These ECAs have established guidelines or adopted generally defined criteria to assess national interest in individual transactions. These criteria include:

a) Using components or raw materials from the ECA country in manufacturing final products abroad;

b) Using design, know-how and expertise from the ECA country in manufacturing final products abroad;
c) Transfer of gross profits to the ECA country;
d) Payment of employees, engagement of carriers and similar service providers
   that pay tax or receive their remuneration in the ECA country;
e) Payment of dividends, licences, royalties or similar payment obligations in
   the ECA country.

The wording of these criteria gives ECAs a lot of discretionary power when
deciding to provide the ECA cover for a particular export credit transaction.
Typically no fixed percentage of foreign content or similar strictly defined
measure is applied when assessing national interest. The decisions based on
national interest are often made on a case-by-case basis because of the variety
of export transactions (Figure 14.3).

When an ECA accepts that an export credit transaction may be covered by
implementing the national interest criteria it does not necessarily mean the
ECA will issue the maximum percentage of cover for the credit risk in the
transaction. ECAs have other instruments for adjusting the ECA cover for these
transactions such as lower percentage of cover, amount of premium and terms
of cover. These elements, combined with the national interest criteria, should
result in a well-balanced ECA decision on providing the ECA cover.

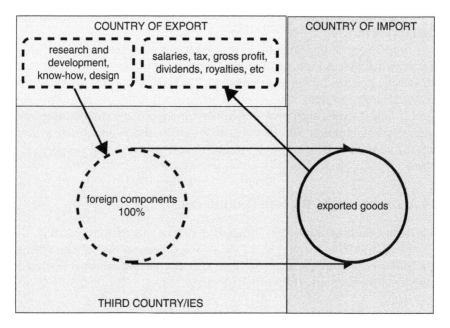

Figure 14.3   National interest of country of export

14.4   Reinsurance as a solution

One solution to the problem of export transactions with foreign content is cooperation between ECAs in the form of reinsurance contracts that allow them to share the risk covered by a primary ECA. Reinsurance contracts are analysed in Chapter 18.

15
Currency

Payments in international commercial and loan transactions are usually made in one of the major trading currencies that are used globally such as the US dollar, euro, Japanese yen, British pound and Swiss franc. These currencies are also called hard currencies. Payment in other currencies such as the currency of the country of export may be agreed upon if the currency is stable and acceptable to both contractual parties. However, the exchange rates between currencies vary on a daily basis, which may negatively affect exporters and banks in their export credit transactions. Their main concern is the risk of receiving lesser value than expected when payment of a credit is converted into another currency. This risk, also called the currency risk, is higher when a payment of credit is agreed in a local currency, which is the term used for the currency of the foreign buyer's country. A local currency may be depreciated or devaluated, resulting in a loss for an exporter or bank.

Exporters, banks and foreign buyers are aware of the currency risk and the need for one or both contractual parties to assume this risk. Assuming the currency risk by contractual parties can be agreed in various ways. The risk can be assumed by the foreign buyer, by the exporter or bank and it can be shared by both contractual parties. There is no universal solution for negotiating and contracting the currency risk because it depends on the bargaining power of the contractual parties. When an exporter with a strong position at the international market sells its goods or services abroad it will accept payment of a credit in a hard currency only. In such a transaction the currency risk is assumed by the foreign buyer whose revenues are earned in a local currency that may depreciate or devaluate in relation to the hard currency. However, some exporters and banks accept payment of a credit in a local currency and assume the currency risk, which sometimes includes even the risk of inability to convert the local currency into a hard currency and transfer the converted amounts out of the foreign buyer's country.

An exporter or bank that assumes the currency risk in a commercial or loan contract with a foreign buyer may seek protection against this risk from third parties. These parties are usually banks that are willing to enter into hedge transactions against unfavourable changes in exchange rates. A hedge transaction is a separate transaction with a third party that is not party to a commercial or loan contract. Since the ECA cover is directly connected with commercial and loan contracts denominated in various currencies it is important to analyse how ECAs deal with currency risks.

15.1 Cover and currency risk

The purpose of providing the ECA cover is to insure against the risk of non-payment of a credit by a foreign buyer. Therefore the majority of ECAs do not provide cover for currency risks only. Another reason for this is that currency risk protection is obtainable from banks and other private financial institutions that would object to competition from the officially supported ECAs in this business. However, when protection against currency risks is not obtainable at the private market, some ECAs may provide a separate cover for currency risks in export credit transactions, without covering credit risks in these transactions.

Even though ECAs do not provide a separate cover for currency risks they are exposed to such risks by covering non-payment of credits in the contracts where payment is agreed in a foreign currency. Covering credit risks in contracts denominated in foreign currencies can be complicated and ECAs deal with the currency issue in various ways. Some ECAs provide cover in their national currency only, while other ECAs provide cover in several foreign currencies and their national currency. Numerous ECAs occasionally provide cover in the local currency of a foreign buyer's country.

Below is description of the ECA cover for credit risks in commercial and loan contracts denominated in various currencies. Solutions for the ECA cover described below are not common for all ECAs and each ECA may have its own policy for providing cover in a particular currency.

15.2 Contract denominated in the currency of the ECA country

When payment of an export credit is agreed in the ECA country's currency, the foreign buyer assumes the currency risk. Therefore the foreign buyer will convert the local currency into the contractual currency in order to make payment of the credit. If the effective exchange rate between the two currencies is unfavourable at the date of conversion, the foreign buyer must pay more than expected for the contractual currency when entering into a commercial or loan contract (Figure 15.1).

If the foreign buyer defaults on payment of the credit denominated in the currency of the ECA country the ECA will indemnify the insured exporter or

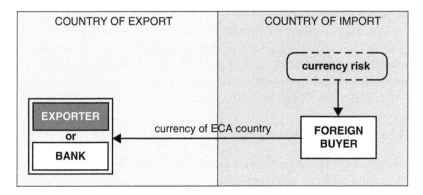

Figure 15.1 Payment of credit in the currency of ECA country

bank in its national currency. By covering the credit risk in this transaction the ECA does not assume the currency risk in case of paying indemnification to the insured. The insured exporter or bank is not exposed to the currency risk in this type of transaction, either when receiving payment of credit from the foreign buyer or being indemnified by the ECA.

15.3 Contract denominated in hard currency

When payment of an export credit is agreed in a hard currency other than the currency of the ECA country, the foreign buyer assumes the currency risk. As with the example above, the foreign buyer will convert the local currency into the hard currency to make payment of the credit. This may result in paying a higher price for the hard currency if the effective exchange rate applicable at the conversion date is unfavourable for the foreign buyer (Figure 15.2).

Some foreign buyers sell their goods or services to customers in other countries and receive their revenues in the same hard currency in which their export credit contract is denominated. In this situation the foreign buyer will pay its credit to the exporter or bank in the same currency without assuming the currency risk. However, these situations are infrequent and the revenues of the majority of foreign buyers are usually earned in their local currencies.

When an ECA covers a credit risk in a contract denominated in a hard currency, the ECA may decide to indemnify the insured exporter or bank in that particular currency. By obtaining this type of cover the insured exporter or bank is protected against the currency risk because the non-paid amount of credit will be indemnified by the ECA in the contractual currency. The currency risk in this type of cover is assumed by the ECA that will purchase the contractual hard currency in order to indemnify the insured and pay for it in its national currency (Figure 15.3).

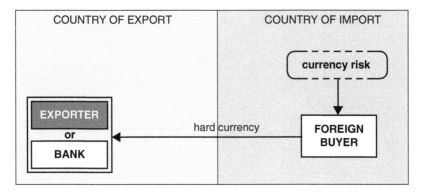

Figure 15.2 Payment of credit in hard currency

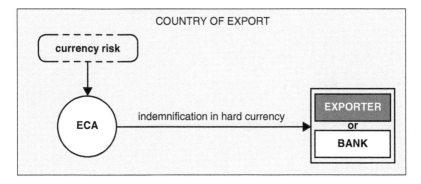

Figure 15.3 ECA indemnification in hard currency

The position of the exporter or bank in this example is almost identical to the position explained in the previous example. The exporter or bank is protected from the currency risk both when receiving regular payments of credit from the foreign buyer and when receiving indemnification from the ECA.

15.4 Contract denominated in other convertible currency

Some ECAs may cover a credit risk in a commercial or loan contract denominated in other convertible currency, usually a currency of an OECD participating country. In this example the convertible currency is distinguished from the ECA national currency, from a hard currency and from the local currency of the foreign buyer's country. Similarly, as in previous examples, the currency risk in this type of contract is assumed by the foreign buyer that will purchase the convertible currency in order to pay the credit (Figure 15.4).

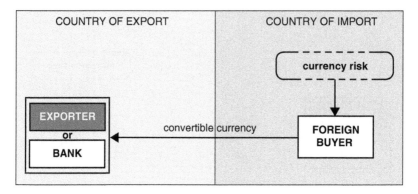

Figure 15.4   Payment of credit in other convertible currency

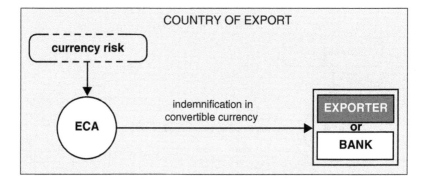

Figure 15.5   ECA indemnification in other convertible currency

When an ECA covers a credit risk in a contract denominated in a convertible currency, the ECA may decide to indemnify the insured exporter or bank in that particular currency. The ECA assumes the currency risk in this type of cover because the ECA will purchase the contractual currency and pay for it in its national currency in order to pay indemnification to the insured (Figure 15.5).

Some ECAs vary this type of cover by limiting the increase in exchange rate between the contractual currency and the ECA national currency. This limitation is applied if indemnification is paid to the insured. The highest increase in the exchange rate is limited to a certain percentage compared with the exchange rate effective on the date of issuing the ECA cover. An ECA may, for example, assume the currency risk up to 25 per cent while the insured exporter or bank assumes the currency risk exceeding this limit. If the effective exchange rate applicable at the date of indemnification exceeds 25 per cent, the insured exporter or bank will be indemnified by the ECA for 25 per cent of the currency exchange loss only. The applicable exchange rate for calculating the indemnification is usually the due date for payment of credit by the foreign buyer.

Depending on their assessment of future currency fluctuations, ECAs may limit the increase of exchange rates in various ways and with various percentages. Some ECAs are willing to provide cover for a higher increase in the exchange rate against payment of an additional premium by the insured exporter or bank.

15.5 Contract denominated in local currency

Some export credit contracts are denominated in a local currency and some ECAs provide cover for the risk of non-payment of a credit in these contracts. In this example the local currency is the currency of the foreign buyer's country distinguished from the hard and convertible currency mentioned in previous examples. In the contracts denominated in the local currency, the exporter or bank assumes the currency risk because the exporter or bank will probably convert the local currency into another currency and transfer it out of the foreign buyer's country (Figure 15.6).

When covering the risk of non-payment of a credit in a local currency, some ECAs do not indemnify the insured exporter or bank in that currency. The indemnification for the non-paid amount is paid to the insured either in the currency of the ECA country or in a hard currency. The applicable exchange rate between the local currency and indemnification currency is typically the exchange rate effective on the due date for payment of the credit by the foreign buyer. ECAs apply this method of paying indemnification because it would be administratively complicated to keep reserves in various local currencies for the eventuality of paying indemnification. Purchasing a local currency for the same purpose could be burdensome administratively and the easiest way to deal with this is paying the indemnification in another currency that is always available to ECAs.

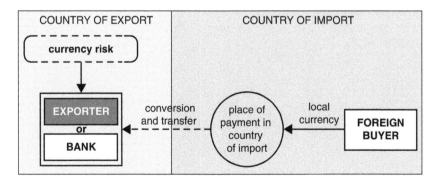

Figure 15.6   Payment of credit in local currency

When issuing cover for non-payment of a credit in a local currency, some ECAs require the insured exporter or bank to include a crystallisation clause in a commercial or loan contract with a foreign buyer. The crystallisation clause provides that, in case of non-payment of the credit by the foreign buyer, the non-paid amount in the local currency will be converted into a hard currency at the exchange rate effective on the due date for payment. Therefore the non-paid amount in the local currency will be replaced by an amount payable in hard currency only. The exchange rate between the local currency and the hard currency will be fixed and the foreign buyer will assume the risk of depreciation or devaluation of the non-paid amount in the local currency. Recovery of the non-paid amount will be in the hard currency calculated according to the crystallisation clause.

Applying the crystallisation clause is a better solution for an ECA that has indemnified an insured exporter or bank than dealing with a local currency when recovering the indemnified amount from a foreign buyer. However, the crystallisation clause is not enforceable in some jurisdictions, even when the foreign buyer has accepted such a clause in a commercial or loan contract. In several other jurisdictions the foreign buyer is required to obtain the exchange control approval for making payment in a foreign currency under the crystallisation clause.

The ECA cover for non-payment in a local currency may exclude the political risk of transferring the local currency out of the foreign buyer's country. This is usually made at the request of the insured exporter or bank when the place of payment agreed in the commercial or loan contract is in the foreign buyer's country. If no transfer of the amount paid by the foreign buyer is intended outside of the foreign buyer's country there is no need to cover the risk of transferring the currency. Excluding the transferring risk from the ECA cover may result in a lower premium rate. The insured exporter or bank does not assume currency risk in such situations since the amount paid by the foreign buyer in the local currency will be used by the insured locally, within the foreign buyer's country.

16
Confidentiality

Confidentiality is important in relations between ECAs, exporters, banks, foreign buyers and other parties that may be involved in providing the ECA cover. The information that is often treated as confidential, which means it cannot be disclosed to third parties, pertains to parties that enter into commercial and loan contracts covered by ECAs, the terms of these contracts and the terms of ECA cover. Such information may be provided by one party to another before entering into a contract or during performance of the contract. Disclosing confidential information to third parties may be prohibited by internal rules of a receiving party or contractual or statutory provisions that exporters, banks or ECAs apply in their work. Therefore it is interesting to analyse how confidentiality applies between an exporter or bank and a foreign buyer, exporter or bank and an ECA, and an ECA and a foreign buyer.

16.1   Confidentiality in relations between exporters, banks and foreign buyers

In practice, exporters and foreign buyers are not willing to disclose information about their commercial or loan contracts to third parties and they often internally classify such information as a business secret in order to prevent its disclosure. When confidential information is provided by a foreign buyer to an exporter or vice versa before entering into a commercial contract, the disclosing party may require the receiving party to enter into a confidentiality or non-disclosure agreement. By entering into such an agreement the receiving party agrees to keep the received information confidential and not to disclose it to unauthorised persons. A confidentiality agreement defines the information that will be treated as confidential, the purpose for which it can be used by the receiving party, and the right of the receiving party to disclose the information to its advisors and auditors, courts of justice, governmental bodies, etc. Later, when entering into a commercial contract, both the exporter and foreign buyer may agree to keep the information about the contract confidential.

The confidentiality of the information a foreign buyer provides to a bank before entering into a loan agreement is usually protected by banking legislation that prevents banks from disclosing information about their customers. This statutory confidentiality obligation is applied both in the negotiating stage and after entering into a loan agreement between a bank and a foreign buyer.

Both banks and companies acting as exporters apply legislation that prohibits the use or disclosure of information with the purpose of preventing insider dealings. This legislation prohibits insiders from taking advantage of confidential information obtained in their work for acquiring or disposing of marketable securities. It also prohibits disclosing of confidential information by insiders to third parties for other purposes such as trade. In addition, disclosing information about individuals is strictly regulated in the legislation of the EU member states and other countries. These statutory provisions protect the confidentiality of the information about commercial and loan contracts between exporters or banks on one side and foreign buyers on the other.

Information that is not usually protected as confidential in contractual relationships between exporters or banks and foreign buyers is about non-payment of a credit by a foreign buyer. It is considered that an exporter or bank has the right to disclose such information when commencing a legal action against a foreign buyer in a court with the purpose of recovering the non-paid amount. Since most court proceedings of this type are not confidential, providing the information about non-payment to the court makes it available to the public as well.

16.2   Confidentiality in relations between exporters, banks and ECAs

When applying for the ECA cover, an exporter or bank is required to provide the ECA with detailed information about the export credit transaction. The information required concerns the foreign buyer, the type of goods or services to be exported, delivery terms, contractual price, credit terms, technical details, etc. The parties to the commercial or loan contract treat this information as confidential and they expect the ECAs not to disclose the information to third parties.

ECAs are aware that disclosing information about commercial and loan contracts to unauthorised parties may cause damage to exporters, banks and foreign buyers. Therefore they classify such information as confidential and protect it by implementing their internal non-disclosure procedures established for this purpose.

In addition, ECAs protect the confidentiality of the information received by applying similar legislation as banks and other parties on preventing insider dealings. ECAs are also obligated to protect information about individuals in the same manner. Some ECAs that have a status of governmental agency apply a special secrecy legislation that is also applied by other authorities of the state. The secrecy legislation is usually strict and these ECAs are not allowed to disclose any information about commercial or loan contracts they receive in the course of their work. When confidentiality obligations are imposed by a statute, some exceptions from the disclosing prohibition are provided to respond to enquiries of courts, tax authorities and other authorities of the state. Courts and other authorities of a state are entitled to require confidential information without prior consent of any party involved.

Most ECAs do not enter into separate confidentiality agreements with applicants for the ECA cover and this is generally accepted by exporters and banks when dealing with ECAs. Given the number of applications ECAs handle on a yearly basis it would be impossible for them to negotiate and enter into a separate non-disclosure agreement with each applicant.

Some ECAs agree to protect the confidentiality of the information received by applicants for the ECA cover by including a non-disclosure provision in their standard terms. These terms are accepted by the applicants when signing applications for the ECA cover, and application forms provided by ECAs usually contain a provision stating that the ECA standard terms will govern contractual relations between the applicant and the ECA.

As with the relationship between exporters, banks and foreign buyers, information that may not be protected by ECAs is related to non-payment of a credit by a foreign buyer.

16.3   Confidentiality in relations between ECAs and foreign buyers

When issuing the ECA cover to exporters or banks, ECAs do not enter into a direct contractual relationship with foreign buyers. They receive the necessary information about foreign buyers from the exporters or banks that apply for the ECA cover and the confidentiality of this information is protected by ECAs as explained above.

However, some ECAs need additional information about a foreign buyer to analyse its business and assess its ability to pay the credit for which the ECA cover was requested. The foreign buyer is then asked to provide additional information to the ECA through the exporter or bank that applied for the ECA cover. The information that ECAs request may include a business plan, especially when assessing project risks where the foreign buyer is a new entity whose ability to pay the credit can be assessed by analysing the business plan only. In other transactions the ECA may request the foreign buyer's last semi-annual financial report that is not available from other sources, information about licences necessary for conducting the foreign buyer's business, information about the foreign buyer's parent company and its financial standing or any other information of importance for the ECA's credit risk assessment.

The foreign buyers that are requested to provide additional information to ECAs often treat this information as confidential and some foreign buyers request ECAs to enter into non-disclosure agreements. This is one of very few occasions where an ECA and foreign buyer enter into any type of agreement with each other. Otherwise they do not have a direct relationship in the process of issuing the ECA cover. While entering into non-disclosure agreements between privately owned companies in their ordinary business is a procedure that normally does not take long time, entering into such agreements with ECAs can involve difficulties and delays.

One possible reason for delay is that foreign buyers may insist on imposing burdensome contractual obligations on ECAs as recipients of confidential information, while ECAs are not always allowed to assume all obligations proposed by foreign buyers due to their status and connection with the state. These differences can result in lengthy negotiations between a foreign buyer and an ECA, causing dissatisfaction of the applicant for the ECA cover because of delays in closing a deal with the foreign buyer. This is especially the case when a foreign buyer works with an ECA for the first time and is not familiar with its way of providing the ECA cover and protecting confidential information.

There are several issues that may arise when ECAs deal with drafts of non-disclosure agreements provided by foreign buyers. Foreign buyers usually propose their national law to govern the agreement and the jurisdiction of their home courts in case of legal disputes. This is not acceptable for ECAs because it is practically impossible for them to learn about all the foreign legal systems with which they have contact. The other reason for not accepting these proposals can be the lack of rule of law in the foreign buyer's country, which makes the national law and the jurisdiction of that country unreliable from an ECA's point of view.

Some ECAs have the status of a governmental agency, which means they are not independent legal entities. When an ECA with this status enters into commercial contracts with other parties, the state or government actually becomes party to the contract. States and governments are restrictive in accepting foreign laws or jurisdictions when entering into commercial contracts with foreign counterparties because it includes waiving the state's immunity from proceedings in foreign courts, which states are reluctant to do.

Some drafts of non-disclosure agreements provided by foreign buyers contain comprehensive and burdensome provisions on liability for breach of the non-disclosure obligation by an ECA such as the liability for the foreign buyer's consequential losses. Most of these provisions are not acceptable to ECAs.

Some foreign buyers include a clause that states the confidential information disclosed to an ECA does not constitute advice and the disclosing party does not guarantee the accuracy of the information in a draft of the non-disclosure agreement. These clauses are acceptable ECAs when the confidential information contains assumptions and business projections that are uncertain by their nature. However, inclusion of these clauses may result in controversy regarding those parts of confidential information that are reasonably expected by ECAs to be accurate such as audited financial reports. What ECAs need in order to assess the credit risk in an export credit transaction is reliable information, and discussions on accuracy of information provided by a foreign buyer may delay processing of the application by ECAs. In general, many ECAs are reluctant to enter into non-disclosure agreements with foreign buyers and, when they do, they accept only such terms that comply with numerous limitations imposed on them by their regulators.

16.4 Transparency requirements

Because ECAs provide cover to exporters and banks with the support of their states, the media and public have increasingly required greater transparency of the ECA business. In order to satisfy the transparency requirements some ECAs publish information about transactions for which they have issued the ECA cover. This information is usually short, containing the name of exporter, the country of import and the value of the contract, but it does not normally contain the foreign buyer's name or the terms of the contract.

The publishing of this type of information by an ECA without the consent of the parties to a commercial or loan contract may constitute a breach of the ECA's non-disclosure obligation and damage the businesses of the parties involved. Therefore the insured exporter or bank must consent to publishing this information. It is not unusual that an exporter or bank does not agree to this and the information about the export credit transaction cannot be published.

An ECA may refrain from publishing information about the cover issued for a particular transaction when providing cover may be an incentive for the foreign buyer to default on payment of credit. For the same reason an exporter may decide not to inform the foreign buyer about the ECA cover for the risk of non-payment of credit. Such situations are rare but an exporter may find it prudent to do so when dealing with a foreign buyer whose willingness to pay the credit, when having financial difficulties, may be negatively affected by the fact the exporter is insured for the risk of non-payment. Neither the insured nor the ECA is obligated to notify the foreign buyer about the ECA cover for the risk of non-payment of the credit.

Some projects where credit risks are covered by ECAs may have environmental or social impacts in the countries of import, giving rise to public criticism. ECAs that apply the OECD Recommendation of the Council on Common Approaches for Officially Supported Export Credits and Environmental and Social Due Diligence are required to disclose publicly information about the ECA cover for the credit risks in some environmentally and socially sensitive projects. This information must be published at least 30 days before the date of issuing the ECA policy and include the project's name, location and description and details of where additional information may be obtained. In practice, this obligation does not cause any difficulties between ECAs and applicants for the ECA cover. Today, exporters, banks and foreign buyers know the OECD requirements and the importance of protecting the environment and local communities, and they typically consent to publishing this information. Chapter 22 describes the OECD requirements regarding environmental and social impacts.

16.5 Confidentiality in relations between ECAs and reinsurers

As explained in Chapter 18, the credit risks covered by ECAs are sometimes reinsured by other ECAs or private reinsurance companies. Some ECAs seek reinsurance to cover an export credit transaction with a considerable percentage of foreign content, to provide capacity for covering new risks in export credit transactions or to balance their portfolios of credit risks by avoiding a concentration of a particular type of risk.

When an ECA approaches a potential reinsurer and negotiates reinsurance of a credit risk, the issue of confidentiality may involve several other parties. Potential reinsurers may request the ECA to provide them with the information necessary to assess the credit risk. The information requested is related to the basic terms of an underlying commercial or loan contract covered by the ECA, including the name of the exporter or bank and the foreign buyer. This information is often treated as confidential and its disclosure to potential reinsurers without consent of the parties involved in a transaction can be prohibited.

In order to comply with its internal confidentiality procedure, contractual or statutory non-disclosure obligation, an ECA must obtain the insured exporter or bank and foreign buyer's consent for disclosing the confidential information to a potential reinsurer. Obtaining the consent from all parties involved in the export credit transaction can be difficult, especially when the ECA policy has already been issued. A foreign buyer may believe its ability to pay the credit is very good and that the ECA does not have any reason for reinsuring that particular credit risk. Some foreign buyers claim that just mentioning the company's name at the reinsurance market as a potential credit risk could negatively affect the company's creditworthiness and damage its reputation. It takes some time to convince a foreign buyer that the reason for reinsuring the credit risk is for the purpose of balancing the ECA's portfolio of risks rather than the ECA's pessimistic projection of the foreign buyer's ability to pay the credit. However, foreign buyers may not consent to disclosure of the confidential information to potential reinsurers.

To avoid that situation, some ECAs require applicants for the ECA cover to consent to disclosing confidential information to reinsurers and provide the same consent from the foreign buyer in the application stage. Such consents are given in written form and they allow ECAs to disclose the confidential information to their potential reinsurers and to the reinsurers' potential reinsurers. Generally it is easier to obtain consent in the early stages of processing an application for the ECA cover than after issuing the ECA policy.

When the applicant for the ECA cover and the foreign buyer have consented to disclosing confidential information to potential reinsurers, ECAs are obligated to protect the information from further disclosure. For this purpose, ECAs enter into non-disclosure agreements imposing the same obligation of non-disclosure on potential reinsurers.

17
Security for Payment of Credits Covered by ECAs

Exporters and banks frequently request security for payment of a credit when entering into commercial and loan contracts with foreign buyers. Foreign buyers also know the importance of security and are often willing to provide security for payment of their credits. In most export credit transactions, security is provided in the form of a non-possessory pledge over the asset purchased on credit terms, but it can come in other forms and in other assets owned by a foreign buyer. The reason behind taking security over the asset purchased on credit terms is that the creditor, who paid for the asset by providing the credit, should have a better right to the asset than other creditors of the foreign buyer. Third parties may provide security for payment of a foreign buyer's credit, either by issuing a guarantee or by providing security in their own assets.

Terminology

> *When a non-possessory pledge is created over an asset purchased by a foreign buyer, the ownership and possession of the asset are transferred to the foreign buyer but the asset is pledged to the insured exporter or bank as security for payment of credit.*

This short description of security indicates that security for payment of an export credit has similar effects to those of the ECA cover. The purpose of both transactions is to protect an exporter or bank from a loss caused by non-payment of a credit by a foreign buyer. Due to this similarity, it can be unclear whether obtaining the ECA cover is necessary in a transaction where payment of credit is secured by security provided by the foreign buyer or a third person. Obtaining security and the ECA cover for the same credit risk must be assessed on a case-by-case basis by taking into account characteristics of the security provided by a foreign buyer and the type of ECA cover obtained for covering the credit risk. Assessing security includes an analysis of the position of a secured exporter or bank when renegotiating a credit, the value of the asset over which security is created, the existence of a secondary market for the asset, the estimated proceeds of enforcing security and selling the asset in an enforcement procedure, the costs of such a procedure, the chances of enforcing security against a particular foreign buyer, the willingness of the foreign buyer to help enforce security, the state of rule of law in the foreign buyer's jurisdiction, etc. On the other hand, assessing the ECA cover includes an analysis of events that may cause non-payment of a credit, the scope of cover and procedures for claiming indemnification from an ECA.

A comparative analysis of differences between security and the ECA cover is a big subject that should be analysed in a separate study; for the purpose of this book, some of these differences are described briefly below.

17.1 Differences between security and the ECA cover

The main difference between security and the ECA cover is the scope of protection against credit risks. While security covers the non-payment of a credit caused by the foreign buyer's insolvency or its unwillingness to pay, the ECA cover includes political events that may prevent payment of credit, such as a decision of a foreign buyer's country to stop transfer of foreign currency out of the country. When the foreign buyer's payment of credit is stopped, the security created over a foreign buyer's asset located in the same country will be of no use. If the insured exporter or bank, acting as a secured creditor, successfully enforces security against the foreign buyer's asset by selling it and receiving some proceeds, the transfer of proceeds will be stopped in the same way as the payment of credit made by the foreign buyer.

If the political risk described above is covered by an ECA, the insured exporter or bank will be indemnified by the ECA for the non-paid amount of credit when the transfer of foreign buyer's payment has been stopped in its country.

The complexity of judicial procedures for enforcing security compared to the simplicity of making a claim and receiving indemnification from ECAs is another important difference. In some jurisdictions, the procedure for enforcing security can be complicated, costly and time consuming, and the financial outcome is highly uncertain. On the other hand, claiming and receiving indemnification from ECAs is a simple procedure without any uncertainty regarding the amount of indemnification and the financial ability of ECAs to make payment.

While security is provided by a foreign buyer or third party at the foreign buyer's request, the ECA cover is issued at the request of an exporter or bank, acting as creditor. An exporter or bank may obtain the ECA cover without involving the foreign buyer and the foreign buyer may not be aware of the existence of the ECA cover for payment of its credit.

17.2 Security and the ECA cover provided for the same risk

When analysing an export credit risk, an exporter or bank may realise that security provided by a foreign buyer is not sufficient protection against the risk of non-payment of a credit. In this situation the exporter or bank may decide to obtain the ECA cover as an additional protection for the same credit risk. Therefore both security and the ECA cover will be in effect at the same time.

It is also possible that an exporter or bank applies for the ECA cover first and requests security from the foreign buyer after being instructed to do so by the ECA, which may require security as a condition for issuing the ECA cover in an individual export credit transaction. ECAs may do this when they find it necessary regardless of whether the foreign buyer previously offered to provide security.

When both security and the ECA cover are provided to an exporter or bank, the question is how these two protections affect each other. This issue is partly analysed in Chapter 13, which explains that providing some types of security may reduce the premium rate charged by an ECA. Another important issue is the enforcement of security by an insured exporter or bank as a condition for receiving indemnification from an ECA. Chapter 19 analyses this issue.

17.3 Effects of security in export credit transactions covered by ECAs

Based on their long experience in dealing with secured credits, ECAs consider several effects of security when assessing a credit risk in a transaction where security is provided for payment of credit. These effects are analysed below in several stages of an export credit contract.

17.4 Security in the initial stage of a contract

When security is created over a foreign buyer's tangible assets such as machinery, land, buildings and similar assets or intangible assets such as receivables and rights, two important effects of security immediately arise. The first effect is that other creditors are prevented from taking security in the same asset; second, the foreign buyer's disposal over the asset is restricted. Releasing security and amending its terms requires the consent of the insured exporter or bank and of the ECA that issued cover for the credit risk. This provides the insured and the ECA with an indirect control over the foreign buyer's business, which is desirable and useful from an ECA's point of view.

Generally, an insured exporter or bank may achieve more comprehensive control of the foreign buyer's business by including financial and negative covenants into the contract, as explained in Chapter 8. However, these types of covenants are typical for international loan agreements but are not common in international commercial contracts where payment is agreed on credit terms. When an exporter in a commercial contract wants to control the foreign buyer's business, and it cannot be achieved in a way typical for international loan agreements, it can be partly achieved by taking security in the foreign buyer's assets.

ECAs are aware of the effects of taking security described above and they consider security an important contractual mechanism in all types of export credit transactions, even when a foreign buyer makes payments of a credit regularly and never defaults.

17.5   Security and renegotiation of credit

Foreign buyers with financial difficulties often request an insured exporter or bank to agree on rescheduling a due date or dates for payment of an export credit. They may request an extension of due dates for payment but they also may request a reduction in the interest rate and sometimes even the principal amount of credit. Generally, and not only in export credit transactions, a secured creditor is in a stronger negotiating position than an unsecured creditor when renegotiating a credit bilaterally. This is especially the case when security is provided over the majority of the foreign buyer's assets or the assets that are necessary for conducting its business on a daily basis. This strong negotiating position is often recognised by foreign buyers because the possibility of enforcing security makes them more willing to agree to a rescheduling solution that is acceptable to a secured creditor.

When a foreign buyer negotiates the restructuring of its total indebtedness in multilateral negotiations with the majority of its creditors, the situation is similar to the bilateral negotiations described above. The foreign buyer and unsecured creditors usually accept a stronger negotiating position and more influential role of secured creditors in the restructuring procedure and in negotiating the restructuring agreement.

ECAs are aware of the advantages of the status of a secured creditor in the situations described above and this is another reason why they require security to be provided in transactions where they consider issuing cover for export credit risks.

After indemnifying an insured exporter or bank that has a status of a secured creditor, an ECA may benefit from the insured's strong negotiating position when trying to recover the debt. Chapter 19 explains rescheduling and restructuring a foreign buyer's credit in connection to payment of claims by ECAs.

17.6   Enforcement of security

In practice, security is not enforced frequently by the secured creditors that have obtained the ECA cover for their credit risks in transactions with foreign buyers because the majority of export credits covered by ECAs are paid regularly and the insured exporters and banks do not need to enforce security. However, security is enforced sometimes, especially when a foreign buyer's financial problems cannot be solved by renegotiating a credit. Security may be enforced before or after commencement of a bankruptcy proceeding against the foreign buyer. Where security is created over a tangible asset of a foreign buyer, it is usually enforced in a judicial procedure that includes taking the asset from the foreign buyer and selling it at a public auction. The proceeds of selling the asset are then paid to the secured creditor and applied against the non-paid credit. Where security is provided in the foreign buyer's receivables or in the form of guarantee for payment of credit, no judicial procedure is required if the foreign buyer's debtor or guarantor are willing and able to pay the insured exporter or bank. If the foreign buyer's debtor or guarantor is able to pay but not willing to do so, the security must be enforced in a judicial proceeding.

An insured exporter or bank acting as secured creditor can be prohibited from enforcing security for a certain period of time after commencement of a bankruptcy or another insolvency proceeding against a foreign buyer. Sometimes called the freezing of creditors' rights in bankruptcy, the prohibition is imposed by bankruptcy legislation in some jurisdictions. This can cause a problem for the insured exporter or bank because the asset over which security is created may lose its value during the freezing period.

Despite the complexity of the enforcement procedure, it is reasonably effective in numerous jurisdictions, especially in countries with stable judicial systems and a high level of rule of law. However, even in such jurisdictions, the financial outcome of a judicial procedure for enforcement of security depends on the value and marketability of the asset over which security is created.

17.7   Uncertainty connected with security

Taking security for payment of an export credit and exercising the rights of a secured creditor can be a straightforward procedure, but it can also be quite complicated because security for export credits is usually provided over assets in foreign countries, where security is governed by local law. Therefore an insured exporter or bank, and even the ECA, must understand the local legal requirements for dealing with security, which is not easy due to the large number of foreign countries with which ECAs deal.

The registration of security, required in some jurisdictions, is considered uncertain, especially when security is created over a tangible asset of a foreign buyer. The registration requirements can be difficult to satisfy and the registration procedure is often connected with payment of fees. Sometimes foreign creditors engage a local law firm or another professional to complete the registration procedure properly. Exporters may be reluctant to register security in their export credit transactions because of the complexity and costs, even where a foreign buyer is willing to provide security over some of its assets.

Assessing the various types of security can be difficult for exporters, banks and ECAs when requested to issue the ECA cover. This is especially the case when they assess types of security that are not used in their countries and with which they are not familiar. Some important types of security such as the English law-based floating charge over a company's assets do not exist in all jurisdictions. Similarly, providing security over future assets of the foreign buyer, sometimes called the after-acquired property, is allowed in legal systems based on English law but not accepted in numerous other jurisdictions.

17.8 Security in intercreditor agreements

Exercising the rights of secured creditors is sometimes regulated in an intercreditor agreement entered into between two or more of a foreign buyer's creditors. Entering into this type of agreement is required when a foreign buyer is a large company that has borrowed substantial amounts of money from banks. An intercreditor agreement provides that all banks must consent before any of them accelerates payment of its loan or takes any legal action against a defaulting foreign buyer. Other provisions in intercreditor agreements provide a decision making method, usually the majority vote, and sometimes a right of veto in favour of one or several creditors.

The enforcement of security by secured creditors is another important issue that is usually regulated in an intercreditor agreement. When security is enforced by an individual secured creditor it may cause bankruptcy of a foreign buyer when restructuring its indebtedness would provide a better financial outcome for all creditors. Therefore intercreditor agreements provide that security can be enforced by an individual secured creditor only if other secured creditors consent to the enforcement. Some intercreditor agreements stipulate that the proceeds of enforcement of security by an individual secured creditor will be shared by all secured creditors. The inclusion of such a provision in an intercreditor agreement is another way to limit the rights of an individual secured creditor and involve other secured creditors in making important decisions that may negatively affect the foreign buyer's business and its existence as a company.

Since existing creditors of a foreign buyer are aware the foreign buyer may need new loans to conduct its regular business, an intercreditor agreement may provide terms for sharing the existing security with new creditors. An insured exporter or bank should report shared security to the ECA because ECAs assess security as it was originally provided and they must reassess the credit risk in a new situation, where security will be shared with other creditors.

When acting as a party to an intercreditor agreement, an insured exporter or bank may have difficulties following an ECA's instructions such as the instruction to enforce security or take a legal action against a defaulting foreign buyer. If other parties to the intercreditor agreement decide that action will not be taken, the insured exporter or bank will be prevented from following the ECA's instruction. Therefore it is important for an exporter or bank to notify the ECA when applying for the ECA cover that its actions against a defaulting foreign buyer may be limited or prevented by provisions of an existing intercreditor agreement.

17.9   Quasi-security

ECAs frequently cover commercial contracts with clauses that do not create security in the formal sense but have very similar effects. These types of contracts are called quasi-security. Quasi-security contracts that ECAs usually cover include lease contracts and sale of goods contracts containing retention of title clause.

In a lease contract, an insured exporter or bank, acting as lessor, has the right to repossess the lease object from a foreign buyer or lessee that has defaulted on a periodical lease payment. Often the right of taking back the lease object is easier to enforce than security, and ECAs see this right as a strong contractual remedy for an exporter or bank against a defaulting foreign buyer.

The retention of title clause provides that the ownership of the purchased goods will be transferred to the foreign buyer when the credit is fully paid to the insured exporter. In a default situation, the insured exporter, acting as owner of the goods, has the right to repossess the goods from the foreign buyer. This is also a powerful contractual remedy, as with the lease contracts described above.

The repossession of goods is usually not a condition for indemnifying an insured exporter by an ECA. When the goods cannot be sold on the secondary market or prices on the secondary market are low, it is better to leave the goods in the possession of the foreign buyer to operate them and pay the credit in the future. In practice, repossessing goods or taking other actions against a foreign buyer should be discussed between the insured exporter or bank and the ECA that issued cover to the insured. Since quasi-security has similar effects as security, ECAs evaluate these types of contracts as security when assessing credit risks in export credit transactions.

Quasi-security in practice

Entering into lease contracts or inclusion of retention of title clause in sale of goods contracts is an accepted custom in the trade with specific types of industrial products. These contracts are often standardised and the ECAs that have more experience with covering export credit risks in such contracts may assume all contracts of a particular exporter always include quasi-security provisions. Therefore it is important to notify the ECA when these provisions are excluded from individual contracts, since this may affect the ECA's assessment of a credit risk in such transactions.

17.10 Negative pledge

When an ECA assesses a credit risk, it may request security be provided as described above, but it may also require the limiting of the foreign buyer's future providing of security for payment of other credits. In international loan agreements this is provided in the negative pledge clause that has become standard in this type of agreement. The title is somewhat confusing because the negative pledge clause usually limits the types of security a foreign buyer may create over its assets, not only pledge. The negative pledge clause limits the foreign buyer from creating new security over its assets without consent of the insured bank acting as a lender in the loan agreement. When this consent is requested by the foreign buyer the insured bank is usually obligated to obtain the ECA's consent. The negative pledge clause is another way to control the foreign buyer's business, one of the main purposes of providing security.

Using the negative pledge clause in loan agreements is also mentioned in Chapter 8.

18
Reinsurance

A primary insurer may decide to transfer one or several of its risks to a second insurer in exchange for payment of a premium, and this is called reinsurance. The second insurer is liable solely to the primary insurer and the primary insurer is liable to the insured and handles all matters prior or subsequent to loss. In a reinsurance contract the primary insurer is called the insurer and the second insurer is called the reinsurer. A reinsurance contract can cover a portfolio of risks or a single risk.

An insurance company may decide to reinsure a risk in order to create more capacity for insuring new risks or to balance its portfolio of risks and protect the company against losses. Reinsuring risks is very frequent in the insurance business, which could not function without reinsurers. The global reinsurance market is dominated by a relatively small number of large multinational reinsurers that specialise in this type of business.

Two types of reinsurance contracts are important in the ECA context. Quota share reinsurance is a type of contract in which the reinsurer receives a percentage of the premium paid to the primary insurer and agrees to pay the same percentage of loss to the primary insurer. In this type of reinsurance, the premium and loss are shared on a pro rata basis. The quota share reinsurance contract is normally used to reinsure single risks. It is called the proportional reinsurance contract because of the pro rata sharing of risk.

Excess of loss is another important type of reinsurance contract by which the primary insurer takes loss or losses up to a specific amount and the reinsurer agrees to pay the loss exceeding that amount. The premium that the primary insurer pays to the reinsurer is not shared on a pro rata basis. This type of reinsurance is also called non-proportional because the premium and loss are shared in a different way than in the proportional type of reinsurance.

18.1   Reinsurance in ECA business

Reinsurance is important for ECAs when issuing cover in transactions where parties from other countries are involved and when managing their portfolios of credit risks. Reinsurance of ECA risks may take two forms, depending on the status of a reinsurer that enters into a reinsurance contract with an ECA as a primary insurer. The first form is reinsuring risks between ECAs and the second is reinsuring ECA risks by private reinsurance companies.

18.2   Reinsurance between ECAs

The ECA reinsurance shares a credit risk between two or more ECAs where part of a credit risk covered by the primary ECA is reinsured by the reinsuring ECA in exchange for payment of a premium. The reinsuring ECA is liable solely to the primary ECA, and the primary ECA is liable to the insured exporter or bank.

The reason for reinsuring credit risks between ECAs is the foreign content in the exported goods or services described in Chapter 14. As a result of economic globalisation, numerous goods for export are manufactured using components from other countries. When these goods are exported on credit terms, the ECA cover is normally requested from the ECA in the country from which the final product is exported. By covering this type of export credit transaction, the ECA from the country of export supports both the national export and exports from the countries from which the components were purchased. Providing cover in this way does not agree with the purpose of ECA business, which is support-ing national export only. The capacity of ECAs to cover credit risks is limited and if they use it to support exports from other countries it may result in their inability to cover credit risks in their national exports. Therefore ECAs are reluctant to issue cover for credit risks in transactions with considerable foreign content, especially in large export transactions that may engage a significant part of their capacity.

In order to facilitate export credit transactions with considerable foreign content, ECAs may enter into reinsurance contracts to share credit risks with other ECAs. This is a contract between the ECA covering the entire credit risk in export of a final product and the reinsuring ECA covering the part of the credit risk proportional to the value of components purchased from the reinsuring ECA's country (Figure 18.1). The premium is shared between the two ECAs proportionally to the share of risk covered.

Reinsurance is the most frequent form of risk sharing between ECAs. The general view is that it provides the best solution for cooperation between ECAs and gives small and medium-sized suppliers of components an opportunity to participate in large export projects and approach new markets.

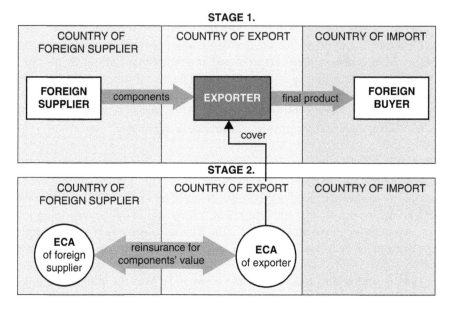

Figure 18.1   Reinsurance between ECAs

A reinsurance contract can take the form of a master contract that governs all future transactions between two ECAs or an individual contract covering a particular credit risk. Reinsurance contracts between ECAs contain definitions of main terms, provisions on rights and obligations of the contractual parties, payment of premium, currency, possible rescheduling of due dates for payment of credit, governing law, etc. Sharing credit risks through reinsurance between ECAs can be used in supplier and buyer credit transactions.

When an ECA reinsures a credit risk, the primary ECA manages the transaction as a whole including issuing the ECA policy and all subsequent stages. The primary ECA may consult the reinsuring ECA on issues related to the credit risk but the final decision on these issues is normally made by the primary ECA. Managing a transaction by the primary ECA has several advantages, such as reducing transaction costs and dealing with the entire credit risk by applying only one set of ECA standard terms.

18.3   Other forms of cooperation between ECAs

In addition to reinsurance, ECAs have developed other forms of cooperation for issuing the ECA cover for transactions where several parties from various countries are involved. These parties may act as exporter, main supplier, sub-supplier, consortium partner, etc. ECAs may cooperate in these transactions through coinsurance, parallel insurance and agreements establishing the percentage of foreign content covered by a single ECA without risk sharing.

18.4   Coinsurance between ECAs

Coinsurance is another model of cooperation between ECAs involved in a joint export credit transaction. Coinsurance can be agreed between two or more ECAs where one exporter acts as a main supplier in relation to a foreign buyer but its final product or service includes deliveries from one or more sub-suppliers from other countries. The sub-suppliers do not have a direct contractual relationship with the foreign buyer and they will be paid by the main supplier if and when the main supplier receives payment from the foreign buyer. However, the ECAs from the countries from which the sub-suppliers make their deliveries are willing to issue cover to sub-suppliers. The exporter, acting as a main supplier, obtains cover from the ECA from the country of export and the coinsurance agreement is entered into between all ECAs involved.

Coinsurance between ECAs may occur in a joint transaction where two or more exporters from several countries of export cooperate in the form of consortium. The consortium agreement provides that only one exporter, the consortium leader, will invoice the foreign buyer, receive payment and distribute it to other consortium partners. Other consortium partners do not have a direct contractual relationship with the foreign buyer and they cannot obtain the ECA cover from their national ECAs. The solution for this situation is obtaining the ECA cover by coinsurance. The consortium leader obtains the ECA cover from its national ECA, which then enters into a coinsurance agreement with other ECAs covering the shares of credit risk of consortium partners.

The coinsurance agreement between ECAs provides that all ECAs involved in the transaction are represented by the ECA that issues cover to the main supplier or consortium leader. This ECA is obligated to notify other ECAs about the foreign buyer's possible payment default, bilateral renegotiating of credit, insolvency, restructuring of the foreign buyer's total indebtedness, recovery, etc. When several ECAs are involved in a single transaction, coinsurance is more effective and simpler than when each consortium partner enters into a separate contract with the foreign buyer for partial deliveries included in the transaction.

The terms under which an individual ECA involved in coinsurance cooperation provides cover to an individual consortium partner can be different and do not need be harmonised between ECAs. The ECAs involved in the coinsurance cooperation are independent in their decision making and their relationship with the individual consortium partners. ECAs do not use coinsurance and the parallel insurance described below very often today because reinsurance contracts solve many situations.

18.5   Parallel insurance between ECAs

Parallel insurance is a model of cooperation between two or more ECAs where two or more exporters or banks from various countries participate in a joint transaction by entering into separate commercial or loan contracts with the same foreign buyer. In this transaction, each exporter or bank may obtain separate ECA cover from the ECA from its country. Participating ECAs will not share the credit risk among them, but may cooperate in dealing with this risk by defining the exchange of information between them. The separate ECA cover issued by participating ECAs remains unchanged and is not affected by the parallel insurance.

18.6 Percentage of foreign content covered by a single ECA

ECAs may agree bilaterally to cover each other's foreign content up to a specific percentage without risk sharing between them. Therefore each contracting ECA agrees to issue cover for the other country's content without involving the ECA from the other country. This bilateral cooperation between ECAs is rarely used today because the reinsurance model provides other solutions for export credit transactions with foreign content.

18.7 Reinsurance between ECAs and private reinsurance companies

This type of reinsurance is different from reinsurance between ECAs because it is based on general principles of reinsurance applied between private insurance companies. Since ECAs are financially supported by their states, which cover any deficit in the ECAs' business, it is interesting to examine why an ECA needs private reinsurance for the credit risks in its portfolio.

There are two main reasons for reinsuring the credit risks covered by ECAs on the private reinsurance market, the first of which is providing additional capacity for an ECA to cover new export credit risks by transferring the existing risks to a reinsurer. ECAs have internal limits for covering credit risks and when these limits are reached they may cover new export transactions only if they increase their capacity by transferring some of their existing credit risks to other parties. The second reason for reinsuring the credit risks is to balance an ECA portfolio of credit risks by avoiding concentration of specific types of risks.

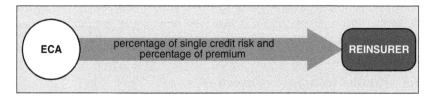

Figure 18.2 Quota-share reinsurance between an ECA and private reinsurer

ECAs may be interested in reinsuring a single credit risk, usually in the form of quota share reinsurance (Figure 18.2). However, an ECA may reinsure several risks from its portfolio of risks in which case the excess of loss reinsurance (Figure 18.3) or a combination of the quota share and the excess of loss reinsurance can be used.

When reinsuring a credit risk from its portfolio, an ECA may decide to reinsure only a part of the credit risk. An ECA may seek partial reinsurance for political risks in a transaction where it has covered political and commercial risks. It may seek reinsurance for a shorter period of risk or a lower percentage of cover than the cover provided to the insured exporter or bank. This depends on the ECA's calculation of effects of a particular risk on its portfolio and on the private reinsurance companies' interest in reinsuring a credit risk under the ECA's terms.

ECAs request the inclusion of specific clauses in reinsurance agreements with private reinsurers. The most important one is the 'follow the fortunes' clause that provides the reinsurer in a reinsurance contact is bound by decisions made by the ECA regarding interpretation of the terms of the ECA policy and payment of indemnification. In other words, the reinsurer is obligated to follow the reinsured ECA in its decision making on these issues. This allows the ECA to make decisions freely, without arguing with the reinsurer about a particular decision. Another important clause is the 'follow the settlement', which provides that the reinsurer is bound by a decision made by the reinsured ECA when settling a claim for indemnification with an insured exporter or bank. When exercising the rights provided in these two contractual clauses and other rights under a reinsurance agreement, ECAs are obligated to act in good faith or utmost good faith, depending on the law that governs the reinsurance contract. The insured's obligation to act in good faith is one of the basic principles of insurance law in general.

Other clauses that are included in the reinsurance contracts between ECAs and private reinsurers are clauses defining the risks covered, payment of premium, procedures for payment of claims, recovery procedures, payment of costs, etc. It is not unusual for ECAs to use the services of insurance brokers when seeking private reinsurance for their risks because many ECAs reinsure their risks only sporadically and they do not have continuous business relations with private reinsurers.

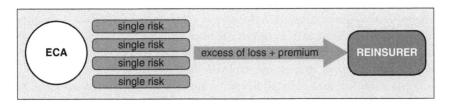

Figure 18.3   Excess of loss reinsurance between an ECA and private reinsurer

19
Claims and Indemnification

The purpose of obtaining the ECA cover is to receive indemnification for a loss caused by non-payment of a credit by a foreign buyer. In practice, there are several stages in claiming and receiving indemnification from an ECA. When a foreign buyer defaults on payment of a credit, the insured exporter or bank is required to notify the non-payment to the ECA. Before paying indemnification for the non-paid amount of credit ECAs apply a waiting period. During this period the insured may be required to enforce the security provided for payment of the credit and take other actions necessary to minimise or avoid the loss. At the end of the waiting period the insured assigns the claim for payment of credit to the ECA and requests indemnification from the ECA. In the final stage, the ECA pays indemnification to the insured exporter or bank.

Some ECAs use the term 'indemnification', while other ECAs use 'payment of claim' when paying losses to insured exporters or banks. Both terms are appropriate for use but this chapter uses 'indemnification' to avoid confusion with other types of claims mentioned in this book (Figure 19.1).

19.1 Notification of non-payment, claim and waiting period

The insured exporter or bank is obligated to notify the ECA about non-payment of a credit covered by the ECA because ECAs do not monitor payment of credits covered by them and the insured's notification is the only way of obtaining this information. The insured is obligated to notify the ECA about non-payment in writing or in electronic form within the time period provided in the terms of ECA policy. Some ECAs provide standardised forms for notification of non-payment that are available on their websites.

Even claims for indemnification can be available in a standardised form, but such a claim can also be made in the form of a simple letter. The letter must contain information about the ECA policy, the due date for payment of the

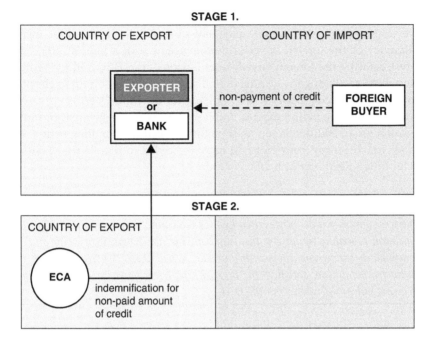

Figure 19.1 Indemnification for the non-paid amount of credit

non-paid amount and the insured's request for payment of indemnification. A claim for payment may be made to an ECA at the same time as the notification of non-payment, or before or after the waiting period expires. Since a foreign buyer may pay the non-paid amount of credit during the waiting period it is practical to await and make a claim for payment of indemnification 5 to 10 days before the end of the waiting period. The ECA claim handling period begins right after the waiting period expires and results in paying the indemnification to the insured without unnecessary delay.

The majority of ECAs do not pay indemnification immediately because they apply the waiting period, which is usually 90 or 180 days after the due date for payment of credit by a foreign buyer. The purpose of waiting period is to determine whether the payment of credit is temporarily delayed due to minor difficulties that can be resolved within a short period of time. The waiting period also gives ECAs an opportunity to examine the case and determine the reason for non-payment. In addition, it may be necessary to assess whether the event that caused non-payment is political or commercial in nature, which is important when percentages of the ECA cover are different for losses caused by these two types of events. In urgent situations the insured or ECA can act to mitigate or avoid loss during the waiting period.

Some ECAs do not apply the waiting period when it is obvious the foreign buyer cannot make the overdue payment of credit. Such situations include bankruptcy of the foreign buyer or commencement of a judicial proceeding for restructuring the foreign buyer's total indebtedness. However, the terms of ECA policies regulating the waiting period vary and it is important to check the terms of an individual policy when applying for the ECA cover.

After the waiting period expires, numerous ECAs delay payment of indemnification for an additional period, sometimes called the handling period. This period, which ranges from 15 to 30 days, is needed to handle the claim and pay an insured exporter or bank.

Terminology

The term 'protracted default' is used by ECAs in connection to claims and indemnification procedure because it includes both the non-payment of credit and its continuance throughout the waiting period. When these two requirements for protracted default are satisfied, the insured exporter or bank becomes eligible for receiving indemnification from the ECA.

19.2   Payment of interest during the waiting period

There are significant differences in the terms of ECA cover that regulate payment of the waiting period interest by ECAs. Some ECAs pay the waiting period interest in all transactions while other ECAs are more restrictive in this respect. Some ECAs charge additional premiums for paying the waiting period interest and the insured exporter or bank may choose whether to pay this premium when applying for the ECA cover. Some ECAs pay the waiting period interest only when the underlying commercial or loan contract provides the foreign buyer is obligated to pay the late payment interest on delayed payments of credit. Since various ECAs apply different terms on payment of the waiting period interest it is important to check the terms of an individual policy when applying for the ECA cover.

Another term that should be checked is whether an ECA pays interest on the indemnified amount when exceeding the period for handling the claim. The majority of ECAs pay this interest if the payment delay was their fault. However, the ECA will not pay any interest when the period for handling a claim for indemnification is extended due to the insured's delay in providing all documents necessary for processing the claim.

19.3   Assignment of claim for payment of credit by insured to ECA

As a condition for paying indemnification, an insured exporter or bank is required to transfer the claim for payment of the non-paid amount of credit

to the ECA. Transferring a claim can be in the form of assignment or subrogation. These terms have different meanings in various legal systems that must
be observed when transferring a claim to an ECA.

In the ECA context, assignment means transfer of the insured's right to claim
payment of the non-paid amount of credit from the foreign buyer from the
insured to the ECA. The assignment is made in writing and if the ECA intends
to recover the non-paid amount directly from the foreign buyer, the foreign
buyer must be notified about the assignment and instructed to make payment
directly to the ECA (Figure 19.2).

ECAs may decide not to notify a foreign buyer about assignment of claim
for payment. A possible reason for not notifying the foreign buyer can be the

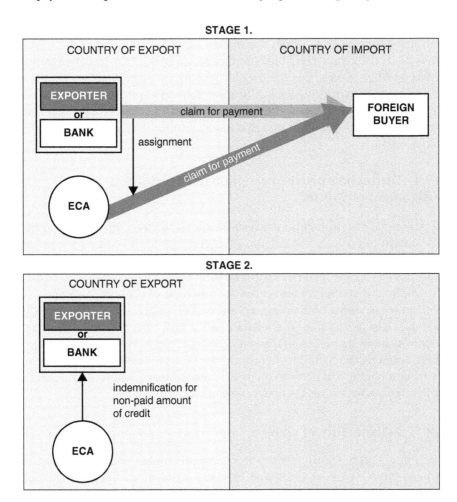

Figure 19.2   Assignment of claim for payment against foreign buyer

exchange control regulation in the foreign buyer's country that requires the ECA to obtain a licence for transferring the payment out of the country. This is because the payment of credit is usually agreed in a hard currency that should be transferred out of the foreign buyer's country to the agreed place of payment. Since obtaining a licence is often complicated and expensive, some ECAs are not willing to engage in such procedures. Instead they allow the insured, having already obtained the necessary licence, to remain as creditor and receive the recovered amount from the foreign buyer. After transferring the recovered amount to the insured's account outside of the foreign buyer's country the insured can transfer this amount to the ECA easily.

The chance for recovery of the non-paid amount of credit from the foreign buyer may be better if the insured exporter or bank continues negotiating recovery or enforcing the claim for payment against the foreign buyer without involving the ECA. When the foreign buyer becomes aware the insured exporter or bank has received indemnification from the ECA, it may negatively affect its willingness to pay the overdue amount of credit directly to the ECA. A foreign buyer with financial difficulties may decide to pay other creditors first and delay payment to the ECA by arguing that the ECA is financially strong, supported by a state, and that it may wait for the payment longer than other creditors.

19.4   Distinction between assignment of claim and assignment of contract

It is important to distinguish between assigning the claim for payment against the foreign buyer from the assignment of contract. Most ECAs do not request assignment of an underlying commercial or loan contract to them because it means replacing the insured exporter or bank as an original party to a contract. Assignment of contract is also called the novation of contract. Assignment of a claim for payment of the non-paid amount of credit to an ECA is limited to a single right arising from the contract, while assignment of the contract as a whole includes transfer of an insured exporter or bank's rights and obligations. After assigning the claim for payment to the ECA, the insured exporter or bank remains a contractual party to the commercial or loan contract and retains all other rights and obligations under the contract.

19.5   Assignability of claim

Assigning a claim for payment of the non-paid amount of credit without the foreign buyer's consent is allowed in many jurisdictions but this right may be restricted in various ways. For this reason an applicant for the ECA cover should investigate whether assignment is allowed according to the governing law agreed upon in the commercial or loan contract and according to the legislation regulating the transfer of foreign currency out of the foreign buyer's country. Where the applicable law requires the foreign buyer's consent for assigning a claim for payment of credit to an ECA it is practical to include a provision in a commercial or loan contract by which the foreign buyer consents to the assignment.

Some commercial or loan contracts provide that the foreign buyer's consent is required for assigning a claim for payment from the insured exporter or bank to any third party, including the ECA. In practice, this means the foreign buyer has the discretion to disapprove assignment of the claim for payment by the insured to the ECA. When this provision is included in the commercial or loan contract the applicant for the ECA cover should notify the ECA about this before the ECA policy is issued.

When a commercial or loan contract expressly prohibits assignment of the claim for payment against the foreign buyer to a third party, including the ECA, the applicant for the ECA cover is obligated to notify the ECA before the ECA policy is issued. In this situation some ECAs may consider waiving the requirement for assigning the claim for payment of the non-paid amount of credit.

19.6 Subrogation of claim

Subrogation is another way to transfer a claim for payment against the foreign buyer from an insured exporter or bank to the ECA. Subrogation means the ECA has the right to take over the claim which is provided in a special provision included in a commercial or loan contract between the insured exporter or bank and the foreign buyer. Unlike assignment of claim, which requires an assignment document, an ECA is subrogated to the claim for payment against the foreign buyer automatically by paying indemnification to the insured exporter. In other words, the ECA steps into the insured's shoes without any additional approval of any party to the commercial or loan contract. When including the contractual provision on the ECA's subrogation right in a commercial or loan agreement, it is necessary to check whether subrogation is valid and enforceable according to the governing law of the contract and the legislation regulating transfer of foreign currency out of the foreign buyer's country.

Sometimes the insurance law of the foreign buyer's country provides the subrogation right, typically as a right of a domestic insurance company to take over the claim for damages against the person that caused a loss. Based on this provision the insurance company is subrogated into a claim for damages after paying indemnification for the loss to its insured. However, it is not clear whether such a legislative provision is applicable to a foreign ECA that has covered a credit risk in an international commercial or loan contract.

Therefore it is better to include the ECA's subrogation right in the commercial or loan contract if the other legislative requirements are satisfied. Finally, the terms 'assignment' and 'subrogation' may mean different things in different legal systems, which must be observed by an applicant for the ECA cover when negotiating and structuring an export credit transaction.

Including contractual provisions on assignment or subrogation in a commercial or loan contract with a foreign buyer can be complicated, especially when the foreign buyer has a strong negotiating position and refuses to accept transfer of any contractual right to a third party. This is especially the case when the foreign buyer is a sovereign or a public entity that applies the public procurement procedure when entering into a contract with the insured exporter or bank. This procedure requires publishing the terms of future contract to make them available to all parties that intend to make an offer or tender. After accepting the selected offer these terms cannot be amended or renegotiated which may prevent transferring claim for payment to an ECA.

19.7   Enforcement of security and indemnification

A foreign buyer or a third person may provide security for payment of credit in transactions covered by ECAs. The most frequently used types of security are the non-possessory pledge created over the goods supplied by the commercial or loan contract and the guarantee issued by a foreign buyer's parent company. However, an insured and a foreign buyer may agree to provide other types of security such as a fixed or floating charge, mortgage, etc. As explained in other chapters of this book, the value of security created over an asset located in a foreign jurisdiction is uncertain and an ECA may assess this value as very low when analysing a credit risk in a transaction for which ECA cover is requested.

When a foreign buyer defaults on payment of a credit for which security is provided, the question is what the insured exporter or bank is required to do with the security before claiming indemnification from the ECA. The question is complex because ECAs may require the insured to act in various ways depending on the type of security, time needed for enforcement, estimation of the enforcement costs and the amount that could be recovered by selling an asset over which security is created.

Most ECAs do not require the insured exporter or bank to exhaust all legal remedies for enforcement of security before claiming indemnification. Enforcement of security can be a lengthy and complicated judicial process that may take several years and it would be unreasonable to let the insured wait to receive indemnification from an ECA. Such a long and uncertain waiting period for indemnifying the insured by an ECA would discourage exporters and banks from requesting security when negotiating their transactions with foreign buyers. It could result in unequal treatment of insured exporters and banks in which the insured whose claim is not secured would be indemnified by the ECA without delay, while indemnifying the insured whose claim for payment of a credit is secured would be delayed until enforcement of security is completed. Therefore the majority of ECAs do not require the insured to exhaust all remedies for enforcing security before indemnification. What an insured exporter or bank may be required to do is begin enforcing security by requesting payment under a guarantee or commencing an enforcement proceeding. Which actions should be taken by the insured depends on the circumstances of each case and consultations between the insured and ECA.

When enforcing security involves selling goods, equipment, machinery, land or buildings, the insured may not be required to enforce security before claiming and receiving indemnification from an ECA. An ECA may decide that no enforcement action will be taken when the asset over which security is created cannot be sold on the secondary market, when the market price is far below the loss caused by non-payment of a credit by a foreign buyer or when the amount that can be recovered by enforcing security is lower than the costs incurred during the enforcement procedure. An example of such situation is selling specially manufactured machinery when the costs of disassembling, transport and storage are higher than the price potential buyers are willing to pay for it.

On the other hand, when security is provided as a guarantee or surety issued by a third party, demanding payment from the guarantor or surety is relatively simple. Therefore many ECAs require the insured to demand payment under a guarantee or surety before claiming indemnification from the ECA. When the payment is demanded and the guarantor does not make it within the deadline provided in the guarantee, the insured becomes eligible to claim indemnification from the ECA. Any further action against the guarantor will be discussed between the insured and the ECA within the recovery procedure.

Enforcing security can be a complex procedure and some insured exporters and banks would rather assign security to ECAs when claiming indemnification. Some exporters and banks believe the fact that ECAs act on behalf of a state would impress a foreign buyer and make recovery of the indemnified amount easier without enforcing security. However, this is not usually the case since a foreign buyer that cannot pay credit to the insured exporter or bank cannot pay it to an ECA either.

When it is decided that security will be enforced, most ECAs instruct the insured to do that without involving ECAs in the enforcement procedure. ECAs indemnify the insured's costs incurred in enforcing security proportionally to the percentage of the ECA cover.

19.8   Assignment of security to ECAs

If security is not enforced by the insured before claiming indemnification, some ECAs may require the insured to assign security to the ECA. This is similar to the ECA requirement for assigning the claim for payment against the foreign buyer, but this is typically not mandatory for receiving indemnification from an ECA. Assignment of security to an ECA can be complicated and several difficulties may arise when trying to accomplish it. Since the assets over which security is created are usually located in the foreign buyer's country, the local law will govern the assignment and enforcement of security. The local law may prohibit assignment of security or require the satisfaction of formalities such as public registration, payment of stamp duties, etc. In some jurisdictions the local law requires the foreign buyer's consent for assignment of security and it must be notarised or certified by a public authority. Obtaining the foreign buyer's consent and satisfying the formal requirements can be a lengthy process that can include payment of fees and stamp duties.

Some local laws require a special licence for operating an asset and creating security over it in the country where it is located. Since a foreign ECA does not hold such a licence, the security created over the asset cannot be assigned to it. When security is created over specific assets operated by foreign buyers that provide public service, the local law can restrict the assignment of security to an ECA. In these situations, a better solution for an ECA is to waive the requirement for assignment of security and let the insured act as a secured creditor.

19.9   Ascertainment of claim

The general view is that ECAs handle claims for indemnifications expeditiously, in a professional manner and without unnecessary delays. ECAs are known internationally as reliable insurers that do not avoid payment of indemnification by using the 'fine print' clauses in their policies. However, ECAs must ascertain claims for indemnification by examining whether claims are justified and due. This includes ascertaining that the foreign buyer has not disputed its payment obligation by alleging the breach of underlying commercial or loan contract by the insured exporter or bank.

ECAs must also ascertain that the insured has assigned its claim for payment against the foreign buyer to the ECA and the claim is made within the time limit. Ascertaining a claim for indemnification and payment usually takes 30 days after the waiting period expires. The ascertainment procedure, also called the claim handling procedure, includes the ECA's internal decision-making process, which may require the approval of a board of directors or similar body within the ECA, especially when dealing with large indemnification amounts. If handling a claim for indemnification by an ECA exceeds the time provided in the ECA policy, the majority of ECAs will pay interest for the late payment of indemnification.

19.10   Scope of indemnification

An ECA policy limits the loss payable to an insured by stating the highest amount of loss and the percentage of cover. When the highest amount of loss is US $100,000 for example, and the percentage of cover is 90 per cent, the ECA will pay the maximum amount of US $90,000 as indemnification to the insured exporter or bank. The majority of ECAs apply the percentage of cover proportionally to any amount of loss, which means the insured is entitled to indemnification of 90 per cent of each dollar of loss. The indemnification of loss payable by ECAs is usually limited to the foreign buyer's regular contractual payment obligation consisting of the principal amount and the contractual interest. The late payment interest, damages for breach of contract by a foreign buyer, tax grossing-up payments, etc., are not usually covered by ECAs.

When the ECA cover is issued by applying the OECD Arrangement, the highest amount of loss that can be covered is 85 per cent of the export contract value as explained in Chapter 21 and elsewhere in this book. The remaining 15 per cent of the export contract value must be paid in advance, which means it cannot be covered by ECAs. In other types of transactions, where the Arrangement does not apply, the highest amount of loss covered by ECAs can be the entire contractual price payable on credit terms by the foreign buyer. No advance payment is required in these transactions.

The risk that an ECA will pay the highest amount of loss is higher when it is agreed that the foreign buyer will pay the entire amount of credit at once as a single payment. If the foreign buyer defaults on a payment, the indemnification paid by the ECA will amount to the highest amount of loss, reduced for the percentage of cover.

The probability that an ECA will pay the highest amount of loss is lower when payment of credit is to be made in several instalments because foreign buyers usually do not default on payment of all instalments of a credit. Therefore the indemnification paid by the ECA can be lower than the highest amount of loss because the ECA will indemnify the insured for the non-paid instalments only. However, it is not impossible that a foreign buyer defaults on payment of all instalments of credit, in which case the indemnification paid by the ECA will amount to the highest amount of loss.

19.11   Indemnification method

When payment of credit is to be made in several instalments falling due in the future, the foreign buyer may default on just one instalment at a time. When covering a credit payable in instalments, ECAs will indemnify the insured exporter or bank for each non-paid instalment as they fall due. When the ECA cover is issued for a single payment of credit, ECAs will pay indemnification to the insured exporter or bank for the entire amount of credit when it is due.

It is important to clarify the connection between the method of indemnification applied by ECAs and the acceleration clause normally included in loan agreements. The acceleration clause entitles a bank to declare due and payable the entire outstanding amount of a loan in case of a foreign buyer's default on payment of a single instalment. Similar clauses are included in commercial contracts between exporters and foreign buyers where payment of a credit is agreed in instalments. If a bank or exporter accelerates payment of all future instalments the question is whether an ECA will pay indemnification according to the original payment schedule or if it will pay the entire outstanding accelerated amount of the credit at once. The answer is that most ECAs will indemnify only due and non-paid instalments according to the original payment schedule, not the entire outstanding accelerated amount of credit. The standard terms of ECA policies usually provide that this particular indemnification method will be applied.

An ECA may instruct an insured bank or exporter to accelerate a loan or credit as a remedy for non-payment of a single instalment by a foreign buyer. However, the acceleration of the export credit initiated by the ECA usually does not result in acceleration of the ECA's indemnification. This is an important distinction between the ECA cover and other types of guarantees issued by guarantors other than ECAs. An example is a guarantee issued by a parent company for repayment of a loan from its subsidiary that is agreed in several instalments. The parent company's guarantee usually provides the entire accelerated outstanding amount of the subsidiary's loan is immediately payable by the parent company.

In special circumstances, some ECAs may agree to indemnify the insured for the entire outstanding amount of credit in the event of non-payment of one or several instalments by a foreign buyer. This method of indemnification is called the early indemnification of the entire outstanding amount of credit. However, the early indemnification is not necessarily the result of acceleration of credit in relation to the foreign buyer and it can be paid by an ECA without accelerating the credit. The early indemnification is an exception from the main rule and it is usually justified by special circumstances. When an ECA applies the early indemnification by paying the entire outstanding amount of credit, the instalments of credit falling due after the indemnification date are usually discounted at an applicable discounting rate.

The majority of insured banks are not interested in receiving an early indemnification from ECAs because it is connected with payment of costs for prepayment of a loan, usually called breakage costs. Breakage costs are usually not included in the ECA cover, which means they will not be indemnified by an ECA to an insured bank. However, an insured exporter may be interested in receiving the early indemnification for all future payments payable by the foreign buyer because exporters do not include breakage costs in their commercial contracts with foreign buyers. Early indemnification depends on the ECA's willingness to make this payment.

19.12 Parties entitled to claim indemnification

The insured whose name is stated in an ECA policy is entitled to claim indemnification from the ECA that issued the policy. The insured is either an exporter that supplied goods or services to a foreign buyer on credit terms or a bank that provided a loan to a foreign buyer for purchasing goods or services from a country of export. In the context of the ECA cover, the insured exporter or bank is normally a legal entity, not an individual. The foreign buyer, acting as a buyer of goods or services purchased on credit terms, or as a borrower in relation to a bank, is also a legal entity.

An insured exporter may assign the right to claim indemnification from an ECA to another party, usually a bank. Such assignments are relatively frequent in transactions where an exporter enters into an export transaction on credit terms and then sells the future claim for payment of credit to a bank at a discount rate. If the exporter has obtained the ECA cover for the credit risk in its commercial transaction, the bank requires the exporter to assign the rights under the ECA policy to the bank. As a result of such assignment the bank becomes the beneficiary under the ECA policy. The ECA must be notified about the assignment and accept the bank as a beneficiary that holds the right to claim indemnification. Even an insured bank may assign its rights under the ECA policy, usually by assigning its rights to another bank.

Assignment of rights under the ECA policy from the insured to a beneficiary provides no better rights to the beneficiary than the insured. Consequently, the ECA's right to deny indemnification remains unchanged after the assignment and it affects the bank the same way as the insured exporter. Therefore, the bank to which the rights under the ECA policy have been assigned would be denied indemnification by the ECA where the foreign buyer has disputed the payment of credit. This may be caused by a breach of the commercial contract by the insured exporter that has assigned its rights under the ECA policy to the bank. The banks to which the rights under the ECA policies are assigned are aware of this risk and they reserve the right to claim repayment of the amount paid to the exporter when purchasing the claim against the foreign buyer. A bank may exercise this right when being denied indemnification from the ECA. This right is also called the right of recourse but it does not concern ECAs since it is agreed between an exporter and a bank without involving an ECA. Chapter 6 analyses assignment of rights provided in an ECA policy.

After assigning its rights under the ECA policy the insured exporter remains in its capacity of the insured in relation to the ECA. Therefore the insured retains all obligations under the ECA policy such as the obligation to avoid or mitigate loss where possible, to disclose relevant information to the ECA, to contribute to recovery of the non-paid amount of credit, etc. As explained in Chapter 6, non-performance of these obligations by the insured may negatively affect the right of the bank to claim indemnification from the ECA.

Before assigning the rights under the ECA policy, the insured exporter or bank must consider whether a particular beneficiary is acceptable to the ECA. The standard terms of some ECAs provide that the rights under the policy may be assigned with their consent only, while other ECAs may accept the assignment of rights without similar requirements.

19.13   Time limitation for claiming indemnification from ECAs

The standard terms of most ECAs provide that the insured's right to claim indemnification for a loss covered by their policies is limited in time. Therefore an ECA is not obligated to pay indemnification to the insured exporter or bank after expiration of the limitation period. The limitation periods provided by various ECAs in their standard terms are between two to five years from the due date for payment of credit by the foreign buyer. The limitation period can be applied for the entire amount of credit when it is agreed the credit will be paid as a single payment or for each non-paid instalment when the payment of credit is agreed in this way.

19.14   Rescheduling of foreign buyer's credit and right to indemnification

A foreign buyer may ask an exporter or a bank to reschedule a credit agreed in a commercial or loan contract covered by an ECA. Sometimes it is unclear whether such rescheduling affects the right of the insured exporter or bank to claim indemnification from the ECA.

An insured exporter or bank is obligated to notify the ECA when asked to reschedule a credit or make any other material amendment of the commercial or loan contract. The standard terms of ECA policies often provide that amendment of due dates for payment of credit or other terms of a commercial or loan contract made without consent of the ECA may release the ECA from its liability. In practice, ECAs know that rescheduling a credit is often the first step when a foreign buyer is experiencing financial difficulties and they usually consent to such requests. Sometimes, the financial situation of a foreign buyer is so difficult that the only alternative to rescheduling credit is bankruptcy, which should be avoided if the foreign buyer has a chance to continue its business.

When an ECA consents to rescheduling the foreign buyer's credit, such consent does not automatically amend the terms of the existing ECA policy for the original payment schedule with the original due dates for payment of credit. Rescheduling a credit means the due dates for payment of credit stipulated in a commercial or loan contract are extended and the foreign buyer will make payments later than agreed originally. On the other hand, the insured's right to claim indemnification from the ECA for the non-paid amounts of credit remains unchanged because the ECA policy covers the original payment schedule. Receiving indemnification from the ECA according to the original due dates was the purpose of obtaining the ECA cover and it cannot be amended without the insured's consent.

Rescheduling the foreign buyer's credit with the ECA's consent may result in other solutions. One possible solution is that no indemnification will be paid by the ECA to the insured as long as the foreign buyer makes regular payments of the credit on the rescheduled due dates. However, if the foreign buyer defaults on payment on a rescheduled due date, the original payment schedule will apply for indemnifying the insured by the ECA. Therefore the ECA will indemnify the insured according to the original payment schedule, including indemnifying all non-paid and due instalments at once and the future instalments as they fall due. In this solution, the indemnification according to the original payment schedule has been temporarily suspended under the condition that the foreign buyer makes regular payments at the rescheduled due dates. This solution is subject to the insured and ECA's consent.

Rescheduling the foreign buyer's credit with the ECA's consent may result in amending the terms of the ECA cover with new rescheduled due dates. Even this amendment of the ECA policy is subject to the consent of the insured and the ECA. When the new payment schedule is included in the ECA policy instead of the original one, the new payment schedule will apply to the ECA. In case of the foreign buyer's default on payment according to the new payment schedule, the insured exporter or bank will be indemnified by the ECA according to the rescheduled due dates.

19.15   Disputed claim for payment against a foreign buyer

ECAs cover various types of underlying commercial contracts where exporters supply goods to foreign buyers such as final products, semi-products, materials, equipment, heavy machinery, technology, consumer goods, etc. Some exporters provide services, engineering works, consultancy and other works where payment is also agreed on credit terms.

It is possible that a foreign buyer is not satisfied with the quality or quantity of the goods delivered or works performed by the exporter. The foreign buyer may claim breach of contract by the exporter and withhold payment of credit, as a contractual remedy, until receiving the complete delivery or performance. It is also possible that the exporter denies any breach of contract, claiming that its delivery or performance satisfies contractual requirements and the foreign buyer is not entitled to withhold payment of the credit. By using this argument the exporter may claim indemnification from the ECA covering its transaction with the foreign buyer for the loss caused by non-payment of the credit by the foreign buyer. When a dispute arises regarding the right of the insured exporter to claim payment from the foreign buyer, ECAs instruct the insured exporter to obtain a judgment of court or an arbitration award proving the exporter's right to claim payment from the foreign buyer. The insured's right to receive indemnification from the ECA and the amount of indemnification will depend on the ruling of the court or the arbitration award.

Due to the nature of loan agreements it is less likely that a foreign buyer, when acting as a borrower, can claim breach of a loan agreement by a lending bank and dispute its obligation to repay the loan. However, if a dispute arises between a bank and the foreign buyer regarding possible breach of a loan agreement covered by an ECA, the ECA would probably instruct the bank to obtain a judgment or arbitration award proving the bank's right to claim payment from the foreign buyer.

20
Recovery

In the ECA context, 'recovery' means collection of a due and non-paid amount of credit from a foreign buyer. Chronologically, recovery follows the indemnification procedure in which an ECA indemnifies an insured for a due and non-paid amount of credit (Figure 20.1). Recovery of debt in the ECA context is similar to recovery of any other debt, except it always takes place in foreign countries. Recovery against foreign buyers is often more difficult than domestic recovery because of geographical distance, lack of information about foreign buyers, cultural differences, insufficiency of legal actions, lack of rule of law in a foreign buyer's country, etc. Since ECAs cover credit risks in export credit transactions with foreign buyers from nearly all countries in the world, they have gained significant experience with recovery procedures in numerous foreign jurisdictions. This experience is useful when assessing credit risks in new export credit transactions for which the ECA cover is requested.

Recovery is not a mandatory procedure in all transactions where indemnification is paid by an ECA to an insured exporter or bank. ECAs decide whether to take a recovery action on a case-by-case basis after analysing all circumstances of a particular credit and chances for receiving any recovery. Sometimes, a foreign buyer is bankrupt and no recovery can be expected from the bankruptcy estate. It is also possible the estimated costs of legal action are higher than the expected amount of recovery, in which case the ECA may decide not to take any recovery action. However, once the recovery procedure is started, ECAs are usually persistent in pursuing it.

20.1 Classes of foreign buyers

The type of recovery action taken by an ECA varies depending on the legal status of a foreign buyer. ECAs distinguish three categories of foreign buyers when issuing the ECA cover and recovering debts. These categories are sovereign, public and private buyers. A sovereign buyer is a foreign state, government,

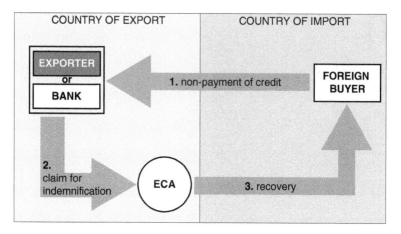

Figure 20.1   Non-payment of credit, assignment of claim and recovery

ministry or another institution that can validly bind a state. The main characteristic of a sovereign state acting as a foreign buyer is that it cannot be liquidated in a bankruptcy proceeding. A public buyer is a company owned or controlled wholly or in majority by a state or government. The public buyer cannot validly bind the state and the company can be liquidated in a bankruptcy proceeding. A private buyer is neither a sovereign nor a public buyer. The private buyers ECAs deal with are nearly always legal entities, organised and registered as companies in the country of import. Private buyers are by far the largest group of foreign buyers with which ECAs work.

20.2   Recovery of debt from sovereign foreign buyers

Recovering debt from sovereign buyers is different from recovering debt from public and private buyers in several ways. Generally, the main difficulty with a foreign state that defaults on payment of a credit to an exporter or bank is that it cannot be sued in foreign courts because of state immunity, an old doctrine in the international public law that was developed when it was seen as an infringement of a state's sovereignty to bring proceedings against it in a court of a foreign country. This doctrine has been modified over the past 30 years regarding commercial contracts between a state and its counterparties. Today, when negotiating a commercial or loan contract with a sovereign counterparty, it is possible to request a sovereign to waive its immunity; some sovereigns do that expressly and accept jurisdiction of a foreign court or foreign arbitration. When a state has not waived its immunity in a commercial or loan contract it is very likely it will claim immunity if sued in a foreign court.

If a sovereign foreign buyer that has contractually waived its state immunity defaults on payment of an export credit, the insured exporter or bank can bring proceedings against it in a foreign court or foreign arbitration. The purpose of the proceeding is to obtain a judgment or arbitration award ordering the sovereign buyer to pay the overdue amount of credit. However, the sovereign foreign buyer may be dissatisfied with a judgment or arbitration award and it may still refuse to make payment. In this situation the foreign judgment or arbitration award must be enforced against the sovereign buyer.

Enforcing foreign judgments or arbitration awards depends on their recognition in the sovereign buyer's jurisdiction or in another jurisdiction where the sovereign buyer has placed some of its valuable assets (Figure 20.2). Sometimes, the recognition can be a straightforward procedure, but it can be a complicated and lengthy judicial proceeding that may result in a negative decision, rendering the foreign judgment or the arbitration award unenforceable.

The next problem that may arise after obtaining a foreign court judgment or arbitration award and their recognition in the jurisdiction of the sovereign buyer is the lack of assets against which the judgment or award can be enforced. An insolvent state may lack liquid assets that can be attached and sold at a public auction in an enforcement proceeding. Some assets of a sovereign foreign buyer are immune from enforcement because they serve the public purpose like the territory of state or other assets that cannot be sold or owned by individuals or legal persons. Therefore only commercial assets owned by a sovereign buyer can be the objects of enforcement. Classification of the sovereign's assets as commercial and non-commercial can be uncertain in some jurisdictions.

If a sovereign buyer's debt is unenforceable for any reason, the insured exporter or bank is prevented from filing for bankruptcy against the sovereign

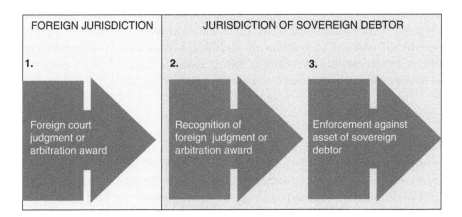

Figure 20.2 Foreign judgment or arbitration award, recognition and enforcement

because sovereign states cannot go into judicial bankruptcy. On the other hand, the state immunity against bankruptcy proceedings can be seen as a positive element when assessing a credit risk before issuing the ECA cover for transactions with sovereign foreign buyers. While a private foreign buyer and a public buyer can be liquidated as legal entities in a bankruptcy proceeding, an insolvent state will continue its existence with at least a little chance to pay its debts in the future.

Finally, a sovereign foreign buyer that has defaulted on payment of a credit can be sued in a domestic court in its jurisdiction. This legal action is always available because state immunity does not apply in domestic courts. However, the foreign creditors are often sceptical regarding impartiality and independence of a sovereign's domestic court and their chances to obtain a judgment against the sovereign in a judicial proceeding. In reality, these chances depend on the state of rule of law in a particular jurisdiction, which should be investigated before bringing a judicial proceeding against a sovereign buyer.

20.3   ECA methods for recovery of debt from sovereign buyers

Since it could be difficult to enforce a debt against a sovereign buyer by legal action it is interesting to see whether there is any other recovery method available to ECAs and insured exporters or banks when a sovereign defaults on payment of an export credit. The general view is that negotiations with a sovereign buyer are the most effective way of recovery. Negotiations can be bilateral or multilateral and both are applied by ECAs when recovering a sovereign debt. When recovery is negotiated bilaterally the outcome of negotiations depends on the ability of a sovereign foreign buyer to pay its debt. In multilateral negotiations, a group of private or sovereign creditors negotiate recovery with a sovereign foreign buyer. Even in this case the outcome of negotiations depends on the ability of the sovereign buyer to pay its debt and the ability of creditors involved in negotiations to agree on a common recovery solution. Possible agreements reached in bilateral or multilateral negotiations with sovereign foreign buyers include rescheduling due dates for payment of credit, reduction of interest rate, debt reduction or a combination of the three.

20.4   The Paris Club

Multilateral negotiations between a debtor state and the states acting as creditors are held in the Paris Club, an ad hoc organisation of governments of creditor states and their ECAs, that began in 1956 to negotiate rescheduling the debt of debtor states. Hosted by the French government, the Paris Club has no charter, firm membership or legal status but it has an established negotiating procedure that the parties are required to follow.

The parties that take part in the Paris Club negotiations are the debtor state and the ECAs and other representatives of the creditor states. ECA claims consist of the claims for payment that the insured exporters or banks assigned to ECAs when receiving indemnification for export credits non-paid by a debtor state.

A debtor state cannot come to the Paris Club to negotiate payment of its debt with its creditors before being invited to negotiations. It will be invited to the Paris Club when it has concluded an appropriate programme with the International Monetary Fund (IMF). This procedure demonstrates that the debtor state cannot meet its external debt obligations and needs a new payment arrangement with its external creditors. The Paris Club creditor states link the negotiations for payment of a sovereign debt to the IMF programme because the economic reforms agreed in the programme are intended to restore a sound macroeconomic framework that will lower the probability of future financial difficulties for the debtor state.

Paris Club decisions can be made only on a consensus among the participating creditor states. Debtor states are expected to prove they need debt relief and they have to provide a precise description of their economic and financial situation. They are also expected to prove they have implemented reforms to restore their economic and financial situation and have a demonstrated track record of implementing the reforms established in an IMF programme. A debtor state that has signed an agreement with its Paris Club creditors should not accept less favourable terms for payment of its debts to private creditors when renegotiating its debts. Private creditors of a debtor state, including banks, other financial institutions and companies, are not admitted to negotiate payment of their claims against debtor states in the Paris Club. The terms agreed for payment of debt of the debtor state to its private creditors will be compared with the terms agreed with the Paris Club creditors.

The outcome of negotiations between a debtor state and its Paris Club creditors is a document called the Agreed Minutes, which is not legally binding. The document constitutes a recommendation to the governments of Paris Club creditors and the government of the debtor state to conclude bilateral agreements implementing the terms and provisions agreed in it. The bilateral agreements between the debtor state and each Paris Club creditor give legal effect to the agreement reached during the Paris Club meeting (Figure 20.3).

20.5   Recovery of debt from public buyers

The term 'public buyer' is used frequently in ECA terminology but other terms such as 'public entity', 'sub-sovereign' and 'autonomous entity separated from the state' are also used. These terms help distinguish the public buyer from the state and indicate the state is connected to the public buyer. The main

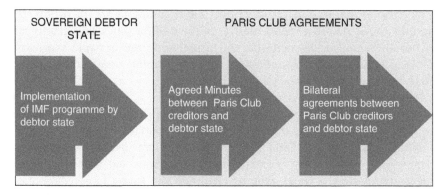

Figure 20.3   Stages in the Paris Club procedure

characteristic of public buyers is that they have their own legal capacity to enter into contracts and assume rights and obligations in their own name, not in the name of the state.

Despite having the capacity described above, public buyers are usually owned or controlled by a state. Some public buyers constitute an important part of the state's infrastructure such as railways, institutions of health care, national air carriers, etc. Public buyers can be financed by governments and managed by government officials, but they can have more autonomy in their business activities. States may own purely commercial companies with broader commercial and decision-making autonomy than public companies, important for the state's infrastructure.

The separation of foreign public buyers from the state is the consequence of their incorporation, usually in the form of a company. A company may come into existence in a regular way, by incorporation and registration in a company register, but it can be established by adopting legislation or by an administrative decision made by a government. When a state acts as owner of a public company it cannot be liable for the company's debts. The same principle is applied to a private company whose shareholders cannot be liable for the company's debts.

However, the state ownership may be important for the ECA recovery of a non-paid credit from a public buyer. This depends on how close the public buyer is to the state and how important its business is for the national economy and public service provided to citizens. Generally, the more important the public buyer's business is, the more likely it is that the state will support it financially to pay its debts. For example, railway traffic is of such importance for each state that the state probably would not allow interruption of the railway traffic because of insolvency of the railway company. Therefore it is likely that the state will make a financial contribution to the railway company to pay a credit to a foreign supplier whose deliveries are of vital importance for operations of the railway company. In this example an ECA may find that the railway's defaulted payments are likely to be recovered with the financial support of the state.

However, this assessment can be wrong if the public buyer has incurred huge debts in foreign currency and the state legislates that these debts will be converted into domestic currency. When this type of legislation is adopted the exchange rates applied to the conversion are usually far below the current exchange rates, which means the payment received by a foreign creditor will be lower than its real value in foreign currency.

These examples show that an ECA's chances to recover debt from public buyers can vary significantly. The state may support the public buyer financially but it also can intervene with legislation that discharges the public buyer's debt at a substantially lower value. The state may decide to restructure the public buyer in a judicial procedure, resulting in reducing its debt, rescheduling its payments or both. It is also possible that the state, acting as the owner of the public buyer, decides the public company cannot be restructured and should be liquidated in a bankruptcy proceeding. This decision can be made when the public buyer does not provide an important public service and is not important for the state's infrastructure.

The term 'public buyer' includes another class of foreign buyers whose status is sometimes misunderstood when analysing the risk of default on their payment obligations. These public buyers are not owned or controlled by the state but administrative entities or units within a state such as municipalities or regional authorities. These public buyers may also enter into export credit transactions acting as a foreign buyer and credit risks in these transactions are sometimes covered by ECAs. When a public buyer of this type defaults on its payment of an export credit covered by an ECA, it would be wrong to assume the state will be liable for its payment obligations or the state will help the public buyer pay its debts. According to a principle established in international public law a long time ago, the states do not have any liability for the debts of administrative entities in their countries.

20.6   ECA methods for recovery of debt from public buyers

The recovery method ECAs apply in relation to public buyers vary depending on the circumstances described above. Negotiations with the public buyer are applied frequently, but the state authority that controls a public buyer has an important role in negotiations. Because the state's controlling authority often makes the final decision as to whether a particular debt of a public buyer will be paid it is useful to negotiate recovery of the public buyer's debt directly with the controlling authority when possible. Negotiations with public buyers may result in an extension of due dates for payment of debt, reduction of the interest rate, debt reduction or a combination of the three.

Enforcing the public buyer's debt can be attempted in a domestic court in the public buyer's jurisdiction. However, the outcome of this judicial proceeding depends on independence of the courts and the state of rule of law in the public buyer's country.

20.7   Recovery of debt from private buyers

The vast majority of foreign buyers in transactions covered by ECAs are private buyers. In the ECA context, a private buyer is a legal entity that is neither a sovereign nor a public entity.

Generally, the recovery methods ECAs apply in relation to private foreign buyers are very similar to the methods applied by numerous other creditors that do not use the ECA cover for credit risks in their export transactions. The main recovery methods applied by ECAs are negotiations with foreign buyers and legal actions.

20.8   Negotiations with private buyers

The recovery method ECAs frequently apply in relation to private foreign buyers is negotiations with the foreign buyer to find a solution for payment of the foreign buyer's credit. Negotiations are the most effective recovery method except when a bankruptcy proceeding is brought against a foreign buyer or when the foreign buyer tries to delay its payment obligation by avoiding negotiations. When trying to recover debts from private buyers ECAs apply various negotiating strategies that are adjusted to a particular foreign buyer and the specific circumstances of an individual transaction. However, the most important factor for involving an ECA in a negotiating process is the amount of export credit covered by it. When an ECA is obligated to pay a large indemnification amount to the insured it is always a strong incentive for its engagement in negotiations with a foreign buyer.

Negotiations with a foreign buyer may be bilateral when an ECA and the insured try to recover a single debt, or multilateral, when the majority of foreign buyer's creditors are involved in restructuring its total indebtedness. The latter is also known as a private work-out, consensual reorganisation or out-of-court restructuring. It does not involve any judicial authority and it results in a private restructuring contract between the foreign buyer and the majority of its creditors.

20.9   Bilateral negotiations for recovery of a single debt

When trying to recover a single debt, an ECA may negotiate with the foreign buyer directly or instruct the insured exporter or bank to do so. Instructing the insured to negotiate is sometimes more practical, especially when the insured exporter or bank has local representatives who have a close customer relationship with the foreign buyer. This recovery strategy can provide a better recovery solution than direct negotiations between the ECA and foreign buyer. When negotiating with the foreign buyer the insured strictly follows the instructions received from the ECA and all agreements reached with the foreign buyer are subject to the ECA's approval. Generally, the recovery negotiations between the foreign buyer, the insured and the ECA are similar to negotiations for rescheduling a credit requested by the foreign buyer before it defaults on payment of credit described in Chapter 19.

An insured exporter may decide not to inform the foreign buyer about the ECA cover for the credit risk in its transaction with the foreign buyer because a foreign buyer having financial difficulties may decide to pay its other creditors first and let the exporter wait for payment, knowing the exporter will receive indemnification from the ECA. If the foreign buyer is not aware of the existence of the ECA cover it would probably treat the insured exporter the same as other creditors when paying its debts or negotiating a solution for their payment. Bilateral negotiations with the foreign buyer may result in the extension of due dates for payment of debt, interest rate reduction, debt reduction or a combination of the three.

20.10 Multilateral negotiations involving the majority of creditors

Multilateral recovery negotiations involve the majority of the foreign buyer's creditors on one side and the foreign buyer on the other. This is a voluntary negotiating process and no judicial authority of state is involved. The negotiating process can be long and burdensome depending on the complexity of the foreign buyer's business, its total indebtedness, number of creditors involved, different rights and interests of various classes of creditors, etc. The ECA's decision to participate in a restructuring process will always depend on its exposure to the foreign buyer or the amount of indemnification paid or to be paid to the insured. ECAs participate in large restructurings by engaging their staff and using the services of external financial and legal advisors. The advisors can be engaged by the foreign buyer or the creditors.

ECAs may be involved in restructuring of a foreign buyer company whose total indebtedness amounts to several billion US dollars. Such huge debts could be difficult to restructure, especially when the foreign buyer is a multinational company with subsidiaries in several countries. A cross-border restructuring of a multinational company is usually a complex, time consuming and expensive procedure.

When a large-scale restructuring is finally agreed on by signing the restructuring agreement it is often confirmed by a court decision. This process, often called pre-packaged restructuring, requires the majority of creditors of an insolvent foreign buyer to accept and sign the restructuring agreement. After that, the foreign buyer company files for the judicial reorganisation that should be allowed by the court according to the restructuring agreement. If the court accepts the pre-packaged restructuring plan its decision is binding on all creditors, even those who have not accepted the restructuring agreement.

Several ECAs may be involved in a large-scale restructuring of a foreign buyer along with creditors such as foreign and domestic banks, bondholders, trade creditors, etc. In this type of restructuring, the interests of various creditors may differ regarding the outcome of restructuring, duration of their engagement in the process, confidentiality of the information about the progress made in the restructuring, willingness to work and contribute to the restructuring, etc. The various groups of creditors that participate in a restructuring process often form committees for promoting their interests and ECAs may do the same by forming an ECA group or a committee for promoting their interests. When involved in a restructuring process, ECAs insist on implementing the principle of equal treatment of creditors and other generally accepted principles of insolvency law. Since ECAs indirectly represent their governments they do not accept restructuring solutions that might jeopardise their good reputation.

In a restructuring process, the conversion of debt into equity may be proposed as part of a restructuring plan. In conversion, a part of total debt of the foreign buyer will be converted into equity, in other words, shares in the foreign buyer company. This solution can be difficult for ECAs to accept because of their legal status and national legislation that prohibits the purchase of shares in foreign companies for any purpose.

A restructuring agreement between the foreign buyer and the majority of its creditors may result in extension of due dates for payment of its debt, interest rate reduction, debt reduction or combination of the three.

20.11   Judicial reorganisation of foreign buyers

A foreign buyer company may be restructured in a court proceeding in which the court makes the final decision on restructuring the company's indebtedness. This decision is binding on all the foreign buyer company's creditors. The judicial reorganisation is provided in legislations of nearly all jurisdictions and the main characteristic of this proceeding is imposing a stay on bankruptcy petitions against the insolvent company and on enforcing security provided to its secured creditors (Figure 20.4). The judicial reorganisation process is usually initiated by the foreign buyer company seeking protection against its creditors, by asking the court to impose a stay on legal actions that creditors can take against it. Judicial reorganisation is not used frequently in insolvency situations and ECAs are involved in these proceedings only sporadically.

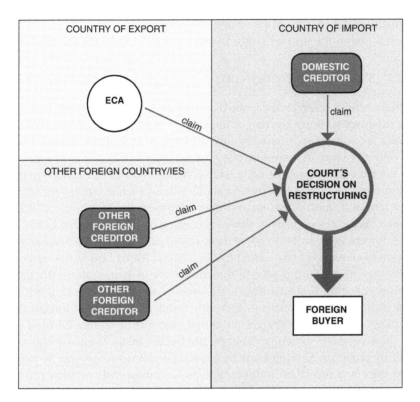

Figure 20.4 Judicial reorganisation of foreign buyer company

20.12 Legal action against foreign buyers

Taking legal action to enforce a claim for payment of credit against a private foreign buyer is another recovery method ECAs may apply. Legal action is taken when a defaulting foreign buyer avoids payment of an undisputed claim and is not willing to negotiate payment of credit with the insured or the ECA. ECAs usually instruct the insured exporter or bank to bring judicial proceedings against the foreign buyer in the insured's name and in its capacity as contractual party. However, an ECA may decide to take legal action against the foreign buyer by enforcing payment of the amount the insured exporter or bank assigned to the ECA when receiving indemnification.

Where a foreign buyer disputes its payment obligation to an insured exporter or bank by claiming breach of contract by the insured, ECAs may instruct the insured to obtain a judgment of a court or an arbitration award to prove its right to claim payment from the foreign buyer. Therefore an ECA will not be involved in a legal action against the foreign buyer and it will await the judgment or the arbitration award and indemnify the insured exporter or bank only if it proves the insured's right to claim payment from the foreign buyer.

20.13   Sharing of recovery costs

Recovery actions taken by the insured and the ECA are nearly always connected with expenses such as the costs of financial or legal advisors, travel costs, etc. Sharing recovery costs is usually regulated by ECAs in their standard terms and only the costs that are necessary for recovery will be shared by the ECA and the insured exporter or bank. However, the costs of the insured and the ECA incurred in carrying on their regular business, such as employees' salaries, office rent and similar costs are not shared between the ECA and the insured. The recovery costs are usually shared according to the percentage of the ECA cover. For example, an ECA will be liable for 90 per cent and the insured for 10 per cent of all recovery costs when the ECA covers 90 per cent of the credit risk.

Recovery of debt from private foreign buyers in large-scale restructurings requires engaging financial and legal advisors that perform comprehensive work necessary for negotiating the restructuring plan with the foreign buyer company. Advisors may charge substantial amounts of money for their work and these costs are sometimes paid by the foreign buyer company and sometimes by creditors. Sharing costs in large-scale restructurings can be complicated since it is regulated in different ways in commercial and loan contracts between the foreign buyer and its creditors. Banks usually include a special clause in their loan agreements stating that the restructuring costs will be paid by the foreign buyer's company. Exporters rarely include such clauses in their commercial contracts with foreign buyers, which may result in the foreign buyer's refusal to pay these costs to exporters. Therefore it is important to find a solution for paying the restructuring costs that is acceptable to all creditors. It is important to do this in the initial stage of the restructuring process and clarify which costs will be paid by the foreign buyer company.

20.14   Application of recovered amounts

When an amount of money has been recovered from a foreign buyer, it may be shared between the insured and the ECA proportionally according to the percentage of the ECA cover. For example, if the ECA cover is 90 per cent of the credit risk, the ECA will receive 90 per cent and the insured 10 per cent of all recovered amounts (Figure 20.5). However, some ECAs provide in their standard terms that they will have priority in relation to the insured so the insured may recover its share after the ECA's share is fully recovered.

Application of the recovered amounts can be complicated if the insured has several claims for payment against the foreign buyer, some of them covered

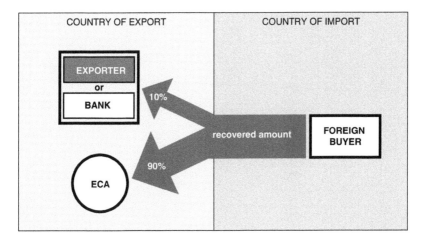

Figure 20.5 Proportional application of the recovered amount

and some of them not covered by the ECA. In this situation, the application of the recovered amounts related to various claims of the insured will be made according to a special priority order provided in the ECA standard terms. The purpose of special provisions is keeping the insured from agreeing with the foreign buyer to pay the insured's non-covered claims first and the ECA covered claim later.

Part IV
Legal Framework

21
OECD and EU Regulations in Terms of ECA Cover

ECA cover is regulated by several international documents, which constitute the international legal framework ECAs apply in their work. Some of these international documents limit the terms and conditions of ECA policies while some of them restrict the provision of cover for credit risks in certain types of export credit transactions. The international legal framework analysed in this chapter is applied by ECAs from the world's major exporting countries, which makes it important for international trade in general.

21.1 OECD Arrangement on Officially Supported Export Credits

The most important international document regulating the ECA cover is the Arrangement on Officially Supported Export Credits adopted by the Organisation for Economic Co-operation and Development (OECD). OECD participating countries have agreed to apply this document, usually called the Arrangement or the Consensus. The Arrangement is a type of international document called a 'gentlemen's agreement', which does not have formal status in law but is considered binding by the participating countries. The countries that participate in the Arrangement are: Australia, Canada, the European Community (including all EU member states), Japan, Korea, New Zealand, Norway, Switzerland and the USA. The Arrangement is voluntarily applied by some ECAs from other exporting countries that do not participate in it officially.

The purpose of the Arrangement is to provide a level playing field where exporters from participating countries compete on the basis of quality and price of exported goods or services, not on the official support received from the state. The Arrangement is also intended to prevent trade distortion and subsidy in the form of tied aid and unrealistic premium rates for providing the ECA cover.

The Arrangement was written in 1978 and it was based on the export credit 'Consensus' among a number of the OECD countries in 1976. Therefore the

Arrangement is also called the Consensus. Before adoption of the Consensus, the lack of rules in this area caused competition among governments to provide the most beneficial financial terms for their exporters, which resulted in state financial subsidies and potential trade distortions.

The Arrangement limits the terms and conditions for providing the ECA cover for export credits such as the minimum premium rates, maximum repayment terms of credits covered by ECAs and minimum cash payments to be made at or before the starting point of credit. It also contains detailed provisions for its implementation. The special parts of the Arrangement, sector understandings, contain provisions for providing official support for the export of ships, nuclear power plants, civil aircraft, renewable energies, water projects and rail infrastructure. Sector understandings are not analysed in this book. Below is a short analysis of the Arrangement's main requirements for issuing the ECA cover.

21.2 Application of the Arrangement

The Arrangement applies to the provision of the ECA cover for credits with repayment terms of two years or more. Under the Arrangement, ECAs from the EU member states are not permitted to cover credit risks shorter than two years when the foreign buyer is from the EU or from an OECD participating country.

Another important feature of the Arrangement is that it does not apply to commercial transactions for export of military equipment or agricultural commodities, or where the commercial contract is an operating lease. The operating lease is excluded from the Arrangement because in this type of contract the lessor transfers only the right of using the leased property to the lessee in return for regular payments. The payments made by the lessee are not seen as payment of a purchase price on credit terms since the lessee is obligated to return the leased property to the lessor at the end of lease period. On the other hand, the Arrangement applies when the underlying commercial transaction is a finance lease because the lessee in this type of lease contract has use of the leased property over most of its economic life. In addition, the lessee usually purchases the leased property by paying a low price for it at the end of the lease period.

The ECAs from the OECD participating countries apply the Arrangement in all their transactions, regardless of whether the foreign buyer's country participates in the Arrangement. The ECAs from the non-participating countries do not apply the Arrangement and they can provide the ECA cover under more favourable terms than those in the Arrangement. In order to neutralise this effect, the Arrangement contains a provision on matching, which allows the ECAs from the OECD participating countries to match the terms of cover offered by the ECAs from both OECD participating and non-participating countries.

21.3 Provisions on down payment, local costs, etc.

The Arrangement provides that some basic requirements must be satisfied when exporters or banks want the ECA cover for credit risks in their commercial or loan contracts. These requirements are related to down payment, export contract value, local costs and starting point of credit that are analysed briefly below.

Down payment

The down payment is a part of total contractual price paid by a buyer to a seller in advance to demonstrate the buyer's commitment to the contract. The basic Arrangement requirement regarding payment of the contractual price is that the foreign buyer must make a down payment of minimum 15 per cent of the export contract value to the exporter at or before the starting point of credit. The down payment is excluded from the rest of the export contract value the foreign buyer will pay on credit terms. Since ECAs cover only the part of the export contract value payable on credit terms, ECAs cannot cover the down payment amount. It is important to distinguish the terms 'export contract value' and 'total contractual price' in this context because the amount of down payment may vary when calculated as a percentage of the amounts defined by these terms.

Export contract value

The export contract value must be determined before calculating the amount of down payment because the export contract value is not always identical to the contractual price. The Arrangement provides that the export contract value is the total amount to be paid by the foreign buyer excluding local costs. When an export credit contract does not contain any local costs, the export contract value is identical to the contractual price in the contract.

Local costs

Local costs are expenditures for goods and services in the foreign buyer's country that are necessary for performing the exporter's contract or for completing a larger project of which the exporter's contract forms a part. After excluding the local costs, if any, the export contract value will be lower than the contractual price. Consequently, the amount of down payment will be lower in a transaction with local costs than in a transaction without such costs. Local costs can be included in the ECA cover up to 30 per cent of the export contract value.

Calculating the export contract value and local costs

Calculating the export contract value and local costs is not simple and it is easier to understand the calculation method from the examples below (Figures 21.1 and 21.2). The two basic parameters for this calculation are:

a) The Arrangement requires a down payment of at least 15 per cent of the export contract value; the 85 per cent remaining can be paid on credit terms and covered by ECAs; and

b) Local costs may be included in the remaining 85 per cent of the export contract value to a maximum of 30 per cent of this value.

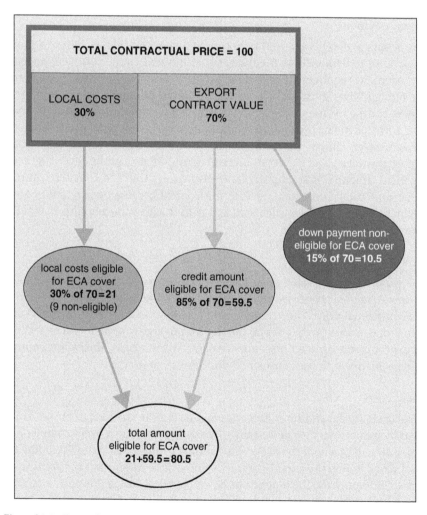

Figure 21.1   Example 1

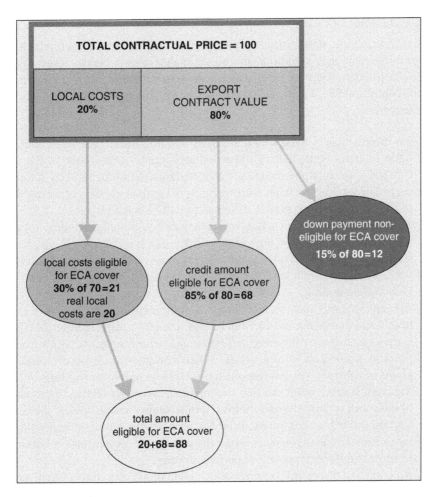

Figure 21.2 Example 2

In Example 1 the amount eligible for ECA cover is higher than the export contract value and includes the maximum percentage of local costs. This makes the ECA cover attractive even for export transactions that include considerable amounts of local costs.

In Example 2, the entire amount of local costs is eligible for the ECA cover and the total amount eligible for the ECA cover is 88. This makes the ECA cover more attractive than Example 1 since the total ECA cover is 88 per cent of the total contractual price. This would not be possible when no local costs are included because the ECA cover would be limited to 85 per cent of the total contractual price.

Starting point of credit

The Arrangement defines the starting point of credit with a comprehensive definition, which is simplified in the short description below. Some words used in the definition are replaced with the terms used in this book for easier understanding. The starting point of credit for various types of goods is defined as follows:

a) For intermediate goods, which are parts or components, the latest starting point of credit is the date of the actual acceptance of the goods by the foreign buyer or weighted mean date of acceptance including services, if applicable. For services the latest starting point of credit is the date of submission of the invoices or acceptance of services by the foreign buyer.

b) For quasi-capital goods such as machinery or equipment, including related services of relatively low unit value and for this type of services, the latest starting point of credit is the same as in (a) above. If the exporter of goods or services is responsible for commissioning, the latest starting point of credit is at commissioning.

c) For capital goods such as machinery or equipment and project services of high value consisting of individual items, the latest starting point of credit is the actual date or the weighted mean date when the foreign buyer takes physical possession of the goods. When the goods consist of complete plants or factories without responsibility of the exporter for commissioning, the latest starting point is when the foreign buyer takes physical possession of the goods. Where the exporter is responsible for commissioning the latest starting point is at commissioning. For services, the latest starting point is submission of the invoices or, when the exporter is responsible for commissioning, the starting point is at commissioning.

d) For complete plants and factories or complete productive units of high value without responsibility of the exporter for commissioning, the latest starting point is when the foreign buyer takes physical possession of the equipment. With construction contracts the latest starting point is the date when the construction is complete. When the exporter is responsible for commissioning, the latest starting point is the date when the exporter has completed installation or construction and preliminary tests to ensure it is ready for operation. In cases of separate performance of individual parts of the project, the latest starting point is the starting point for each separate part or the mean date of those starting points. For services the starting point is the same as in c) above.

The description above is not identical to the wording of the definition of the starting point of credit provided in the Arrangement because some terms have been amended and some parts of the definition have been simplified. Therefore it is necessary to read the wording of the Arrangement provisions. There are two terms that need additional explanation. The first term is 'acceptance of goods or services by the foreign buyer' and the second one is 'commissioning'.

Acceptance of goods or services

Acceptance of goods or services is described as the foreign buyer's communication to the exporter that the goods or services have been accepted. This is the usual way of accepting the goods or services but the foreign buyer may accept them by retaining them for a reasonable period of time without communicating to the exporter that they have been rejected.

Acceptance is related to the delivery of goods or services by the exporter. Delivery of goods can be done in different ways and at various places such as the exporter's place of business, a designated port, a designated place at a border, the foreign buyer's place of business, etc. Delivery terms are important for the contractual parties since the ownership of the goods and the risk for their loss or damage usually passes from the exporter to the foreign buyer when delivery is completed. Completion of delivery by the exporter corresponds to the foreign buyer's acceptance of goods or services. It may be agreed in international commercial contracts that the foreign buyer's obligation to pay the contractual price arises when delivery is completed. When the payment is agreed on credit terms the delivery and acceptance date often constitute the starting point of credit in the meaning provided in the Arrangement.

Commissioning

Commissioning is usually described as a procedure by which an equipment, facility, or plant is tested to verify its functioning after it has been installed according to the contract, design and specifications. It may include training the staff that will operate the equipment, facility or plant. The term 'commissioning' comes from shipbuilding where it has the same meaning.

21.4   Maximum terms for payment of export credits

The Arrangement contains provisions that regulate the maximum duration of credits covered by ECAs. These provisions provide two alternatives that are applied depending on the classification of the buyer's country in Category I or Category II.

If a foreign buyer's country is classified in Category I, the maximum payment term of a credit covered by an ECA is five years. It is possible to extend this maximum period up to eight-and-a-half years but the ECA that intends to provide cover for a credit longer than five years must notify other ECAs participating in the Arrangement about this extension. If a foreign buyer's country is classified in Category II, the maximum payment term of the credit covered by an ECA is ten years.

Category I countries are those on the World Bank's graduation list available on the OECD website, while all other countries are in Category II. This classification is determined by per capita gross national income as calculated by the World Bank to classify borrowing countries. Classification of countries in Category I and II should not be confused with another classification of countries used by ECAs for calculation of minimum premium rates. This particular classification, where countries are classified in categories from nil to seven, is analysed in Chapter 13.

21.5   Payment of principal and interest

The Arrangement regulates that the principal of credit covered by an ECA must be paid in equal instalments. The principal and interest can be paid in instalments, no less frequently than every six months and the first instalment consisting of principal and interest must be paid no later than six months after the starting point of credit. These payment terms are the Arrangement's basic requirements.

The Arrangement's provisions on payment of principal and interest can be disregarded by ECAs when an action is taken to minimise loss in a transaction for which the ECA cover has been issued. This is possible only when the foreign buyer is insolvent and rescheduling or restructuring a credit is needed to avoid or minimise the loss to the ECA involved.

21.6   EU regulation

The European Union adopted several documents regulating the provision of ECA cover by the ECAs from the EU member states. The most important of these documents is the Communication of the Commission amending the period of application of Communication of the Commission to the Member States pursuant to Article 93(1) of the EC Treaty applying Articles 92 and 93 of the Treaty to short-term export-credit insurance (2010/C 329/06). In this notice, which amended previous notices on the same issue from 1997 and 2005, the EU regulated the provision of the ECA cover for marketable risks. The marketable risks are short-term export credit risks with duration of credit less than two years. The short-term export credit risks are agreed in a commercial or loan contract entered into between two parties in the EU, or between an exporter or bank from the EU and a foreign buyer from an OECD country. According to this notice, the ECAs from the EU member states are restricted from covering marketable risks. The purpose of imposing this restriction was to remove distortions in this type of cover when private export credit insurers were competing with ECAs supported by their states. The medium- to long-term export credit risks are not classified as marketable and ECAs are free to cover these risks when a foreign buyer is from an EU or OECD country.

The second EU document of importance is the Council Directive 98/29/EC on harmonisation of the main provisions concerning export credit insurance for transactions with medium- to long-term cover. This directive contains provisions on characteristics of the supplier and buyer credit cover and definitions of the commercial and political risk. It also contains definitions of credit risk and manufacturing risk, provisions on the scope of the ECA cover, indemnification of claims, etc. Several provisions in this directive are analysed in other chapters of this book.

The third document of importance for providing the ECA cover within the EU is the Commission Notice on the application of Articles 87 and 88 of the EC Treaty to State aid in the form of guarantees (2008/C 155/02). This notice applies to the ECA cover for contract bonds and guarantees, interconnected bonds and guarantees, counter-indemnity cover issued to exporters, pre-shipment cover issued to banks, cover for confirmed letter of credit and cover for payments under an operating lease contract. With this notice, the ECAs from EU member states are allowed to provide cover to no more than 80 per cent of the highest amount of risk in these transactions.

22
Other OECD Regulations and International Sanctions

The second part of the international framework ECAs apply is the OECD regulation on combating bribery in international business transactions, environmental and social impacts and sustainable lending practices. This regulation is agreed upon internationally and it has become increasingly important for ECAs because ECAs may be prevented from issuing the cover in transactions that do not satisfy all international requirements. This regulation refers to other international documents that provide principles, criteria and requirements that must be satisfied in transactions for which ECA cover is requested. ECAs may have other requirements and apply criteria that are provided in their national legislation or agreed internationally. In addition to the OECD regulation and the international documents to which this regulation refers, ECAs also implement international sanctions imposed multilaterally or unilaterally. The issues analysed in this chapter are very broad and should be analysed in a separate study. However, this book addresses them in this chapter only.

22.1 Combating bribery in international business transactions

Corruption is a phenomenon that is often connected with international business transactions including trade and investments. Bribery, the most widespread form of corruption, has existed as a criminal offence for a long time and has been prosecuted in national courts around the world. However, the existing national legislation on bribery as a criminal offence does not always provide legal ground for prosecuting bribery of foreign public officials in international business transactions. The OECD recognised the need to combat bribery on the international level by adopting the OECD Convention on Combating Bribery of Foreign Public Officials in International Business Transactions in 1997. The OECD Convention provides a broad definition of bribery and introduces foreign bribery as a criminal offence under national laws of the countries that ratified this convention. Some 40 countries, including those that participate in the OECD, ratified the convention and implemented it into their national laws. The role these 40 countries have in global export and their commitment to prosecute foreign bribery makes this convention very important for all those involved in international trade.

The OECD Convention deals with 'active bribery', which is committed by the person who promises or gives the bribe, while 'passive bribery' is the criminal offence committed by the official who receives the bribe. Bribery is very broadly defined as the promise or giving of undue payment or other advantages, whether directly or through intermediaries, to a public official for himself or for a third party to influence the official to act or refrain from acting in the performance of his or her official duties in order to obtain or retain business. A foreign public official is any person holding a legislative, administrative or judicial office of a foreign country or in an international organisation, whether appointed or elected, or any person exercising a public function or task in a foreign country.

When processing applications for the ECA cover and dealing with transactions for which ECA cover is issued, the ECAs from countries that have ratified the OECD Convention are required to apply strict procedures to prevent bribery. In the application stage for issuing the ECA cover these ECAs are required to:

a) Inform applicants about the legal consequences of bribery in international business transactions under the national legal system of the ECA, including its national laws prohibiting such bribery, and encourage them to develop, apply and document appropriate management control systems that combat bribery;

b) Require applicants to provide a declaration that neither they nor anyone acting on their behalf, such as agents, have been engaged or will engage in bribery in the transaction for which the ECA cover is requested;

c) Verify and note whether applicants are listed on debarment lists of the World Bank Group, African Development Bank, Asian Development Bank, European Bank for Reconstruction and Development and the Inter-American Development Bank;

d) Require applicants to disclose whether they or anyone acting on their behalf in connection with the transaction in question are currently under charge in a national court or, within five years preceding the application, have been convicted in a national court or been subject to the equivalent national administrative measures for violating laws against bribery of foreign public officials of any country;

e) Require that exporters and other applicants disclose, on the ECA's demand, the identity of people acting on their behalf in connection with the transaction in question and the amount and purpose of commissions and fees paid, or agreed to be paid, to such people.

If bribery has been proved in connection to a transaction for which the ECA cover is already issued, ECAs are obligated to deny payment of indemnification if claimed by the insured. Today, ECAs from countries that ratified the OECD Convention apply these rules on a regular basis.

22.2   Environmental and social impacts

Protecting the environment and local communities directly affected by export credit transactions is closely related to the work of ECAs. Many projects that affect the environment and people in local communities could never be realised without providing the ECA cover. When assessing an application for ECA cover, ECAs have become increasingly cautious when analysing the effects a business activity might have on the environment and social conditions in a foreign buyer's country or other countries that may be affected by the activity.

The OECD recognised the need to protect the environment and local communities by adopting The Recommendation of the Council on Common Approaches for Officially Supported Export Credits and Environmental and Social Due Diligence ('Common Approaches'). This document regulates ECAs' actions when providing cover for export credit transactions with repayment term of two years or more. The Common Approaches that were revised in 2007 and 2012 are applied by the ECAs from the OECD participating countries. This is not a legally binding document but it is implemented in practice and the ECAs concerned are expected to do their utmost to fully implement these rules. The Common Approaches are available on the OECD's website.

According to the Common Approaches, ECAs that apply this document will screen applications for the ECA cover and classify projects that include the export of goods and services. Applications for the ECA cover are classified into categories A, B and C. This classification is made according to their potential environmental and social impact.

The projects in Category A have the potential for significant adverse environmental and social impacts in areas broader than the facility sites. This category also includes projects in sensitive sectors or located in or near sensitive areas. The Common Approaches contain an illustrative list of Category A projects with examples of projects in this category. The list is comprehensive, but it is not exhaustive, which means that other projects may be classified in Category A. Examples of projects in Category A include crude oil refineries, thermal power stations, installations for production or enrichment of nuclear fuels, installations for extraction of asbestos, construction of motorways, pipelines, terminals and other facilities for gas, oil and chemicals, sea ports, waste processing and disposal installations.

Even if a project does not appear in the list it may be classified in Category A if it is planned for a sensitive location or is likely to affect its location. Examples of sensitive locations are national parks, forests with high biodiversity value, areas of archaeological or cultural significance, etc. Projects involving the involuntary resettlement of a significant number of affected people are also included in the list of Category A projects.

The projects in Category B have potential environmental and social impacts that are less adverse than projects in Category A. These effects are usually site-specific, few of them are irreversible and mitigation measures are more readily available. No illustrative list for the Category B projects is attached to the Common Approaches. Projects classified in Category C are likely to have minimal or no adverse environmental and social impacts.

22.3   Reviewing potential environmental and social impacts

ECAs use these classifications when reviewing a project to decide whether to provide the ECA cover for an export credit transaction within the project. In order to evaluate a project's potential environmental and social impacts, an ECA will require information from the applicant including an environmental and social impact assessment (ESIA). The ESIA is mandatory for Category A projects and it cannot be made and reviewed by the same party. The scope of review of the potential environmental and social impacts of Category B projects may vary. No ESIA is required if a project is classified in Category C.

ECAs are required to disclose publicly information about Category A projects at least 30 days before issuing an offer or final commitment to provide the ECA cover for such project. The project information should include the project name, location, description of project and details about where information may be obtained.

When reviewing the potential environmental and social impacts of projects for which ECA cover is requested, ECAs should benchmark projects against relevant aspects of the international standards applied to the project. In addition, projects must be benchmarked against the relevant aspects of all ten World Bank Safeguard Policies. The World Bank issued these environmental and social policies to support sustainable poverty reduction by preventing and mitigating undue harm to people and their environment in the development process.

The World Bank Safeguard Policies are related to environmental assessment; natural habitats; by considering the conservation of biodiversity avoiding the use of harmful pesticides in rural development and health sector projects; ensuring that indigenous peoples participate in and benefit from projects and that adverse impacts on them are avoided or minimised; avoiding or mitigating adverse impacts on physical cultural resources; avoiding involuntary resettlement of people to the extent feasible; reducing deforestation and enhancing the environmental contribution of forested areas; preserving the safety of dams and international waterways; and avoiding projects in disputed areas.

The projects will also be benchmarked against the International Finance Corporation's (IFC) performance standards, which are: social and environmental assessment and management system; labour and working conditions; resource efficiency and pollution prevention; and community health, safety and security.

It is obvious from the short list of the World Bank Safeguard Policies and IFC Performance Standards that the environmental and social impacts of various projects for which the ECA cover is requested must be evaluated, but human rights aspects also must be considered. ECAs are aware of the need for human rights protection and are careful not to support projects where child labour is involved or where people are resettled without sufficient and fair compensation for their properties, for example.

22.4   Sustainable lending practices

The history of borrowing huge amounts for investment in developing countries has positive and negative effects. This borrowing contributes to the economic and social development of borrowing countries but it can hinder development if resources are not used well. This is especially important for low-income countries trying to reduce their poverty and existing debt.

However, in order to develop their economies, low-income countries continually need foreign credits. Providing new credits requires analysis of whether the new borrowing will generate positive effects and foster sustainable development. When providing the ECA cover for new credits taken by the low-income countries, it is important to avoid unproductive expenditures, preserve debt sustainability and support good governance and transparency.

In order to achieve these goals the OECD issued its Principles and Guidelines to Promote Sustainable Lending Practices in the Provision of Official Export Credits to Low-income Countries. This document applies when the ECA cover is requested for credits of sovereign and public buyers and publicly guaranteed buyers. These categories of buyers are the central, regional and local governments and public enterprises whose credits would be assumed or guaranteed by a government in the case of default.

By implementing these OECD principles, the ECAs from the OECD participating countries will obtain reasonable assurances that their credit decisions are not likely to contribute to debt distress of the low-income countries. The OECD principles apply to the ECA cover for export credits with a payment period of one year or more.

22.5   International sanctions

International sanctions imposed against states, organisations or persons constitute a part of the international legal framework ECAs apply. The effect of international sanctions on export credit transactions should be distinguished depending on whether sanctions are imposed before or after issuing an ECA policy.

When international sanctions are imposed after issuing the ECA policy they may constitute a political event covered by the policy. Chapter 3 describes international sanctions as political events that may cause non-payment of a credit by a foreign buyer. ECAs usually cover political events of this type, which means an ECA will indemnify an exporter or bank for a loss caused by an international sanction imposed after issuing the ECA cover.

However, an international sanction may be imposed before an ECA policy is issued, and this sanction may prevent an ECA from issuing the ECA cover. Therefore an ECA will not issue the ECA cover when an international sanction prohibits the export of specific goods or services or when a sanction prohibits selling goods or services to a particular person or entity. Sometimes international sanctions do not prohibit export of particular goods or services but prohibit issuing ECA cover for these transactions; in this case the exporter is allowed to pursue its transaction with the foreign buyer without obtaining the ECA cover for the transaction's credit risk.

International sanctions may be imposed multilaterally or unilaterally. Multilateral sanctions are decided by several states such as the member states of the United Nations, the European Union or other international organisations. Unilateral sanctions are imposed by a single state against another state, organisation or person. The international sanctions ECAs are concerned with usually address trade and economic sanctions banning certain types of commercial or financial transactions. A sanction can be imposed in the form of an arms embargo or a ban on the export of specific goods or services, financing in the form of grants and loans, providing the ECA cover, etc. International sanctions may be imposed against specific persons, entities or state institutions.

23
Selected Standard Terms of ECA Cover

As mentioned in previous chapters, nearly all ECAs use standard terms when providing the ECA cover. This means the same terms regulating the rights and obligations of an ECA and an insured are included in all ECA policies as a part of a policy document. Using standard terms saves time for processing a huge number of applications and contributes to equal treatment of applicants for the ECA cover.

The standard terms used by ECAs are similar although written and structured in various ways and governed by various national laws. The ECA cover may be issued in the form of insurance or guarantee but the essential elements of the ECA policies are similar. Therefore, a guarantee issued by an ECA in one country can be characterised as an insurance policy in another and vice versa.

The similarity of commercial and loan contracts covered by ECAs has also contributed to the similarity of the ECA standard terms. The commercial and loan contracts used internationally are often standardised or written in a way that makes entering into these transactions easier and cheaper. When ECAs provide cover for the risk of non-payment of credits agreed to in standardised transactions, the ECA standard terms mirror the terms of the underlying commercial and loan contracts.

Another reason for the similarity of the ECA standard terms is the international cooperation between ECAs based on the idea of creating a level playing field for exporters and banks involved in export transactions. Today this cooperation occurs through the OECD, EU and Berne Union, which is an international organisation of ECAs and a forum for professional exchange between its members.

The long use of the terms included in ECA policies has contributed to their standardisation and broad acceptance. Some of the standard terms have remained unchanged for a long time, providing similar rights and obligations in ECA policies issued in various countries and governed by various national laws.

However, it would be wrong to assume that the ECA standard terms are identical. Some standard terms are extensive documents containing detailed provisions while others are short documents comprising a few pages. It is necessary to understand all terms of an individual ECA policy because it may contain amendments and modifications of the terms described in this book. Additionally, individual ECA policies may contain several special terms provided for covering an individual export credit.

The majority of ECA standard terms such as definitions of political and commercial events, types of the ECA cover, terms of payment of premium, indemnification, recovery procedures, etc., have been analysed in previous chapters of this book. Therefore the following analysis of selected standard terms of the ECA cover is limited to terms that are not analysed in previous chapters.

23.1   Compensation of loss

Provision of the ECA cover is based on the concept that the insured exporter or bank will be compensated for the loss incurred by non-payment of a credit by a foreign buyer. This means that a bank that has provided a loan or an exporter that has supplied goods or services to a foreign buyer on credit terms has interest in obtaining the ECA cover. Other parties do not have such insurable interest and are not eligible to obtain the ECA cover. The concept of compensation of loss is taken from insurance law and the ECA cover does not differ in this respect from insurance contracts.

Compensation of loss is an element that distinguishes the ECA cover from other types of contracts used to transfer credit risks and other types of risks. These contracts are often called contracts for differences where two contractual parties agree that one party will pay the difference between the current value of an asset and its value stipulated in the contract to the other party. The terms of ECA cover do not provide such possibility because the indemnification payable by an ECA is limited to the specific amount of loss incurred by the insured exporter or bank.

23.2   Disclosure of information to ECAs

When applying for the ECA cover and in any communication with ECAs the applicants are under obligation to disclose to ECAs all material facts about an underlying commercial or loan contract. Material facts are difficult to define since every fact may be classified as material if it affects assessment of risk made by an ECA when deciding whether to issue the ECA cover. National laws that govern ECA policies usually provide that exporters and banks must act in good faith or in the utmost good faith when disclosing information to ECAs.

In order to make disclosure of information easier for applicants, many ECAs have included a number of questions in the application forms they provide to exporters and banks. These questions are about an underlying commercial or loan contract for which the ECA cover is requested, particularly about payment and delivery terms agreed in the contract, ability of the foreign buyer to pay the credit, previous experience of an exporter or the bank with dealing with a foreign buyer, etc. When required, exporters and banks are under obligation to disclose other information about their commercial or loan contracts with foreign buyers to ECAs.

Another important question is whether an applicant has knowledge about all material facts an exporter or bank is normally expected to have about its future contract with the foreign buyer. The general view is that an applicant should have information about all terms and facts that are usually known to contractual parties when entering into a particular type of contract. If an applicant does not have such information when applying for the ECA cover the best way to proceed in such situation is to inform the ECA about that.

The obligation to disclose information to an ECA continues even after issuing the ECA policy. An insured exporter or bank is obligated to disclose information indicating a deterioration of the foreign buyer's financial standing, risk of insolvency, or a possible dispute between the insured exporter and a foreign buyer regarding the exporter's performance of its obligations under a commercial contract and similar circumstances. The reason for imposing this obligation on the insured is that ECAs do not have direct communication with foreign buyers and the insured exporters and banks are their main source of information about the credit risks covered by ECAs. After issuing the policy it is very important for an ECA to receive information about changes in the foreign buyer's financial standing. An early warning about a foreign buyer's financial difficulties that affect its ability to pay the credit may enable the ECA to take an action or instruct the insured to act in a particular way in order to mitigate or avoid the loss.

Sometimes it is unclear how information should be communicated by the insured to an ECA. When the information is given to an ECA verbally it may be understood as less important by the ECA and not properly recorded. It could also be difficult to prove conveyance of verbal information to the ECA if it is not documented. Communicating with an ECA in a written or electronic form is probably the best way for an insured or applicant for the ECA cover to provide information.

23.3   Increase of risk after issuing the ECA offer

When an offer for covering a particular export credit risk is issued and communicated to the applicant for the ECA cover it is legally binding for the ECA for the period of time stated in it. This means that the offer cannot be withdrawn by the ECA before the expiration of that period. However, if the risk for non-payment of the credit increases before the expiration of the offer, ECAs usually have the right to withdraw the offer. This right is often limited to situations where the risk has increased substantially before expiration of the offer and this term is usually included in the offers issued by ECAs to applicants for the ECA cover. When a risk is not substantially increased it would not result in the withdrawal of an ECA offer. An example of a substantially increased risk that would result in the withdrawal of an ECA offer is outbreak of war in the foreign buyer's country that will unavoidably affect the foreign buyer's business in a negative way, and its ability to pay the credit. It is important to explain that ECAs withdraw their offers very rarely.

Before an ECA offer is communicated to an applicant for the ECA cover, the applicant may receive information about a substantial increase of the credit risk for which the offer issued. Since ECAs are not involved in negotiating commercial or loan contracts, it is likely that the ECA that has issued the offer will not receive the same information. The question is whether the applicant for the ECA cover is obligated to disclose information about the increased risk to the ECA, even if it would result in withdrawal of the ECA offer. The general understanding is that the disclosure obligation described above includes even such situations despite the risk that disclosure may result in withdrawal of the ECA offer.

23.4   Permits for performance of commercial and loan contracts

Performance of commercial or loan contracts covered by ECAs is often connected with obtaining various permits for import, currency transfer, building permits, etc. Some permits must be obtained before entering into a commercial or loan contract while others can be obtained during performance of the contract. The majority of ECAs provide in their standard terms that an insured exporter or bank is obligated to ascertain that all permits necessary for the performance of a commercial or loan contract have been obtained. This is because ECAs do not have the knowledge or ability to control obtaining all permits that might be necessary for performance of various commercial or loan contracts in foreign countries. If a commercial or loan contract covered by an ECA cannot be performed due to an insured's failure to obtain the necessary permits, the loss caused by such a failure is usually not covered by ECAs.

23.5   Variation of commercial and loan contracts

In transactions covered by ECAs, an insured exporter or bank sometimes agrees with a foreign buyer to amend some terms of a commercial or loan contract. Such amendment must be approved by the ECA if it affects the credit risk covered by the ECA or if it does not comply with the terms of the ECA policy. Some ECAs provide in their standard terms that amending a commercial or loan contract without their consent will discharge the ECA from its obligations under the ECA policy. It may also result in reduction of the amount of indemnification payable by the ECA. This standard term is usually limited to amendments of the material terms of a commercial or loan contract, especially the terms regulating the foreign buyer's payment of a credit and providing security for the payment. Rescheduling the due date or dates for payment of credit, which is analysed in the Chapter 19, is probably the most frequent amendment of commercial and loan contracts covered by ECAs.

In some export credit transactions foreign buyers provide security for payment of their credits in the form of a charge over their assets or in the form of a guarantee issued by a third person. Security for payment of a credit constitutes part of an underlying commercial or loan contract covered by an ECA and it cannot be released or amended without the ECA's consent. Releasing of security or amending its terms by the insured without the ECA's consent may also discharge the ECA from its obligations under the ECA policy or result in reduction of the amount of indemnification payable by the ECA.

23.6   Obligations of the insured at increased risk

In a situation where the risk for non-payment of a credit covered by an ECA has increased, the insured is obligated to try to avoid or minimise the loss for the ECA. When considering an action for avoiding or minimising the loss, the insured is usually obligated to consult the ECA about the appropriateness of such action. Some standard terms provide that in case of disagreement between the ECA and the insured exporter or bank regarding the intended action, the ECA's decision will prevail. The reasoning behind this provision is that the ECA will take the final loss and has the right to decide what action should be taken to avoid or minimise the loss. This situation may arise only before the loss has incurred and it should be distinguished from recovery procedures that are analysed in Chapter 20.

23.7   Retaining the non-covered percentage of risk by the insured

Some ECAs provide in their standard terms that an insured exporter or bank must retain the non-covered percentage of risk, also called the residual risk. The reason for this requirement is that ECAs want the insured to be continuously involved with the credit risk in order to avoid or minimise the loss where possible.

Some ECAs are flexible on this issue and they allow transfer of the residual risk to a limited number of third parties, usually specified in the standard terms of an ECA policy. Transferring the residual risk to other parties that are not specified in this way is not always possible, even if such parties are acceptable for ECAs regarding their status, reputation and good standing.

Some ECAs stipulate that they have a discretionary right to allow transfer of the residual risk to a third party on a case-by-case basis. However, ECAs may be reluctant to consent to such transfer for the reason of involving the insured in avoiding or minimising the loss. Some ECAs allow transfer of residual risk without limits, but such ECAs are very few.

23.8   Waivers and amendments of the ECA standard terms

ECAs handle a huge number of applications for the ECA cover and it would be impossible for them to negotiate and draft individual terms for each individual policy they issue. Therefore the majority of ECAs apply standard terms that save time and are practical. By providing the standard terms ECAs expect exporters and banks to negotiate and structure their transactions with foreign buyers in compliance with these terms.

However, the transactions covered by ECAs are not identical and standard terms do not always fit an individual transaction. For this reason it is not always possible to comply with all ECA standard terms and some individual standard terms need to be waived or amended in order to match the transaction for which the ECA cover is requested. When requesting a waiver or amendment of a standard term, the insured exporter or bank must be aware that ECAs are reluctant to waive or amend those terms that constitute basic requirements for providing the ECA cover. Another reason for this is that ECAs conduct their business with the official support of their states and they are generally expected to treat all exporters and banks equally, even when waiving or amending their standard terms.

Some ECAs do not read commercial and loan contracts when handling applications for issuing the ECA cover and they do not analyse whether the provisions of these contracts comply with the ECA standard terms. In such a situation the exporter or bank is obligated to analyse whether a commercial or loan contract complies with the ECA standard terms and request waiver or amendment of a particular ECA standard term when necessary.

23.9   Governing law and jurisdiction for ECA policies

ECA policies are nearly always governed by the national law of the ECA country because the majority of insured exporters and banks are from the same country as the ECA that provides cover for their commercial or loan contracts with foreign buyers. When both contractual parties are from the same country they normally choose their national law to govern their contract. When a bank from a third country provides a loan to a foreign buyer and obtains the ECA cover from the ECA in the country of export, ECAs are reluctant to accept any other law or jurisdiction but their own. This is not a problem for multinational banks involved in such transactions because they have experience dealing with ECAs from various countries of export.

Bibliography

Delphos, W.A. (2004) *Inside the World's Export Credit Agencies* (Ohio: Thomson South-Western).

Gianturco, D. (2001) *Export Credit Agencies: The unsung giants of international trade and finance* (Westport: Quorum Books).

Goode, R. and Gullifer, L. (2008) *Goode on Legal Problems of Credit and Security*, 4th edn (London: Thomson Reuters Sweet & Maxwell).

OECD: http://www.oecd.org/tad/xcred/arrangement.htm

Stephens, M. (1999) *The Changing Role of Export Credit Agencies* (Washington: International Monetary Fund).

Velmurugan, P.S. and Palanichamy, P. (eds) (2009) *Export Credit Insurance (Opportunities & Challenges)* (New Delhi: Serials Publications).

Wood, P.R. (2007) *International Loans, Bonds, Guarantees, Legal Opinions*, 2nd edn (London: Sweet & Maxwell).

Wood, P.R. (2007) *Principles of International Insolvency*, 2nd edn (London: Sweet & Maxwell).

Index

Note: Bold entries refer to figures.

acceleration clause, 176
acceptance certificates, 78
acceptance of goods or services, and
    starting point for credit, 202, 203
account receivables cover, 63–**4**
advance payment, 5
advance payment guarantee, 93
amendment of ECA standard terms, 217
amendments to contracts, 215–16
anticipatory breach of contract, 27
application process for ECA cover, 118–20
arbitrary repudiation, 27–8
Arrangement on Officially Supported
    Export Credits, 8, 197–8
and application of, 198–9
and buyer risk categories, 125–6
and classification of export credit
    risks, 35
and down payments, 42, 51, 80, 81, 89,
    108, 199
and ECA direct loans, 108–9: interest
    rates, 109
and exclusions from, 198
and export contract value, 199:
    calculation of, **200–1**
as 'gentleman's agreement', 197
and lease contracts, 198
and local costs, 199: calculation of,
    200–1
and matching provisions, 198–9
and maximum duration of credit, 42,
    44–5, 80, 81, 109, 203–4
and medium- to long-term cover, 42,
    52, 80, **81**, 198
and participating countries, 197
and payment of principal and interest,
    204
and percentages of ECA cover, 175
and premium rates for ECA cover, 123:
    minimum rates, 124–5; mitigation
    techniques, 126–7; providing security,

127–8; reducing minimum rates, 126;
    third party payment guarantee, 126
and project finance cover, 44–5
and provisions of, 198
and purpose of, 197
and requirements of, **42**, 44–5
and sector understandings, 109
and short-term cover, 38
and starting point for credit, 202–3:
    acceptance of goods or services, 202,
    203; commissioning, 202, 203
and tied aid, 113
assignment of claim, 14–15, 54–5, 56,
    58–9, 122, 177–8
and account receivables ECA cover,
    63–**4**
and claiming indemnification, 168–**9**,
    170: notifying foreign buyer, 169–70
and determining allowability of, 170–1
and distinction from assignment of
    contract, 170
and medium- to long-term cover, 41
and right of recourse, 177
and risks assumed by bank, 56–7
and short-term cover, 38
assignment of contract, and distinction
    from assignment of claim, 170

bankruptcy procedures, 6, 27, 156, 188
banks
and buyer credit cover, 77
and changes in, 9
and confirmed letter of credit cover, 95–**6**
and contract bond and guarantee cover,
    92: counter-guarantee cover, **94**;
    interconnected bonds and guarantees,
    93–4; justified and unfair calling,
    92–3, 95; types of contract bonds, 93
and definition of, 6
as ECAs (export credit agencies), 9
and ECA direct loans, 110–11

banks – *continued*
  and export credits, 5
  and exporter's assignment of claim,
      54–5, 56, 58–9: account receivables
      ECA cover, 63–4; risks assumed by
      bank, 56–7
  and loan agreements: acceleration
      clause, 176; Arrangement
      requirements, 80; bank-to-bank
      loans, 81–2; branches of
      multinational banks, 86–7; ECA
      requirements, 80–1; funded loan
      sub-participation, 84–5; loan
      participation, 83–4; payment of loan
      amount to exporter, 78–9; purpose of
      loan, 78; separation from commercial
      contracts, 79; syndicated loans, 82–3;
      unfunded loan sub-participation,
      85–6
  and meaning of term, 13–14
  and medium- to long-term cover, **41**
  and multinational banks, 14
  and pre-shipment cover, **91**
  and promissory notes: ECA cover, 61–2,
      63: purchase of, 61
  and purchasing bills of exchange, 58:
      ECA cover, 59–**60**, 61; position under
      ECA policy, 58–9
  and purchasing claims for payment, 53–4
Berne Union, 4, 212
bid bond or guarantee, 93
bilateral investment treaties (BITs), 106
bills of exchange, 58
  and banks' purchase of, 58: position
      under ECA policy, 58–9
  and ECA cover for, 59–**60**, 61
breach of contract, 19, 26, 57, 59, 63–4,
      79, 89, 92, 93, 100–1, 177
  and disputed claims, 179–80
  and repudiation, 27–8
breakage costs, 176–7
bribery, and Convention on Combating,
      119, 206–8
buyer credit, 5
  and definition of, 77
  and distinction from supplier credit, 77
  and money for money transactions, 50
buyer credit cover, 77, **78**
  and limitations of, 79
  and loan agreements: bank-to-bank

loans, 81–2; branches of
      multinational banks, 86–7; funded
      loan sub-participation, 84–5; loan
      participation, 83–4; payment of loan
      amount to exporter, 78–9; purpose of
      loan, 78; separation from commercial
      contracts, 79; syndicated loans, 82–3;
      unfunded loan sub-participation,
      85–6
  and manufacturing loss cover, 90–1
  and medium- to long-term cover, 41:
      requirements for, 80–**1**
buyer risk credit enhancement, 127–8

civil disturbance, and foreign investment
      cover, 100
claiming indemnification, **167**
  and ascertaining claims, 174
  and assignment of claim to ECA, 168–**9**,
      170: determining allowability of,
      170–1; distinction from assignment
      of contract, 170; notifying foreign
      buyer, 169–70
  and claim for payment, 166–7
  and claim handling procedure, 174
  and definition of, 8
  and disputed claims, 179–80
  and handling period, 168
  and interest on delayed payments, 168
  and method of indemnification,
      175–7: acceleration clause, 176; early
      indemnification, 176–7
  and notification of non-payment, 166
  and parties entitled to claim, 177–8
  and protracted default, 168
  and rescheduling of foreign buyer's
      credit, 178–9
  and scope of indemnification, 175
  and security: assignment to ECA, 174;
      enforcement of, 172–3
  and stages of, 166
  and subrogation of claim to ECA, 171–2
  and time limits, 178
  and waiting period, 167–8: payment of
      interest during, 168
coinsurance, and cooperation between
      ECAs, 163
combined policies, 90
commercial interest reference rates (CIRRs),
      109–10

commercial risks, 7
  and arbitrary repudiation, 27–8
  and assessment of, 31–2
  and comprehensive definitions of,
    17–18
  and consequence of classification as,
    47–8
  and distinction between insolvency and
    payment default, 26–7
  and distinction from commercial
    events, 16
  and insolvency, 24–6: guarantors, 25–6;
    private buyers, 24–5
  and payment default, 26
  and percentages of ECA cover, 46
  and refusal of goods or services, 28
  and time of occurrence, 17
commissioning, and starting point for
    credit, 202, 203
Common Principles for Export Credit
    Insurance (EU), 18
  and definitions of commercial
    events: arbitrary repudiation, 27–8;
    distinction between payment default
    and insolvency, 26–7; insolvency,
    24–6; payment default, 26; refusal of
    goods or services, 28
  and definitions of political events:
    decision by ECA's, insured exporter's
    or bank's country, 20; decision of a
    third country, 18–20; force majeure,
    23; legal provisions in buyer's
    country, 23; moratoriums,
    20–1; place of payment, 22;
    prevention or delay in transfer of
    funds, 21–2
compensation of loss, 213
confidentiality, 145
  and confidentiality agreements, 145,
    148–9
  between ECAs and foreign buyers,
    147–9
  between ECAs and reinsurers, 150–1
  between exporters, banks and ECAs,
    146–7
  between exporters, banks and foreign
    buyers, 145–6
  and insider dealing, 146
  and secrecy legislation, 147
  and transparency, 149–50

confirmed letter of credit cover, 95–**6**
Consensus, *see* Arrangement on Officially
    Supported Export Credits
consortiums of exporters, 66
  and coinsurance, 163
construction contracts, 50, 65
contract bond cover, 92, **93**
  and counter-indemnity cover, 94–5
  and interconnected bonds, 93–4
  and justified and unfair calling of
    bonds, 92–3, 95
  and types of contract bonds, 93
contracts for differences, 213
Convention on Combating Bribery of
    Foreign Officials in International
    Business Transactions, 119, 206–8
corruption, and Convention on
    Combating Bribery, 119, 206–8
counter-guarantee, 92, 94
counter-indemnity, 92, 94
  and cover for, 94–5
country risk classification, 125
  and mitigation techniques, 126–7
covenants, 154–5
  and breaches of, 26
  and loan agreements, 80–1
credit, and definition and forms of, 5
credit reports, 31
credit rescheduling, *see* rescheduling
    foreign buyer's credit
credit risk, *see* export credit risk
credit terms, 5
creeping expropriation, 99–100
crystallisation clause, 144
currency risk, 138–9
  and contract in convertible currency,
    141–2, 143
  and contract in currency of ECA
    country, 139–**40**
  and contract in hard currency, 140–**1**
  and contract in local currency, **143**–4
  and crystallisation clause, 144
  and hedge transactions, 139

developing countries
  and ECAs in, 132–4
  and sustainable lending practices, 210
direct loans, *see* ECA direct loans
disclosure of information, 213–14
  and increased risk, 215

disputed claims, 179–80
documentation risk
  and distinction from legal risk, 29
  and exclusion of liability for, 28–9
domestic transactions in foreign country
  and difficulties in covering credit risks,
    71–2
  and recovery from end buyers, 74
  and reinsuring domestic insurer, 75
  and shifting credit risk through
    guarantees, 73–**4**
  and use of 'if and when' payment
    terms, 72–**3**
down payments, and Arrangement
  requirements, 42, 51, 80, 81, 89, 108,
  199

early indemnification, 176–7
ECAs (export credit agencies), 3
  and classification of, 9–10
  and cooperation between, 162:
    coinsurance, 163; cover of foreign
    content, 164; parallel insurance,
    163–4; reinsurance, 161–2
  and international legal framework, 10
  and organization of, 7–8
  and origins of, 10
  and purpose of, 10, 134
  and standard terms used by, 212–13,
    217
  and state support for, 7–8, 9–10
ECA country credit policy, 30
ECA cover, **3**
  and account receivables cover, 63–**4**
  and application process, 118–20
  and bills of exchange, 59–**60**, 61
  and confirmed letter of credit cover,
    95–**6**
  and contract bond cover, 92–3, 94–5
  and definition of, 7
  and firm size, 3
  and framework cover, 36–**7**, 51
  and guarantees, 92–3, 94–**5**
  and importance for international trade, 4
  and letter of interest, 117
  and line of credit cover, 37
  and manufacturing loss cover, 89–91
  and national interest, 135–**6**
  and offer of, 118, 120–1: increase of risk
    after, 214–15

  and official support, 11
  and partial cover, 45–6, 103–4, 124
  and percentage of, 46–7, 103, 175
  and pre-shipment cover, **91**
  and process of issuing, 117–18
  and project finance cover, 44–5
  and promissory note cover, 61–2, 63
  and purpose of, 75, 166
  and special policies, 88
  and users of, 9, 12
  see also buyer credit cover; foreign
    investment cover; medium- to long-
    term cover; premium for ECA cover;
    short-term cover; supplier credit cover
ECA direct loans, 10
  and application process, 110
  and Arrangement provisions, 108–9
  and banks, 110–11
  and definition of, 107
  and exporters, 111–12
  and interest rates, 11–12, 108:
    commercial interest reference rates,
    109–10
  and misconceptions about, 108
  and offer of loans, 110
  and official support, 11–**12**
  and premium for credit risk, 112–13
  and purpose of, 107–8
  and recourse against bank or exporter,
    112
  and repayment terms, 108
  and tied aid, 113
ECA policy, 14, 121–2
  and amendments, 121–2
  and assignment of rights, 14–15, 122
  and beneficiary of, 14
  and early cancellation, 122
  and expiration of, 122
  and governing law, 217
  and issuing of, 118, 121
  and scope of indemnification, 175
  and terms for, 117
  and waivers or amendments of terms,
    217
ECA products, 11
environmental and social impacts,
    149–50, 208–9
  and environmental and social impact
    assessment (ESIA), 209
  and reviewing projects for, 209–10

escrow accounts, 127, 128
European Union
and regulation of ECA cover, 97, 204–5
and restrictions on short-term cover,
38–9, 204
see also Common Principles for Export
Credit Insurance (EU)
exchange rates, *see* currency risk
export contract value, 80, 199
and calculation of, **200–1**
export credit agencies, *see* ECAs
(export credit agencies)
export credit, and definition of, 5
export credit insurance and guarantees,
and definition of, 7
see also ECA cover
export credit risk, 3
and basic classification of, 35–6
and consequence of classification of,
47–8
and definition of, 6
export credit subsidies, 107
exporter
and changes in, 9
and definition of, 6
and ECA direct loans, 111–12
and meaning of term, 12–13
exporter's certificate, 119
export-import bank model, 9
exports, and bans on, **20**
expropriation, and foreign investment
cover, 99–100

firm size, and availability of ECA cover, 3
force majeure, 23
foreign buyers
and definition of, 6
and loan contracts, 77
and private buyers, 7, 182
and public buyers, 6–7, 182
and sovereign buyers, 6, 181–2
foreign content of exported goods or
services, 38, 132, **133**
and determination of, 134–5
and distinction from local cost, 132
and inadequacy of term, 135
and multinational companies, 132–4
and reinsurance, 137, 161
and short-term supplier credit cover, 51
and variety of rules on, 134–5

foreign investment cover
and assignment of claim, 104–5
and bilateral investment treaties, 106
and calculation of losses, 105–6
and definition of, 98
and duration of, 104
and eligible investments, 102: equity
investments, 101–2; investment
loans, 102
and eligible investors, 102–3
and highest amount of cover, 103
and indemnification, 105–6
and legal status of investment projects,
102
and limitations of, 98
and obligations of insured investor, 106
and partial cover, 103–4
and percentage of cover, 103
and political events, 98, 99: breach
of contract by government, 100–1;
breach of unconditional payment
obligation by government, 101;
currency inconvertibility, 100;
delay in transfer of funds, 100;
expropriation and nationalisation,
99–100; social instability, 101; war,
civil disturbance and terrorism, 100
and premiums, 104
and waiting period, 104
foreign subsidiaries as importers
and exporter's control of subsidiary, 76
and supplier credit cover, **70–1**, 74:
difficulties with, 71–2; global cover,
75–6; issuing guarantees, **73–4**;
political risks, 76; recovery from
end buyers, 74; reinsuring domestic
insurer, 75; use of 'if and when'
payment terms, 72–3
framework cover, **36–7**
and supplier credit cover, 51
funded loan sub-participation, 84–5

global supplier credit cover, 75–6
governing law, 217
government agencies, as ECAs
(export credit agencies), 10
guarantee cover, 92, **93**
and counter-guarantee cover, **94**
and counter-indemnity cover, 94–5
and interconnected guarantees, 93–4

guarantee cover – *continued*
  and justified and unfair calling of
    guarantees, 92–3, 95
guarantees as security, 152, 156, 172
  and enforcement of, 173
guarantors, and insolvency, 25–6

handling period, 168
hard currencies, 138, 140–**1**
hedge transactions, and currency risk, 139
human rights protection, 210

'if and when' payment, 67, 69
  and domestic foreign transactions, 72–3
imports, and bans on, 18–**19**
increase of risk, 214–15
  and obligations of insured, 216
indemnification
  and definition of, 8
  and foreign investment cover, 105–6
  and methods of, 175–7: acceleration
    clause, 176; early indemnification,
    176–7
  and parties entitled to claim, 177–8
  and scope of, 175
  see also claiming indemnification
insider dealing, 146
insolvency, 16, 24–6
  and distinction from payment default,
    26–7
  and guarantors, 25–6
  and private buyers, 24–5
insurance, and restrictions in foreign
  countries, 71–2
insured under an ECA policy, 7, 14
interconnected bonds and guarantees,
  93–4
intercreditor agreements, and security,
  157–8
interest rates, and ECA direct loans,
  11–12, 108: commercial interest
  reference rates, 109–10
intermediaries and supplier credit cover
  intermediary in import country, 67–**8**,
    69
  intermediary in third country, 69
International Finance Corporation (IFC),
  210
international legal framework, 10, 197, 206
  and classification of risks, 35

and Convention on Combating Bribery,
  119, 206–8
and environmental and social impacts,
  149–50, 208–9: reviewing projects for,
  209–10
and international sanctions, 210–11
and medium- to long-term cover, 42
and project finance cover, 44–5
and short-term cover, 38–**9**
and sustainable lending practices, 210
see also Arrangement on Officially
  Supported Export Credits; Common
  Principles for Export Credit Insurance
  (EU); European Union
International Monetary Fund (IMF), 185
international trade, and ECA cover, 4
Isabella clause, 79

judicial reorganization of foreign buyer
  company, 190–**1**

lease contracts, 50, 158
  and Arrangement, 198
legal risk, 29
letter of interest, 117
letters of credit cover, 95–**6**
line of credit cover, 37
loan agreements, 77
  and acceleration clause, 176
  and bank-to-bank loans, 81–2
  and branches of multinational banks,
    86–7
  and foreign buyers, 77
  and limitations of buyer credit
    cover, 79
  and loan participation, 83–4: funded
    loan sub-participation, 84–5;
    unfunded loan sub-participation,
    85–6
  and payment of loan amount to
    exporters, 78–9
  and pre-shipment cover, **91**
  and purpose of loan, 78
  and requirements for: ECA
    requirements, 80–1: medium- to
    long-term ECA cover, 80
  and separation from commercial
    contracts, 79
  and syndicated loans, 82–3
  see also ECA direct loans

local cost, 199
  and calculation of, **200–1**
  and distinction from foreign content,
    132
local currency
  and currency risk, 138, **143–4**
  and payment in, **23**, 127

manufacturing loss cover, 89
  and buyer credit cover, 90–1
  and calculation of manufacturing loss,
    89–90
  and manufacturing period, 89
  and supplier credit cover, 90
medium- to long-term cover
  and Arrangement requirements, **42**, 52,
    80, **81**
  and assignment of rights, 41
  and banks, **41**
  and buyer credit cover, 80
  and characteristics of, 40–1
  and individual processing of
    applications, 40
  and international regulations, 42
  and supplier credit cover, 52
  and time taken to arrange, 40
  and unattractiveness to private insurers,
    40
medium- to long-term credit transactions,
  and characteristics of, 40
mitigation techniques, and premium
  rates for ECA cover, 126–7
money for money transactions, 50
money laundering, 119
moratoriums, 20–1
multinational banks, 14
  and buyer credit cover, 86–7
  and legal status of local branches, 86–7
multinational companies
  and complex export transactions, 13, 65
  and difficulties in obtaining ECA cover,
    132–4
  and global supplier credit cover, 75–6
  see also foreign subsidiaries as importers

national interest
  and criteria for determining, 135–**6**
  and ECA cover, 135
nationalisation, and foreign investment
  cover, 99–100

negative pledge, 80, 159
non-possessory pledge, 152, 172
novation of contract, 170

offer of ECA cover, 118, 120–1
  and increase of risk after, 214–15
official support
  and definition of, 8
  and provision of ECA cover, 11
  and provision of ECA direct loans,
    11–**12**
Organisation for Economic Co-operation
    and Development (OECD)
  and Convention on Combating Bribery,
    119, 206–8
  and environmental and social impacts,
    149–50, 208–9: Common Approaches,
    208
  and sustainable lending practices, 210
  see also Arrangement on Officially
    Supported Export Credits

parallel insurance, and cooperation
    between ECAs, 163–4
Paris Club, 184–5, **186**
partial cover, 45–6, 124
  and foreign investment cover, 103–4
payment default, 26
  and distinction from insolvency, 26–7
payment of indemnification, *see* claiming
    indemnification
payment on delivery, 5
performance bond or guarantee, 93
performance for money transactions, 50
permits for performance of contracts, 215
place of payment, 22, 66
political risks, 7
  and assessment of, 30–1
  and breach of contract by government,
    100–1
  and breach of unconditional payment
    obligation by government, 101
  and comprehensive definitions of,
    17–18
  and consequence of classification as, 47–8
  and currency inconvertibility, 100
  and decision by ECA's, insured
    exporter's or bank's country, 20
  and decision of a third country, 18–20
  and delay in transfer of funds, 100

political risks – *continued*
  and distinction from political events, 16
  and exporter-subsidiary transactions, 76
  and expropriation and nationalisation,
    99–100
  and force majeure, 23
  and foreign investment cover, 98, 99
  and highest amount of cover, 103
  and indemnification, 105–6
  and legal provisions in buyer's country,
    23
  and moratoriums, 20–1
  and non-payment by a state, 17
  and partial cover, 103–4
  and percentage of cover, 103
  and percentages of ECA cover, 46–7
  and place of payment, 22
  and prevention or delay in transfer of
    funds, **21–2**
  and social instability, 101
  and time of occurrence, 17
  and war, civil disturbance and
    terrorism, 100
premium for ECA cover
  and additional premiums, 129
  and buyer risk categories, 125–6
  and country risk classification, 125
  and definition of, 8, 123
  and elements in calculation of, 124
  and foreign investment cover, 104
  and increased rates, 128–9
  and indication of rate, 131
  international regulation, 123
  and minimum rates, 124–5
  and payment of, 122, 129
  and purpose of, 123
  and reducing minimum rates, 126:
    mitigation techniques, 126–7;
    providing security, 127–8, 154; third
    party payment guarantee, 126
  and repayment of, 129
  and shifting costs to foreign buyers, 130
  and short-term cover, 37–8
  and types of cover, 123–4
  and waiting period interest, 168
  and website calculators, 131
pre-shipment ECA cover, **91**
private buyers, 7
  and definition of, 25, 182
  and insolvency, 24–5

  and recovery of debt from, 188:
    bilateral negotiations over single
    debt, 188–9; judicial reorganization,
    190–1; legal action, 191–2;
    multilateral negotiations, 189–90;
    negotiations, 188; restructuring
    process, 189–90
private insurance companies, 11
  as ECAs (export credit agencies), 9–10
  and medium- to long-term cover, 40
  and short-term cover, 40
project finance cover
  and characteristics of, 44
  and complexity of, 44
  and international regulations, 44–5
  and processing applications, 44
project finance transactions
  and characteristics of, 43–4
  and duration of, 43
  and loan repayments, **43**
  and project companies, 43
promissory note cover, 61–2, 63
protracted default, 168
public buyers, 6–7
  and administrative entities, 187
  and definition of, 25, 182
  and financial support from state, 186–7
  and recovery of debt from, 185–7:
    methods, 187–8
  and relationship with the state, 185–6

quasi-security, 158–9

recourse, right of, 177
recovery of debt, 181, **182**
  and application of recovered amounts,
    192–**3**
  and difficulties with, 181
  and legal status of foreign buyer, 181–2
  and private buyers, 188: bilateral
    negotiations over single debt,
    188–9; judicial reorganization,
    190–1; legal action, 191–2;
    multilateral negotiations, 189–90;
    negotiations, 188; restructuring
    process, 189–90
  and public buyers, 185–7:
    administrative entities, 187; financial
    support from state, 186–7; methods,
    187–8; relationship with state, 185–6

and sharing of recovery costs, 192
and sovereign buyers, 182–3,
    184: bilateral negotiations, 184;
    multilateral negotiations, 184;
    Paris Club, 184–5, **186**
refinancing, 53
refusal of goods or services, 28
reinsurance
    and confidentiality, 150–1
    and definition of, 160
    and domestic foreign transactions, 75
    between ECAs, 161–2
    between ECAs and private reinsurance
        companies, **164**–5: 'follow the
        fortunes' clause, 165; 'follow the
        settlement' clause, 165
    and excess of loss reinsurance, 160, **165**
    and foreign content in export
        transactions, 137, 161
    and non-proportional reinsurance, 160
    and proportional reinsurance, 160
    and quota share reinsurance, 160, 165
    and reasons for, 160, 164
repudiation, 27–8
rescheduling foreign buyer's credit, 178–9
    and restructuring agreements, 190
    and security, 155
residual risk, 46, 82, 216–17
restructuring, and recovery of debt from
    private buyers, 189–90: judicial
    reorganization, 190–1; sharing costs
    of, 192
retention of title, 158
risk, *see* commercial risks; currency risk;
    export credit risk; political risks
risk assessment, 29–30
    and commercial risks, 31–2
    and political risks, 30–1

sanctions, 210–11
security, 152–3
    and assessment of, 153, 157
    and assignment to ECA, 174
    and control of foreign buyer's business,
        154–5
    and credit renegotiation, 155
    and definition of, 8
    and differences from ECA cover, 153
    and effects of, 154
    and enforcement of, 155–6, 157, 172–3

and guarantees, 152, 156, 172, 173
and intercreditor agreements, 157–8
and local legal requirements, 156–7, 174
and negative pledge, 159
and non-possessory pledge over asset,
    152, 172
and premium rates for ECA cover,
    127–8, 154
and quasi-security, 158–9
as requirement of ECA cover, 154
and retention of title, 158
and security and ECA cover for same
    risk, 154
and similarities with ECA cover,
    152–3
and uncertainty connected with,
    156–7
selling of claims, 53
    and bills of exchange, 58
    see also assignment of claim
short-term cover
    and characteristics of, 36–8
    and foreign content in exported goods
        and services, 38
    and framework cover, 36–7
    and international regulations, 38–9
    and premiums, 37–8
    and supplier credit cover, 38, 51–2
short-term credit transactions, and
    characteristics of, 36
small and medium-sized business, and
    ECA cover, 3
social instability, and foreign investment
    cover, 101
sovereign buyers
    and definition of, 6, 25, 181–2
    and non-payment by, 17
    and recovery of debt from, 182–3,
        184: bilateral negotiations, 184;
        multilateral negotiations, 184;
        Paris Club, 184–5, **186**
state, the
    and ECAs (export credit agencies), 7–8,
        9–10
    and immunity of, 182, 184
    and official support, 8
    and public buyers, 185–7
    see also sovereign buyers
subrogation, 169, 171–2
sub-suppliers, 67

supplier credit, 5
  and definition of, 49
  and distinction from buyer credit, 77
supplier credit contracts, 50
  and complex transactions, 65
supplier credit cover, 49
  and account receivables cover, 63–4
  and bank's purchase of bills of
    exchange, 58; ECA cover, 59–60, 61;
    position under ECA policy, 58–9
  and bank's purchase of promissory
    notes, 61; ECA cover, 61–2, 63
  and complex transactions, 65: contracts
    between exporters and sub-suppliers,
    66–7; intermediary in import
    country, 67–8, 69; intermediary in
    third country, 69; several parties on
    exporter's side, 66; subsidiaries acting
    as importers, 70–1
  and domestic foreign transactions,
    74: difficulties in covering credit
    risks, 71–2; issuing guarantees,
    73–4; recovery from end buyers, 74;
    reinsuring domestic insurer, 75; use
    of 'if and when' payment terms, 72–3
  and exporter's assignment of claim,
    54–5, 56, 58–9: risks assumed by
    bank, 56–7
  and exporter's obligations, 55–6
  and global cover, 75–6
  and limitations of, 50–1
  and manufacturing loss cover, 90
  and medium- to long-term cover, 52
  and short-term cover, 38, 51–2
  and types of, 51
suspension of payments, 26–7

sustainable lending practices, 210
syndicated loans, 82–3

terrorism, and foreign investment cover,
  100
third country decisions, and political
  risks, 18–20
third party payment guarantee, and
  premium rates for ECA cover, 126
tied aid, 113
transfer of payment
  and place of payment, 22
  and prevention or delay of, 21–2, 66,
    100, 125, 153
transparency, 149–50

underwriters, 120
unfunded loan sub-participation, 85–6
United Nations, 20, 22, 211

variation of contracts, 215–16

waiting period
  and foreign investment cover, 104
  and payment of indemnification,
    167–8
  and payment of interest during, 168
waiver of ECA standard terms, 217
war, 16
  and foreign investment cover, 100
whole turnover cover, 36–7
World Bank, 125, 204
  and Safeguard Policies, 209
World Trade Organisation (WTO),
    and Agreement on Subsidies and
    Countervailing Measures, 123

Printed and bound by CPI Group (UK) Ltd, Croydon, CR0 4YY